BROKEN TO BULLETPROOF

BECOMING GOD'S TRUE MAN

TD Wilcox

Other Titles by TD Wilcox

Break It Now! The Secret to Living in Freedom from Bad Habits, Negative Patterns and Addiction
Nails (a novel)
The Joseph Scroll (the sequel to "Nails", coming soon!)
Tickle Spiders – A Frightfully Fun Bedtime Rhyme (Children's)

BROKEN TO BULLETPROOF

BECOMING GOD'S TRUE MAN

Broken to Bulletproof

Copyright © 2016 by Tony D. Wilcox and Atomic Media Works, Inc. All rights reserved, including the right to reproduce this book, or portions thereof, in any form.

Author's Blog & Promotional website:
www.brokentobulletproof.com

Author's website:
www.tdwilcox.com

ISBN: 978-0692650950
First Edition: August 2016
Printed in the United States of America

For my Bulletproof Brothers:
Mike, Tim, Mark, Jerry & Dan

All of you...Bulletproof Strong

ACKNOWLEDGEMENTS

Special thanks to my "Bulletproof Brothers:" Mike, Tim, Mark, Jerry & Dan – I am forever grateful and indebted for your friendship. This book could not have been written without you and your love for Jesus and for me. Thanks to my long-time friend Dr. Kent Denmark who gave me a bed, some food, a pair of sandals, counsel and love the day after my rock bottom. To Pastor Matt Brown, Dan C., Brian M., Adam A., Andrew B. and the whole staff at Sandals Church in Riverside, CA – for helping me learn how to be real with myself, God and others - THANK YOU! To my friend Paul D. - I am grateful to have you in my life and for helping me find a new way to live. Thank you to Carol Kelley for selflessly offering your editing and proofing skills. To my brother, Tim – thank you for being everything a brother should be and more. Mom and Dad – thank you for patiently standing by me always during the good, the great, the bad and the awful. I love you both tremendously. To my daughters: Tori, Abby, Mattea and Terra – you are beautiful lights in my world and precious gifts from the Lord. I am SO grateful for you all. To my wife, my love, Celeste – you are my "Brave One," my soul-mate and very best friend in the whole world. I am so thankful you stayed to fight alongside of me. Finally, to Gunner, the Wonder Dog – you taught me lessons of loyalty and helped my heart heal when I needed it the most....♪ ♪ "Ohhhh, the Gunny!" How could a dog become such a good friend?

TABLE OF CONTENTS

Preface
Introduction
For Group/Individual Study

Jabbok
Grenade!
Broken to Bulletproof
The Secrets
Worthship
Veritas
Deceitful Desires
The Magpie
The Diamond
The Shamed
Carrying My Cross
The Mask
The Jailers
The Brave One
Fur, Teeth & Knives
War
Out of Order
Thwarted Efforts
Sex & Golf
The Pain
Appeasement
Everything Broken
Bulletproof Glass
Bulletproof Brothers
Bulletproof Strong
In Jesus, I Am
Bulletproof Manhood
Epilogue - The Next Step

Bibliography
Resources
The Author

PREFACE

As the different pieces of this project began to come together, I found myself thinking, "I probably shouldn't even be ALIVE right now, much less living such an amazing life. I've made some really terrible choices, awful mistakes, took so many rebellious actions with tons of negative consequences. But I've learned so much and God has restored things in such amazing ways, revealed things to me I never would have understood before and given me a life I never dreamed I could have. Maybe others could really benefit from what I've learned along the way, from my mistakes. Maybe God could use my experiences to help others struggling with the same kinds of things I struggled with."

I felt like a prisoner of war that had been rescued from captivity in a foreign land and brought back home. The thought reminded me of a term I had read in a recent news article – "HUMINT".

HUMINT is short for "human intelligence" in military terminology. It is term that describes the information collected from human sources such as a recovered hostage or prisoner of war. This information is used by military personnel to create strategy for future operations. It lets them know how the enemy works, when they perform operations, what weapons they use, what is their primary mission, etc. It is valuable information in warfare.

I am one of the fortunate souls, a captive that was *rescued* and extremely fortunate – no *blessed* - to make it out alive. Sadly, I know so many others like me that did not. If you'll allow me to run with this analogy a bit further...during my many years in "captivity", I became keenly aware of the enemy's operations. Where it hides out, how it uses camouflage for cover, how its methods look and feel, what are its strengths that we should be aware of and how we can exploit its weaknesses. All of this information is HUMINT about the enemy that held me captive...

Addiction.

I had wandered through life without a map and without a team and had walked right into a trap. What had started out as innocent curiosities for me as a kid progressed later in life to full-blow addictions that I COULD NOT STOP. Before I knew it, the door slammed shut behind me and I was held captive by multiple addictions - to alcohol, pornography, pills, sex. I lived for many years in this captivity and eventually reached a point in life where I realized I was completely powerless. I had no way out.

Here was the trap I found myself in: I was stuck between being "addicted" to substances and behaviors AND the fear of allowing others to see my real, personal failures, struggles and shortcomings. BOTH of these options were anathema to MY plan of success. I had become someone I didn't want to be. I may have looked like a free man, but in reality, I was in a spiritual jail cell. In this state of captivity, there was only one thing I knew how to do – HIDE. So I developed my own strategy to live life undercover.

But it was really even deeper than that. Even an evil warlord like addiction reports to a higher authority. The true source of addiction and the root of most of the problems in our world today:

SELFISHNESS and SELF-CENTEREDNESS.

The truth is, almost everything I did in life was designed to benefit ME, promote ME, bring pleasure to ME. I lived a completely self-centered, selfish life in pursuit of success, money, pleasure and recognition. And the world cheered me on all along the way.

I think I'm a fairly intelligent person as the world would consider it. I have a college degree. I've run a couple of different multi-million dollar companies during my career. I own my own relatively successful business. I've written a few books. Most people would look at me and think I'm a fairly smart and successful person. Well, here's the truth about how smart I am: my BEST thinking, planning and strategizing in life only brought me misery, shame and despair and landed me in spiritual captivity. As smart as I may have been, I couldn't "outsmart" addiction.

The more men I am able to share my story with, the more I find that I am not alone. Pornography is pandemic in our culture and the rest of the world – even in the church. One recent survey of *Christian men between 18 and 30 years old revealed that...*

> *79 percent look at pornography at least monthly.*
> *36 percent view pornography on a daily basis.*
> *32 percent admit being addicted to pornography (and another 12 percent think they may be).*

For middle-aged Christian men (ages 31 to 49)...

> *77 percent looked at pornography while at work in the past three months.*
> *64 percent view pornography at least monthly.*
> *18 percent admit being addicted to pornography (and another 8 percent think they may be).*

Even married Christian men are struggling with pornography and have had extramarital sexual affairs:

> *55 percent look at pornography at least monthly.*
> *35 percent had an extramarital sexual affair while married.*

Source: http://www.charismanews.com/us/45671-shocker-study-shows-most-christian-men-are-into-porn

Porn, adultery, chronic masturbation, alcoholism, pill and illegal drug abuse, the pursuit of money and other similar struggles – these currents run strong like riptides against the hearts of men trying to *find life* in the world today. They are currents that draw us away from the shore of what it means to be a TRUE man in God's eyes and sets us adrift in an ocean of despair, frustration and shame. It's NOT the way God intended for men to lead and live. It is NOT the way God designed us originally. It is IN-AUTHENTIC, FALSE manhood. I refuse to live like that anymore.

So this book, Broken to Bulletproof, is my own personal file of HUMINT, the classified information I collected during my time in captivity behind enemy lines. It's a treasure trove of the spiritual and emotional lessons learned through many years of secret struggles, addiction, marriage, fatherhood and friendship. It's also a collection of trials, mistakes, willful and rebellious sins and tragedies as I stumbled through life learning how to find my true self. It is my own personal deep dive into the dark depths of my heart in search of the TRUE man that God originally had in mind when He created me. I come up gasping for the air of honesty with self, God and to you, the reader, as to what I found there. This is me *finally* being REAL with myself, with God and others.

Mostly though, Broken to Bulletproof is a love story of rescue, restoration and redemption.

So why would I bear my own heart and soul to people like you reading this book around the world? Because I want my life, my experience and even my *failures* to be **worth** something. I want to offer something to this world that will help others that struggle the way I did. I want to share what I've learned about the way human beings are made, how we struggle in our natural condition and how we can be set free. This world needs more REAL men. And I'm not talking about guys that sit around drinking beer, watching ESPN and go on hunting trips. And certainly not men that are bound up in the shackles of addiction. The world needs men that are courageous enough to take the dangerous journey into the darkness of their own hearts and are *willing to become what their Creator originally intended when He designed them.*

The world needs men that are courageous enough to take the dangerous journey into the darkness of their own hearts.

If you struggle in any of the ways that I did, my prayer is that these pages will be helpful to you in planning *your own* escape. Look, jail SUCKS - I don't care if it is a physical jail cell (yes, I've been there) or a spiritual one. Jail is an absence of *freedom.* My passion, my mission in life is to *help men find the true man God originally created them to be.* But the fact is, so many of us…maybe even MOST of us are held in bondage to *some kind of addiction (whether we'll admit it or not)* and we'll never discover our true selves from the inside of a spiritual jail cell.

Before we can become the true men that God created us to be, we must *find freedom.* We have to find a way to unlock the door of the spiritual jail cell that is holding us in bondage. We can't fulfill God's purpose for our lives when we are held in spiritual captivity. *Broken to Bulletproof* is my story of escape. I share it with you now, regardless of what your own captivity may look like, with the hope of helping other men like me get their own hands on the keys.

TD Wilcox
Southern California
January 2016

FORWARD

"In my career as a physician working in the field of Addiction Medicine I have met over 24,000 people who struggle with chemical dependencies. When I meet a patient for the first time they will tell me how much they want to change but for many reasons they are not ready to change and continue to struggle. My hope, for you the reader, is that you <u>are</u> ready to change. My prayer is that you will not just read what Tony has written but DO what he teaches and practices himself. Then, as Tony testifies, you will be blessed and find that freedom you are so desperate for and that God is so eagerly ready to give."

Dr. Doug Richards, MD, MPH
Southern California
January 2016

INTRODUCTION

Real men are an endangered species.

What do you think of when you hear that phrase, *"real man?"* Do you think of someone you know personally and think, "That guy is a real man"? Do you think of a Hollywood celebrity or a soldier or maybe a professional athlete? Do you think of a person you've heard about in the news recently? Or maybe you think of a mythical character in a book or movie? Whose *image* comes to mind when you hear the question, **"What is a real man?"**

What are the characteristics of a *"real man?"* What kinds of things do "real men" do which might define them? What kinds of things will they NOT do? Do you know one or have you ever met one personally? How is a *real man* made or how does he come to be?

And here's maybe the most dangerous question of all..."Are YOU a *real man?"*

Now stop for a moment and do a self-assessment. How exactly does this question make you "feel?" Wait - do *real men* talk about their feelings?

What is the self-talk going on in your head right now?
Does it make you feel angry or offended?
Confused or unsure?
Has someone or something told you that you're NOT a real man?

Do you want to answer with a resounding, "Hell yes I'm a real man!" but you find yourself pausing, questioning that response...doubting?

Are you thinking something like, "Well, I really *want* to be a real man, but I have no idea how to do that or even what that means?"

Or maybe you're thinking, "I would be able to say I know that I'm a real man if I could only stop _____" or "I could say I'm a real man if I could accomplish _____."

Maybe you have made so many mistakes, been so beat down, suffered so much disappointment, failed so many times in life that there's really no question...you can answer definitively, "No. I am definitely NOT a *real* man." I've felt like that.

Sadly, the truth is that in today's world, REAL MEN are simply in short supply. We look around in search of one and we have to sift through scores of men that have walked out on their wives and families, abandoned their responsibilities as fathers, are held captive by secret addictions to things like pornography, sex, drugs or alcohol, compromised their values at work, drove their girlfriends to the abortion clinic or passively just "exist" in a loveless marriage. And then there are the truly evil ones that lie, cheat, hate, murder, rape, rob and destroy. Surely these are not the REAL MEN of our world today.

Or is there something different? Is there something better? Is there something bigger for us to aspire to?

Who really gets to define what a REAL MAN is anyway? Popular culture? Mom or Dad? The government? A wife? A boss? A friend? A lover? My CPA? Or is a REAL MAN defined by his actions? His past? His physical strength? His looks? His bank account? The kind of clothes he wears or the car he drives or the watch on his wrist? His job? His power over others? His accomplishments? The number of sexual conquests he's had? The number of followers he has on social media? I could go on and on about the myriad confusing ways from which we are tempted to draw our value as men.

There was a time in my own life that I would have said I was SURE I was not a real man. I had put up such an amazing façade and worked my strategy of deceit and misdirection so well that almost everyone *saw* me as a successful, happy, disciplined, church-going husband, father, and friend *(a REAL man, perhaps?)*. No one knew what I was REALLY like because I wouldn't let them see my true self. *I projected what I wanted others to see and I was wicked good at it.*

This kind of duplicity was killing me though. I realize now that I had been chasing what I thought were the things that would make me a real man, but deep inside I knew a real man *wouldn't do the things I did*. A real man would have self-control. A real man would have integrity. A real man would be faithful, loyal. A real man would have courage. Those are selfless characteristics of mythical heroes. I didn't have ANY of those things. Truth be told, I reached a point in my life when I really wasn't sure WHO I was. When I looked at myself in the mirror, I certainly didn't like what I saw staring back...

An addict
An alcoholic
A liar
An adulterer
A fraud

Not the marks of what I thought was anything resembling a REAL MAN. In the deepest depths of my soul I TRULY WANTED to be one, but the problem was, I had no idea how to become one and I felt like the things I had done had disqualified me from *ever* becoming one.

So, at 47 years old, I was faced with a choice: lose everything I held dear (wife, kids, career, reputation, health, friends, etc.) by continuing to live a false life of pretense, hiding my secret behaviors, wallowing in addiction, shame and deceit...

OR *die*.

Awesome.

So I took the easy way out and chose death. No really - I'm serious. Let me explain.

There is a passage in the Bible penned by the half-brother of Jesus himself that used to frustrate me to no end. It reads,

"Grieve, mourn and wail. Change your laughter to mourning and your joy to gloom."   - James 4:9

I have always struggled with this passage. It didn't seem to mesh with the rest of scripture. Doesn't God want me to be happy? Have an abundant life? If so, why would he command me to mourn, to be filled with gloom? I didn't get it.

Today, I understand this verse. It makes all the sense in the world to me. But I had to die (in a spiritual sense) to fully understand it though. I had to come to the very end of myself, my own power, my own resources, in order to understand this verse. I had to hit "rock bottom" – twice, actually.

The very first step in recovery from addiction is to grasp the fact that we are *powerless*.

STEP 1: *"We admitted we were powerless over our addiction and that our lives had become unmanageable."*

I was certainly powerless and my life had definitely become unmanageable. I sat in my first few AA meetings while I was in rehab, way in the back of the room against the wall (the old timers affectionately call this back row of chairs "death row") and I tried to hide with my baseball cap pulled down low. I listened to the stories of others, spilling out their lives, their regrets, their heartaches and their own personal destruction...and in their stories, I heard my own. I felt like my life was over. I realized, "I'm just like these people. God, what have I become? I'm an alcoholic." I sat back there filled with gloom and I wept.

I grieved. I mourned. I wailed. That's when I understood what James was saying.

"Grieve, mourn and wail. Change your laughter to mourning and your joy to gloom."

Think about it. What is that verse describing? When is really the only time that it is proper, appropriate, necessary and acceptable to *grieve, mourn, wail and wallow in gloom?*

When someone DIES.

Death row was EXACTLY where God wanted me to be. This is the point in a man's life when he gives up fighting, when he finally relents and stops struggling, striving and wrestling with God. When he concedes that his own plans to run his own life successfully have failed miserably. The very point of this kind of spiritual death IS so that we can fully realize our own **powerlessness.**

You see, it isn't until we accept and acknowledge our own death (both spiritually and our physical mortality) that we are truly in a position to receive help from God. BEFORE we get to this point, our own strategies and plans for life are blocking us from receiving what God is so willingly offering each one of us. This is exactly where James is trying to lead us with this verse, trying to get us to understand that we MUST DIE before we can receive the life God has for us. There are many verses in the Bible about this...

"Whoever finds his life will lose it, and whoever loses his life for my sake will find it." (the words of Jesus) - Matt 10:39

"Truly, truly, I say to you, unless a grain of wheat falls into the earth and dies, it remains alone; but if it dies, it bears much fruit. (the words of Jesus) - John 12:24

"And whoever does not carry their cross and follow me cannot be my disciple." (the words of Jesus) - Luke 14:27

"For to me to live is Christ, and to die is gain." (the words of the apostle Paul) - Philippians 1:21

I had to learn the lesson of these verses the hard way. I sat there in the back of an AA meeting and acknowledged that my best thinking had failed to bring me the life I wanted, but instead it brought me to death row. So I admitted that I, too, was powerless and that my life had become unmanageable. I was ready to get help. I was ready to start living differently, ready to turn-around and travel in the opposite direction. Ready to give up the life I had been living. I was ready to die.

Do you see? God knew that I *had* to die...so that I could be resurrected. You can't be resurrected if you don't die first! That's the only way He could begin the process of making me into the man HE had intended for me to be all along.

Look, I'm not for one second going to try to convince you that I'm a REAL MAN now and if you do these 10 simple things you can become one too. It's not for me to decide who is or isn't a REAL

MAN. God decides that because He is the one that created us. And he created each of us in vastly different ways. There is no cookie-cutter version of true manhood that can be applied to every man, although our culture certainly tries to jam us all into one (think Rambo and Indiana Jones, James Bond, Jason Bourne, Hugh Hefner, Laird Hamilton, Kobe Bryant, Peyton Manning, etc.). What about the man that God gifted with musical talent or amazing artistic creativity or culinary skills? Are they somehow excluded from authentic manhood? Of course not.

What I CAN tell you is that, before, I KNEW I was not a real man. I was living a lie. I was a fraud, a fake, a façade. I was something false, a human being *pretending* to be a real man. Today, I am something very different. Today, I am able to let people see THROUGH me. I can let the world see who I really am with all my faults, failures and shortcomings. I have learned how to take down the façade and to live my life with *transparency.* It is the defining characteristic of my life now. I don't do it perfectly, but I am always striving for it. It's a way of life that is consistently *moving towards* becoming what God wants me to be, consistently *moving towards* becoming the TRUE person that He intended for me to be all along. I am daily being made into something new...something **true, *authentic* and *real*...and I will let you see me exactly the way I am in the process.** God is making me into what He wants me to be *through the process of transparency.* That is the only way that His light can shine.

"No one lights a lamp and puts it in a place where it will be hidden, or under a bowl. Instead they put it on its stand, so that those who come in may see the light."
                                                            - Luke 11:33

My friends that know what I've been through, know the things I've done, how I've lived – they see me now and they can't believe my story. They can't believe that my wife and I not only stayed together, but that we have a stronger, more intimate marriage today than we ever could have imagined. Most people, most marriages don't survive the kinds of hell I put us through, much less THRIVE afterwards. There's only one reason I survived the hell of my addictions...BECAUSE I WAS WILLING TO DIE.

Isn't that crazy talk? But that's exactly what happened to me. Death is a *pre-requisite* for resurrection. Dying is the only state in which a man can take no credit for the miracle that God is about to do.

Dying is the only state in which a man can take no credit for the miracle that God is about to do.

At the beginning of this introduction, I asked whose "image" comes to mind when you think of the phrase "real man?" When God made man and placed him in the garden of Eden, He made us "in His own image." We were designed to bear His image through our lives. He gave us the charge to "be fruitful and multiply." This is the gift of "causation," the ability to create change in the world. It is the gift of power in our lives in which we have the free will to choose how we will discharge it in the world. Will we obey his command to "be fruitful and multiply?" Will we invest this power bestowed on us in ways that create growth, promote righteousness and bear His image TRULY to the world in which we live? Or will we selfishly direct this power towards destruction, our own pleasure and present a FALSE image to the world?

This is the challenge for us as men.

So this book is not about a destination, it is about a direction, a process...a journey. It is about understanding and accepting our own *brokenness* so that we have the reference point from where we begin our journey. It is about placing a tombstone in the ground at the place where the old, false, broken man DIES. And it is about having the spiritual courage to take steps *towards becoming a TRUE MAN, an AUTHENTIC man...a* <u>REAL MAN</u>.

Still waiting for me to give you my definition? Here's what I've come to understand what a REAL MAN is:

A REAL MAN is the TRUE man that God intended for you to be all along.
Nothing more, nothing less.

This book is my personal story about this journey in my own life. It is a privilege to share it with you and to point the way towards that TRUE man that God had in mind when He formed his very first thoughts...*of YOU.*

"The night is nearly over; the day is almost here. So let us put aside the deeds of darkness and put on the armor of light."
- Romans 13:12

FOR PERSONAL/GROUP STUDIES

If you intend on using this book as the centerpiece for your own personal study or with others as a group, here are some additional thoughts and suggestions that you should consider as you move forward.

HONEST IN, UP AND OUT

At the end of each chapter, you'll find a section entitled *"Bulletproof Glass Challenge."* It includes several questions designed to help you reflect on the content and take a truly honest look from three different perspectives – self, God and others. I call this being *"Honest In, Up and Out."*

Being **"Honest IN"** describes self-reflection. It is when you honestly examine *your own* feelings, thoughts, habits, and motives and compare them with your values and true beliefs and with God's righteous standard. It is an introspective assessment as to *if you are being true to yourself or not.*

Being **"Honest UP"** describes honest communication *with God* in which we pray and confess areas of our hearts and lives where we see in-congruency with the true person God created us to be. God knows our deepest thoughts, dreams and desires - this is where we spend time examining them with Him, expressing our struggle to Him and listening for His response.

Being **"Honest OUT"** describes true, honest communication and relationship *with others* where we share and discuss these difficult things that God has revealed to us so that *we can hear more from Him through our close, trusted friends*...our "Bulletproof" brothers.

BULLETPROOF BROTHERS/COMMUNITY

Having the willingness to allow God to speak into our lives THROUGH other trusted individuals is essential to spiritual formation. I want to encourage you to pray that God will bring other godly men, trusted friends that will walk this journey with you and to be *willing* to keep your eyes open for them. I did this during the difficult times I'll describe in this book and I asked God to bring me a "Jonathan" into my life - someone that is loyal, devoted, brave and kind..."knit to my own soul"...like King David's friend in the Bible (see I Samuel 18). God answered that prayer by developing my relationship with several men that I would now count as my closest friends in the world. We meet multiple times a week and I talk to one or more of them at least once a day by phone or text. I call these men my "Bulletproof" brothers. They are the guys that will someday carry my casket when I die. I love them with the love of Christ. They each represent a unique conduit of God's love, wisdom and power into my life...and I into theirs.

Part of becoming the true man that God created you to be will include a new life in community with others like I've just described. We weren't created to live life alone and we certainly can't find true healing and authentic manhood without the help of other friends we can trust.

"As iron sharpens iron, so one man sharpens another."
– Proverbs 27:17

EMPATHY/SAFE RELATIONSHIPS

A "Bulletproof" brother is a special, unique person. They will be someone that possesses the characteristic of "empathy." Empathy is *"the ability to understand and share the feelings of another."* An empathetic friend is someone who doesn't rush to "fix" a problem or difficult situation you are in but is willing to listen to the details of it and *experience the discomfort with you.* Empathetic friends are the ones who understand that simply "being" with you in a difficult time may be the best thing they can do for you rather than offering empty platitudes or quick-fix solutions. They are friends that you know are "safe" for you to share even your deepest hurts, failures, struggles and fears with because they will respect what they hear and willingly enter into that struggle with you.

I want to encourage you to consider your different relationships and gauge the level of empathy of each of them. The friends that listen well and are empathetic in their communication are likely candidates to be a "Bulletproof" brother to you. Ask yourself if you would trust this person with an intimate detail of your life. Would they respond respectfully and give honor to your struggle? Would they willingly join with you in your emotional discomfort and relate to your pain? If so, they are probably a safe relationship that you should pursue developing. If they are not emotionally mature enough to respond safely and can only deflect, minimize, excuse or mock your behavior or feelings then they probably are *not* a safe relationship to pursue. Pray. Ask for wisdom and ask God to bring one or more "Jonathans" into your life and to surround you with a group of men that will form a worthy "Bulletproof" brotherhood. God will honor that prayer.

WILLINGNESS

Discussing and digging into this material honestly with a group of trusted friends takes a spiritual determination called *"willingness."* Willingness is a spectrum that measures the quality or state of your ability to do something, readiness. It describes your level of commitment to move forward in the process of becoming the true man God designed you to be. Are you truly *willing* to talk about difficult subjects with other men? Are you truly *willing* to be honest with yourself, God and others about your own personal thoughts, behaviors, habits, negative patterns or addictions? Are you truly *willing to do whatever it takes* to develop into the true man that God created you to be?

When I work personally with other men that are struggling in their own lives, I've found that I can give them my own personal story, my experience, my knowledge and wisdom, my opinion, my encouragement and my prayers - all of that can be helpful to others. But what I CAN'T give them, and something that is truly CRITICAL to making progress, is the spiritual component of "willingness." Many times it takes a challenging or tragic life circumstance to put us in a place where we become truly willing to change. For those struggling with addiction, it usually takes an event that brings us to "rock bottom" in our own personal lives...but it doesn't HAVE to. If you find yourself with a smoldering desire to change but you lack willingness, here is the best advice I can give you: PRAY. Ask God for willingness. I've found that you can't generate willingness on your own if you don't already have it - God is the only one that can give it to you.

In order to fully benefit from this material and to make valuable progress towards becoming the true man that God created you to be, you will need a heavy dose of "willingness." If you're NOT willing, you won't make progress. That would be like saying you are going to climb Mount Everest but never starting your training by going on even a short hike in your local hills. In many of the Bulletproof Challenge questions I've included a question specifically designed for you to do a personal *willingness check*. These are important questions to pause and truly consider your level of willingness and commitment to move forward in the journey God is calling you into. Before you take that next step, ask yourself, "Am I *truly willing* to discover what God has for me if I take this journey?" If so, you are in for an amazing, life-changing adventure.

SPIRITUAL FORMATION

The process and practice of spiritual formation is the development of spiritual maturity that leads to a deeper devotion and relationship with God. The Bible calls this the process of *"sanctification"* in most translations. It is the way in which God moves us, changes us, refines us into the true person that he originally had in mind when He created us - that is our goal. That's what this book is about and it should be the goal of any group that uses this book as a study tool.

Broken to Bulletproof is specifically about the spiritual formation of men – not that women can't benefit from the very same concepts and principles. I've been told by women that reading this book gave them a special insight into their man's life and struggle that they were previously unaware of. But the book is written from a man's point-of-view and with men in mind as the primary reading audience.

I believe God created men to be leaders and godly stewards of His gifts in our families, communities and the world in general. The fact is, we aren't born with an inherent knowledge of how to accomplish that, so it requires that we go through a rigorous process to learn, a process that goes AGAINST our culture and AGAINST the broken human nature we are born with. We are like fish swimming upstream in this worthwhile pursuit of TRUE, godly manhood. My personal mission is to call and lead men into this process of spiritual formation with the goal of achieving godly, authentic manhood – becoming the TRUE men that God created.

TD Wilcox
Southern California

CHAPTER ONE

JABBOK

Several years ago, a little over a year before I finally hit rock bottom and got sober, I was awakened in the middle of the night by a dream. Actually, it was more like a "sentence" rather than a dream. Like one of those songs you get stuck in your head and you can't stop singing it to yourself, but it wasn't musical. It was just this phrase being repeated over and over in my mind. It wouldn't stop. I rolled over for fifteen minutes or so in bed, but it was relentless. It was this phrase:

> "Jacob I loved, but Esau I hated."
> "Jacob I loved, but Esau I hated."
> "Jacob I loved, but Esau I hated."

I couldn't find the off button and so it repeated like a broken record. I knew it was from the Old Testament, but I couldn't remember where. I finally relented, got up and went downstairs to my computer and searched the term. I found the story of Jacob and Esau and read the story of Jacob's ladder. I learned that Jacob's name means "heel grabber" or "the lowest of the low". It can also mean "insidious" or "deceitful".

Jacob was a liar.

Why would God love a liar? I was even more perplexed now, so I continued searching.

That's when I stumbled on an article entitled, "Jabbok."[1]

It was an intriguing word to say the least. I clicked the link and was instantly drawn in. It was the transcript of an old sermon (from 1999) by Pastor David Wilkerson. He is noteworthy because of a book he had written back in the 70's called "The Cross and the Switchblade." It was later made into a memorable movie starring Pat Boone and Erik Estrada. I remembered seeing it as a kid.

The Jabbok sermon is a lengthy, interesting and convicting text, especially for someone struggling with secret sins. It is based on the story in Genesis 32. Here's what I learned about Jabbok. Jabbok was the place where Jacob wrestled with God...

> "Jabbok is the place where Jacob wrestled with the Lord. It is where he made his total surrender to God. It is where he got his new character, and new name - Israel. It was the place where he cast down his last idol, and won his greatest victory."
>
> "Jabbok means 'a place of passing over.' It also stands for struggle; to empty and pour out. What a glorious truth is revealed in this place called Jabbok. It has everything to do with us today. It is the place where God's people discover the secret of power over every besetting sin. It represents a life and death crisis - one that leads to absolute surrender."
>
> "There can be no glorious victory over self and sin until you go to Jabbok. There comes a time we must "have it out with God." We must face ourselves and be emptied of all evil desires and selfish ambitions."

Evil desires and selfish ambitions. I was certainly familiar with those. These were convicting words to me. And as if that wasn't convicting enough, I read on...

> "But this humble, obedient, praying, God-fearing, truth-loving servant of God was still into **appeasement!** That means, "giving in to a dangerous power to avoid trouble." Peace at any cost includes compromise!"

"Instead of trusting God in his crisis, he worked angles. He tried to think his way through his problem. He divided his cattle into separate droves, sending them on ahead to soften his brother's heart. He would bombard Esau with wave after wave of gifts of goats, camels, bulls, sheep, donkeys, and rams."

"For he said, I will **appease him**..." (v. 20).

"**Appeasement!** That is what multitudes of Christians are into! They give in to a dangerous power, because they are afraid they are helpless! You hear it everywhere nowadays "I just can't help it! I don't want to do it. I hate my sin. But in spite of all my super efforts, I give in and fail!"

"So over and over again, we appease! We sin and confess, weep and confess, try to think our way out. Oh, the angles, schemes, justifications, excuses, plans - all in vain. We seem powerless against overwhelming needs and desires."

I could relate to ALL of this. It was as if God had shaken me awake from my sleep to wrestle with me over this specific message. I was convicted to the core. Because of the fear, anxiety and stress in my life, I was doing exactly what the sermon text said - *"giving in to a dangerous power to avoid trouble."* Appeasement. I don't think I had ever paid attention to the word, but I understood it. Appeasement for me came in the form of "medicating" the spiritual and emotional pain and shame I was feeling. I was hiding secret sexual sin. I was secretly viewing pornography. I was secretly visiting massage parlors for illicit sexual encounters. I was hiding and abusing alcohol and prescription pills. I was appeasing my troubled heart with everything and anything...except God.

This sermon has so many rich, truthful analogies that it was hard for me to take it all in - powerful. If you want to check out the entire sermon, I have an audio recording on the media page of my website:

http://www.brokentobulletproof.com/media

I didn't sleep the rest of the night. I got showered and dressed and headed to work early. I knew something had to change. I had been hiding my sinful behaviors, covering up, evading, pretending, excusing and minimizing them for many, many years now. **I was lying to myself, to God and to everyone else.** I was hiding behind a mask designed to make others think I really had it all together. As much as I hated the behavior, the truth was, I couldn't stop. While I wouldn't have been able to say it then, I can say it now – I was an addict and an alcoholic; a slave to many different addictions at once.

I knew something had to change, but I didn't see a way out. I wanted my own Jabbok, to cross over, but I had no idea what that meant in practical terms. There were things I had done that I was SO ashamed of I had vowed to *never tell anyone;* to take them to the grave. Those things were eating away at my heart and soul like a wicked, black spiritual cancer. Paul's words in Romans 7 rang out in my heart...

"I do not understand what I do. For what I want to do I do not do, but what I hate I do...For I have the desire to do what is good, but I cannot carry it out. For I do not do the good I want to do, but the evil I do not want to do—this I keep on doing...What a wretched man I am! Who will rescue me from this body that is

subject to death? Thanks be to God, who delivers me through Jesus Christ our Lord!"   - Selections from Romans 7

When I got to my office, I sat down at my computer and started writing out a letter to God. Surely he would rescue me from this hell, right? I want to share this very private, personal letter to God with you – this is part of how I live now, being "Honest OUT" – authentic with others. I know some of what you will read here will sound silly, immature, but I want to share it as I wrote it as an example of just how troubled I was. Please keep in mind that, when I wrote this, I was in a very spiritually and emotionally sick state, addicted to multiple things, covered in shame, guilt and selfishness. I share this in the spirit of vulnerability with the hope that it will help others that are struggling like I was. This is what I wrote...

Lord Jesus, my Savior, my friend, my God,
Last night, you woke me around 3 a.m. I was restless and the one thing that kept running through my mind was "Jacob I loved, but Esau I hated." I couldn't get that out of my head. I finally relented and got out of bed around 3:30 and went to your word. I read the story of Jacob and Esau and of Jacob's ladder. I did some research online and read a couple of commentaries about the subject of sanctification (the best I read was by Spurgeon) and divine election. But I think you more wanted me to end up here, at Jabbok. I ran into the word online and it sounded familiar, so I searched it in Google and ended up at the sermon by David Wilkerson about the place. You have lead me most literally to my own personal Jabbok – "the crossing." I choose today to cross over.
I have some secret sins, Jesus. I know they are no surprise to you. I want to write about them, confess them on paper to

you...and then cross over to repentance and BURN the writing as an offering to you. My secret sins have been:

        Pornography   Drunkenness   Sexual Immorality
                    Adultery   Idolatry

    I am at a spiritual crossroads. I want to fight, but the fact is...I am lacking the supernatural power of your Holy Spirit. I have lost most of my battles because I have tried to accomplish it in my own flesh. I NEED YOUR SUPERNATURAL POWER, JESUS!!!! I'm desperate! I pray for your Holy Spirit to be poured out on me. Not because of my own merit – I don't deserve ANYTHING good from you, Lord. You have blessed me with so many wonderful gifts that I don't deserve! I only ask for an outpouring of your Spirit so that I can overcome the evil one. I cannot overcome his power without your HOLY SPIRIT. I cannot physically stop doing the things I have been doing WITHOUT YOUR HOLY SPIRIT. I need you, Jesus.

    I ask right now, in the name of my Savior, my Redeemer, my Lord, Jesus Christ of Nazareth, that you allow me to cross over my own personal Jabbok and give me the supernatural power that I need to conquer the enemy's work in these areas of my life, breaking the strongholds of drunkenness, pornography, sexual immorality, adultery and idolatry. I am ready to do battle, Lord...but this battle is YOURS. Please fight it in me, through me – empower me to overcome. Please do whatever it takes to make me well!

    Today, with the reading and testifying of this letter...and the ceremonial burning of it, I cross over Jabbok into my own personal promised land of freedom from these besetting sins and the bondage of them. I am NOT a coward...but a CONQUEROR...even MORE than a CONQUEROR in the name of Jesus, my Savior and Lord!

    AMEN!

This was a hard letter to write. I put on paper, in a general way, the secret sins I had vowed never to tell anyone. Because the crushing amount of guilt and shame that I was under, this was the closest thing I could do to a "confession." I printed out one copy and then I password protected the file on my computer. I didn't want ANYONE to ever read those words and know the awful things I had done.

Surely God would answer this prayer, right? I dated it and signed it. I thought about actually signing it in blood. If there had been a notary present, I think I would have had it notarized, except I would have been too ashamed for the notary to read it in order to notarize it. I wanted it to be official, but more than anything, I WANTED IT TO WORK! I needed it to work. Really, this strategy was my last hope.

I took the letter with me, hopped in my truck and drove 30 miles or so out to a campground I knew of way up in the hills. It was during the week, so there wasn't really anyone around. I found a quiet spot, parked and went to sit down by the fire pit. I looked around to make sure no one was around to hear me because I was so paranoid of being found out. Once the coast was clear, I stood up and read the letter out loud to God...and wept.

It was the most heartfelt prayer I had ever prayed. I was desperate to get well...**_as long as nobody else ever knew about it._** The shame I carried was devastating, crushing. I pleaded with God to save me, release me, heal me. Surely this would work. And guess what?

It DIDN'T.

I don't know what I was expecting. Maybe the Holy Spirit to drop down on me and I'd collapse and start speaking in tongues? A flash of light? A burning sensation in my hands? Maybe I'd just hear a whisper of God's voice? Something! But no, nothing happened. I didn't *feel* any different. So I burned the letter in the fire pit, made sure the words could not be read by anyone, stamped out the ashes...and drove back to my office.

Looking back now, while I didn't believe the prayer had worked, it turns out that this was actually the most dangerous and effective prayer I had ever prayed. I still didn't tell anyone anything about my secret struggles. I would continue wearing a mask and pretending to be the guy that had everything all together - lying to myself, God and everyone else...at least for a while.

BULLETPROOF GLASS CHALLENGE:
Honest IN (Being authentic with myself, self-assess) –
- What strategies do you find yourself using to APPEASE the spiritual forces of fear, shame, anger, etc.?
- What would it feel like for you to NOT use those strategies and just SIT in the discomfort of those spiritual forces? Is that something you would be willing to try?
- Can you think of a time when you've actually done this or would you say you've never been able NOT to appease?

Honest UP (Being authentic with God, pray, confess) –
- Do you have secrets that you've "stuffed" or "ignored" and that you're not even willing to discuss openly with God, much less with anyone else?
- Is God calling you to "cross over" in any sense, to leave behind a way of life that is displeasing to Him?

Honest OUT (Being authentic with others, share, discuss) –
- What things have you been keeping secret that you need to confess to someone else, a trusted friend or family member?

- WILLINGNESS CHECK: Are you truly willing to be real and authentic with your struggles or failures with them, regardless of how they will respond...or not?
- Who do you have in your life that you can trust to respond in grace and truth when you talk to them about these kinds of things?

CHAPTER TWO

GRENADE!

I had everything.

No, really – I did. I had the American dream. I had the wife, the kids, the house, the cars, the job, the income, the friends, the health, the good looks, the college education. I HAD it. And then one day I set off the grenade that blew it all to hell.

I had just walked out of a two-hour meeting with my wife. Her best friend and my best friend were also in attendance for emotional support. After 22 years of marriage, I had just confessed to them all that I had been living a secret life that included a long-term addiction to pornography which had led to unfaithfulness along with the serious abuse of alcohol and prescription drugs. I had outlined every sordid detail of my addictions that I could remember since I was in high school. It was in a word; brutal.

My wife was devastated. It was literally as if I had pulled the pin on a grenade and blown up all of our lives.

I had been lying to my wife, my friends, my family and hiding my behaviors from everyone since I was in college. *I was so ashamed of my secret addictions and behaviors that I couldn't bear to tell anyone.* Over the years, there were brief instances when I had been partially truthful to my brother or to my roommates in college or maybe to a close friend or a pastor...but I was NEVER completely transparent. It was just way too unbearable. I had made a vow to myself that there were simply things I had done in my life that NO ONE would ever know, things I would take to the grave. It felt like, if I told someone, anyone what I had done, what I was STILL struggling with...I would die.

...if I told someone, anyone what I had done, what I was STILL struggling with...I would die.

REWIND TO ABOUT A WEEK PRIOR to this meeting when I confessed to my wife. I had just returned from, of all places, a weekend missions trip with some guys from my church. While I was away, my wife had found evidence of pornography on my iPad. When I returned, she gave me an opportunity to confess, but I couldn't. I lied. I denied it. I minimized it. She called me on it and showed me the proof. There was no getting out of it. But what she had found was only the tip of a very large, very old iceberg. She didn't know the half of what was REALLY going on in my life.

She knew I had struggled with pornography because we had had this conversation before, but this time she found more - things to make her believe my problem may be bigger than just pornography...and it was. This time she asked me point blank, *"You haven't actually ever gone further than pornography and been with someone else, have you?"* I remember thinking to myself, "This is it, man. You can't keep lying. You have to tell her the truth. It's OVER." My pornography addiction had escalated over the years to the point that I had actually physically been with other women multiple times.

Time stood still and it felt like all of the air got sucked out of the room. I hung my head, nodded and said, "yes."

She ran out of the house in tears. I packed a bag and drove to the mountains with a six pack of beer and a bottle of vodka.

She ran out of the house. I packed a bag and drove to the mountains with a six pack of beer and a bottle of vodka.

I didn't know if I would ever come back. As far as I was concerned, the previous life as I had known it – the one with the wife and the four beautiful daughters and the good job and the income and the house and the friends – that life was OVER. I was headed straight into a new life of misery, drunkenness, debauchery, pain, sorrow and regret that surely would eventually end in death. While my wife still didn't know the details, she knew there was more to be revealed. The pin was now out of the grenade and I was holding the lever closed...at least for the meantime.

I spent the next several days in a haze of alcohol and prescription drugs and a trip to a strip club. I needed to escape myself, but I couldn't. I tried to medicate the deep, spiritual pain I was experiencing with every vice I could conjure, but none of them worked anymore. I went completely off the grid. My phone was blowing up, my voicemail was full. My wife, my friends, my brother, my parents, my employer – they were all calling me, texting me. I didn't answer any of them...for days. My wife was sure I was on my way somewhere to commit suicide. Everyone was rightfully scared for my life. And so was I.

After the third or fourth day holed up in a ratty hotel room up in the mountains, I had an epiphany...

"Why don't you just tell the truth?"

Huh? Sad to say, but this is NOT something I had realistically considered until then. At this point, what did I have to lose? My wife had already seen the tip of the iceberg. Is it possible that by telling the truth, doing the very thing I felt would KILL me that I might actually regain my life in some manner? Is it possible I could set off a grenade in my life and survive? Is it possible that by telling the truth...doing the very thing I felt would KILL me...that I might actually regain my life?

I remember this clearly: I'm sitting alone in my silver GMC Yukon on a gravel lot up in the mountains. I've already downed a full six pack of beer. I've got a bottle of vodka sitting between my legs. My cell phone is vibrating wildly in the cup holder – text messages from my wife, my friends, my parents, my brother. No one knows where I am. I'm contemplating what it would be like to die. I wasn't planning to kill myself, but I WAS considering what it would be like to be dead. I just wanted the emotional and spiritual pain I was feeling to STOP. I had never thought or felt like this before. It was the very darkest moment of my life.

That's when I heard the whisper.

Now, I have had experiences with God before, mind you. As deep into sin as I had been most of my life, I still knew what God's voice sounded like when I heard it. I knew what his presence felt like when he showed up. I had been a "Christian" since I was 17. But I had never heard God's voice *like this*. It was not an audible voice, but it was still as clear as a bell to me. The still, small voice inside said...

"Tony, you have a choice to make."

I knew what He was talking about. He was saying that it was time for me to choose between a life of sin, darkness, alcohol, sex, pornography – pursuing my own selfish, evil desires (READ: IDOLS) or...I had to choose God. It was that simple. I nodded my head in agreement. I understood completely. I couldn't speak. Snot and tears dripped from my face.

"If you choose me, I will give you life. If you don't, you are going to die."

I knew He was right. I KNEW that if I kept on pursuing my own selfish desires that it would end up killing me. I was out of control. I would end up getting in a car wreck, a bar fight, dying drunk in a gutter somewhere, having a heart attack or worse...committing suicide. If I chose wrongly, I was going to die, no doubt. I knew this to be true. This was a literal crossroads for me.

I yelled back to the whisper and said, out loud, "I don't want to die! But Lord, I don't know how to tell the truth! That's what will kill me! I'm afraid I'll die if I tell the truth!"

But Lord, I don't know how to tell the truth!

I sobbed the deepest sobs I had ever sobbed. What was I going to do? I didn't want to die in a life of sin and drunkenness, to leave my wife and my kids, my parents and friends...but I didn't have the courage to tell the truth either. There was NO WAY I could let anyone know how bad off I really was, how BAD I had really been. I was WAY TOO ASHAMED to tell the truth. I took a long pull on the bottle of vodka and it burned all the way down. I had no idea how to be truthful and at that moment, I thought I was now condemned to a very brief life of lying and deceiving others about who I really was.

"Follow me and I will give you the courage you need to tell the truth."

Wait, what? Did I hear that right? The voice whispered again...

"Follow me and I will give you the courage you need to tell the truth."

Something changed in me at that moment. This was my moment of clarity. This was the voice of my God. I KNEW I could trust this voice. This was the voice of Jesus. I made up my mind right then and there to tell the truth and to trust God with the consequences.

I drove back to my hotel room and opened up my laptop and I started writing what I called my "manifesto." I made up my mind to tell the truth and I trusted Jesus that he would give me the courage and the strength to do it. I took him at his word. I spent the rest of that evening writing out every sordid detail of my hidden, sinful addictions as far back as I could remember. I would find out later that what I was actually doing was my own, unguided attempt at one of the steps of addiction recovery - *STEP 4: a searching and fearless moral inventory.* I stayed up well past 2 a.m. working on the "manifesto".

The next day after I had sobered up a bit, I called a close friend – someone I had been "partially" transparent with over the years and I said, "I'm in trouble. I need you to get some guys together as soon as possible. I am deep into sin and I need to talk to some guys and confess it." He understood completely as he had been in a similar place in his own life in the past. This is how recovery works – one broken person helping another. Within the next hour he had assembled a group of five of our friends including himself and set a meeting for the next day. I called my wife and told her…

"Tomorrow, I'm meeting with some of my friends. I'm going to tell them the truth about what has been going on with me. I'm going to tell them everything. After that, I'd like to meet with you to tell you the same things. You deserve to know."

She said she wanted to meet, but she didn't think she would be ready to face me tomorrow. She was already hurting and scared and she knew I was going to drop a bomb – or bombs. She told me she wanted to schedule it for the following day and that she wanted a friend to sit in with her *(not only to offer her emotional support, but more so to be a voice of reason to her in case she tried to kill me!)*. I told her I thought that was a good idea and that I would like to have a friend there with me also.

I met with my friends the next day and read my "manifesto" to them, word for word. It included all of the deepest, darkest secrets I had held since I was a young boy up to the present time… every rebellious sin, every despicable act, every moral failure. I shared with these men all the secrets that I had sworn to myself I would take to the grave. I told them everything. They patiently listened…and then offered me grace, forgiveness and wise counsel. I also realized later that this was a form of the FIFTH STEP of recovery - *STEP 5:* **"Admitted to God, to ourselves, and to another human being the exact nature of our wrongs."** These guys did not minimize my sin, but acknowledged it for what it was, and they did not shame me.

The next day, I met with my wife and her closest friend, and my best friend also sat in for emotional support. These are the first words I spoke at the start of that meeting...

"Celeste, I love you and I am so very, very sorry. I expect that you will want to divorce me. You have every right to. I have broken my vow to you. I have failed you and our four beautiful daughters. I have betrayed your trust and lied to you many, many times ever since we've dated. You deserve SO MUCH MORE, SO MUCH BETTER. Please do not wear my failure as your own. This IS NOT ABOUT YOU. This has NOTHING to do with your value. This is about me and about how I view myself. This is about MY failure, MY bad decisions and MY sin. This is NOT about you or our family. You are a warrior princess in every sense and I do not deserve to even KNOW someone as beautiful, devoted, strong and faithful as you. You deserve a man that will honor all of your beautiful, godly qualities and treat you with the love of Christ.

The things I am about to reveal to you I am ashamed of. I am grieved almost to the point of death by them. John 10:10 says "the enemy comes to steal, kill and destroy." He has achieved this mission in my life. He has stolen my joy, killed my integrity and destroyed my confidence and relationships. He has reduced me to a heap of flesh.

I have lied about these things for most of my life, but here is the complete, ugly truth."

After that, I spent the next two hours telling my wife and our two friends, in detail, about my long-hidden, fierce addictions and abuse of pornography, sex, pills and alcohol, about my infidelity and everything I had told the men I had met with the previous day. We all cried many tears over those two hours. When we finished, I fully expected my wife to tell me she wanted a divorce. I would also find out later that what I was doing in this meeting is the *5th STEP of recovery: We admitted to God, to ourselves, and to another human being the exact nature of our wrongs.*

As far as I was concerned, I had pulled the pin on the grenade and it had exploded, destroying my marriage, my family, my friendships, my career, my health, my finances…my very heart and soul. Darkness set in.

As I drove away from that meeting, headed back up to the mountains to the hotel room I was staying in, my wife sent me a text. It read this:

"I have never been more proud of you as a man than I am today. Thank you for having the courage to give me the truth."

"I have never been more proud of you as a man than I am today. Thank you for having the courage to give me the truth."

While I knew I still had a very long, painful road ahead of me and I had no idea what it would look like (divorce was still a very real possibility), I immediately understood Jesus' words to me a few days before when he told me, *"Follow me and I will give you the courage you need to tell the truth."*

Indeed he had.

I was starting to realize that God was bigger than my marriage and my own petty life strategies. God would show up in a powerful way once again after this meeting as I was driving the dark, winding mountain road back to the hotel where I was staying. This time he would speak words that would change me at the very core of my being and set the course of my life off into a completely new direction.

BULLETPROOF GLASS CHALLENGE:
Honest IN (Being authentic with myself, self-assess) –
- How does this story about confessing hidden, secret sins make you feel and why?
- Do you have any secret behaviors that you feel shame about?

Honest UP (Being authentic with God, pray, confess) –
- If God were to speak to you today about your own secret behaviors, what would He say?
- Do you have any secret behaviors, thoughts or fantasies that you need to confess as sin to the Lord?

Honest OUT (Being authentic with others, share, discuss) –
- What things do you need to discuss with a trusted friend or with your Bulletproof brothers?
- WILLINGNESS CHECK: Are you truly willing to listen and consider how they will respond…or not?
- Are you afraid you would be rejected or treated differently if your trusted friends or close family knew about these behaviors?

CHAPTER THREE

BROKEN TO BULLETPROOF

I had just confessed years of hidden, secret, sinful behavior, including a fierce pornography and sex addiction as well as secret alcohol and prescription pill abuse. It was like detonating a grenade in the middle of my life. My marriage of 22 years was now in serious jeopardy. I was ashamed of myself in every way possible. My heart was riddled with the bullet holes of fear, shame, guilt, regret, disappointment, disloyalty, deceit, addiction and a host of other spiritual wounds.

"...in addition to all, taking up the shield of faith with which you will be able to extinguish all the flaming arrows of the evil one."
- Ephesians 6:16

To me, I equated the "flaming arrows of the evil one" to BULLETS and I felt spiritually like I had been living under enemy fire for years...and years. My soul was riddled with the bullet holes of shame, fear, anger and resentment.

Doubt set in. While I knew I was acting in obedience to the words I heard from God, I was feeling like I had made a terrible mistake as I drove back up the dark, winding mountain road to the hotel where I was staying. I knew I had now set in motion something that could not be reversed and I had no idea what it meant for my life going forward. I had an empty pit in my stomach and I was scared.

It was difficult navigating the road at night, trying to see through teary, swollen eyes...my head pounding from crying so hard with my wife over the last several hours. I knew I had crushed her heart, shattered all her dreams and there was nothing I could do about it. I wanted to drink so badly, but drinking was part of what had gotten me in the mess I was in now. I pounded on the steering wheel and tried to keep my SUV between the lines. What had I just done? I felt even more alone and desperate than I ever had before.

I cried out to God...

"Jesus! What am I going to do now? I just crushed my wife's heart! She is going to divorce me! I don't know how to live life without her! Without my kids! Please help me!"

Now, I don't want to sound wacky here and I don't want to give the impression that this is an everyday occurrence for me by any means. I said earlier that I'm familiar with being in the presence of God. I've experienced him before, so I know what it's like. But this was something all together different, even different than just a couple of days before when I had heard God's voice. This was a rare, personal encounter with the God of the universe. At what was now my very lowest moment, it seemed as if He invaded the cabin of my SUV and I became suddenly aware that He was there, whispering a message that cut through the darkness...

"You are now like a clear sheet of glass."

A clear sheet of glass? My life had been so dark, so full of lies and deceit. I had worn a mask for most of my life, pretending to be someone and something I was not. It was as if my confession had wiped that slate clean, but I still didn't like it. I yelled back at God...

"I don't want to be a sheet of glass! Glass breaks! I'm tired of being broken, Lord! I don't want to break anymore!"

I pounded on the steering wheel and screamed out loud and I meant it. I was broken beyond repair and had no interest in ever experiencing that kind of pain again. I thought about drinking...that would stop this pain. If EVER I needed a drink, it was right now.

That's when He whispered again...

"As long as you keep telling the truth, you will be a clear sheet of BULLETPROOF GLASS."

Bulletproof glass. Now that's an entirely different deal. That was good. I loved it. It's unbreakable; a symbol I could hang onto. It is a symbol of strength and protection. It's transparent so that light *shines through it.* Nothing is hidden, but all is safe behind bulletproof glass. It is like armor of light for my heart, my soul.

A verse came to mind...

"The night is nearly over; the day is almost here. So let us put aside the deeds of darkness and put on the armor of light."
- Romans 13:12

Hope.
This imagery from God gave me hope in a desperate time of hopelessness. The thought that God would use my vulnerability to create a shield of transparent protection from the spiritual and emotional pain I was suffering gave me tremendous hope. Just tell the truth and I am safe. Beautiful.

I knew my life was set on a new course now and, even though I had no idea where it would take me, this idea of living my life with transparency, authenticity...this was an exciting new proposition. Suddenly, long-forgotten verses from the Bible came flooding to mind with new meaning...

> *"To gain your life, you must lose it."*
> *"All things are possible with God."*
> *"My power is made perfect in your weakness."*

This exchange gave me courage to *accept and embrace* my brokenness. I made the rest of the trip up the mountain with a new-found hope and a heart so grateful it overcame the fear that had engulfed me. The desires to drink and medicate the pain of my shame and fear faded away - those bullets couldn't penetrate now. I felt a shield around my heart that was impenetrable so that I didn't have to lie to protect it any longer. It was a new beginning with a new way to live life - a path away from the pain of brokenness and heartbreak into a new life of transparency behind a clear sheet of bulletproof glass; from Broken...to Bulletproof.

BULLETPROOF GLASS CHALLENGE:
Honest IN (Being authentic with myself, self-assess) –
- How does the concept of living like a "clear sheet of bulletproof glass" make you feel and why?
- What spiritual wounds are you carrying from your past because of things you've done or things that have been done to you or happened to you?

Honest UP (Being authentic with God, pray, confess) –
- If you told God how you are feeling about these wounds, what would He have to say in response?
- Is there sin you need to confess in relation to these wounds that might be the first step in healing from them?

Honest OUT (Being authentic with others, share, discuss) –
- WILLINGNESS CHECK: Are you truly *willing* to discuss these wounds with a trusted friend? Why or why not?
- In what ways do you need to be "transparent" like a "clear sheet of bulletproof glass" with your friends and family that love you the most?

CHAPTER FOUR

THE SECRETS

Shame is the San Quentin for your heart - a prison where a man's heart will probably rot and die. This prison's cell guard is the foul spirit from Hell that says, *"You're not good enough"* or *"Who do you think you are?"* It whispers accusations of *insignificance, incompetence and impotence.* Shame is an epidemic in our culture.

Shame is a misplaced focus on self. It's different from guilt, which is a focus on behavior. Guilt says, *"I did something bad. I'm sorry I made a mistake."* Shame says *"I did something bad. I <u>AM</u> bad."* For men, the message from shame is *"Don't be perceived as weak. You don't need to ask for help."* That's the message of impotence. Sadly, in our culture today, most men would rather stuff their emotions and true feelings at the cost of their own personal serenity than fall on their own swords by *being vulnerable, open and honest* in front of their woman - it's too painful. When men reach out and are vulnerable to their woman, they typically get the crap beat out of them. Being truly vulnerable with a woman can be frightening, brutal work.

But that doesn't absolve men of the responsibility to be vulnerable. We are called by Jesus to "lay down our lives," and to "carry our cross." There is no exception that says "unless you're wife is going to be pissed and yell at you." Here's the truth, men: vulnerability is not weakness, it is *spiritual courage.* So much of what I've learned about shame and vulnerability comes from the work of best-selling author Brene' Brown. She is a PhD and calls herself a "shame and vulnerability researcher and story-teller." She is the author of several best-sellers including my favorite, *Daring Greatly* and most recently, *Rising Strong.* Her Ted talk entitled *"The*

Power of Vulnerability"* has racked up over 24 million views as of the time of this writing *(you can view it on the media page of my website, www.brokentobulletproof.com)*. Here's Brown's take on vulnerability: Vulnerability is the ANTIDOTE to shame.

Vulnerability is the ANTIDOTE to shame

Shame was a MASSIVE part of my own personal "brokenness." Much, if not most of my healing has come through learning to withstand shame, to live transparently as behind that protective sheet of bulletproof glass I discussed in the previous chapter. Seriously working through the 12-steps of recovery with a friend to guide me helped me to learn how to be vulnerable and develop "shame resilience."

My wife is such a strong woman, a Godly woman. She does NOT back down from a fight - spiritually and emotionally speaking. This is one of the things I love most about her and that attracted me to her in the beginning. In her own vulnerable moments, she'll confess that one of her core struggles is with anger. Before we were married, going through pre-marital counseling, she revealed to me that her greatest fear was that her husband would someday cheat on her (which would only serve to validate the lie the enemy had whispered to her since childhood - *"you're not beautiful enough"* - the message of *insignificance*). This is why I HID the fact that I was already struggling with pornography before we got married - because of SHAME. I lacked the spiritual courage to tell her for fear of losing the relationship because of how I expected her to react.

Brene' Brown defines shame as *"the fear of disconnection."* Shame says, "If you truly knew me the way I am, you won't accept me. You will reject me." Couple that with shame's two allies, DECEIT and FEAR and you have a deadly recipe for A SECRET. I believed the lie (deceit) that my wife wouldn't love me if she knew of my pornography and sex addiction. I hid my behavior from her (deceit) because I was afraid (fear) that she would leave me if she knew. This is shame. This is why I hid my addiction for so many years - from almost EVERYONE. Shame is a powerful motivator for hiding and lying – a LACK of transparency. It is at the root of addictive behavior and it encourages us to wear a mask, to present a false-self to the world instead of our TRUE selves.

Recently, I read a news article about an adult cheating website being hacked and having all of the private information of its users stolen. Their tag line read, *"Life's short. Have an affair."* This hack not only included names, addresses and credit card information with which the hackers threatened to use to expose the website's clients, but also the secret sexual fantasies and fetishes of its clients. A company like this one leverages the power of shame to make a profit – its message is "have an affair, don't tell anyone and we won't either. We'll *protect you* from shame and allow you to carry out your own evil desires." This website encourages the "deceit" of presenting a false-self, hiding what is really going on. The hackers have threatened to expose this lie under the threat of shame by revealing a list of the website's users to the public. Shame is crouching at the door for every client of this company. I read another story a few weeks later about the president of a Christian university whose name was on that list and he was exposed. He had a loving wife, beautiful and successful adult children, friends and colleagues that respected him…and when he found out he had been exposed, he committed suicide. The adult cheating website company didn't kill this man. The hackers didn't kill him. SHAME killed him. Ironic that the website's home page features an image of a woman with her index finger over her pursed lips - the image of "keeping a secret."

Over our first 22 years of marriage, my own personal struggle with pornography progressed and developed into deeper, darker sin and I hid it from everyone. Sometime around our third year of marriage, I was already compromising my principles and acting out sexually – the details are not important, but at this point I was definitely being disobedient to God and behaving in ways that were severely damaging my marriage even though my wife was completely unaware. I hid these experiences, not only from my wife, but from my closest friends as well, for the most part. About the only one that knew about any of it was my brother. Even though I felt like I could tell him anything (and still do), I didn't want to because I didn't want to smash his perception of me as his older brother to whom he looked up to.

Here's another lie that most men believe when we're wading into these waters – "I'm not hurting anyone so this is ok." Men are so good at compartmentalizing this stuff that we actually believe our own bullshit most of the time. To me, when I made my marriage vows, I didn't fully understand the spiritual commitment I was making – keeping my vow to my wife simply meant keeping my pecker in my pants as far as I was concerned. At the time I believed that, as long as I didn't cross THAT line and PHYSICALLY enter in with another woman, I was keeping my vow. Not so. The reality is, the TRUTH is, every time I viewed pornography and/or acted out somehow sexually I was being DISLOYAL in my heart to my wife and violating my marriage vows. Jesus KNEW men were like this. That's why he tells us in scripture...

> *"But I tell you that anyone who looks at a woman lustfully has already committed adultery with her in his heart."*
>
> *- Matthew 5:28*

Adultery is a heart issue. The actual breaking of trust happens far before a man is ever with another woman physically. Even though I had convinced myself that I wasn't really hurting anyone, I was. I was hurting my wife, my marriage, my kids, myself...not to mention any other woman I may have acted out with. This progressive behavior was crushing my intimacy with my wife – spiritually AND physically. I was trapped in a hellish prison of shame. None of my friends knew. I was masterful at presenting myself behind a mask of "I've got it all together" to my co-workers, friends, family and my wife. I did this for years, living a double-life, masquerading as a successful, Christian man, loving husband, spiritual leader, godly friend, worship and bible study leader at church and dedicated father. *It was all a complete lie.* I HATED what I was doing and I HATED who I was. The prison door of shame was closed and locked and the lights were turned out. While I may have been presenting something acceptable on the outside, in my heart, darkness was setting in – the solitary confinement of my soul.

I remember a time when my brother and I were away on a weekend fishing trip (which usually involved as much or more drinking as it did fishing). This was a few years before I confessed to my wife and the guilt was weighing heavy on me. I was drinking alcoholically to numb the shame, I was taking pills, I was addicted to porn and acting out sexually, hiding and lying to everyone. I was desperate for a way out. Maybe, just maybe, God would give me a chance, the courage to tell him while we were on our trip and that would alleviate the pressure enough for me to live, to move forward. Maybe that's what I needed to help me stop. I hoped and prayed for the right time that I might have the courage to tell him and possibly relieve the shame.

The moment came while we were walking through a field, from the river in which we had been fishing, back to the car. I said, "I've got something I need to confess. Something that needs to go in the lock box." He said, no problem and was ready to listen. We sometimes asked each other to put things in the "lock box" - that was code for "this secret is so nasty, you can NEVER betray me by telling anyone about it." It was our brotherhood covenant of trust. "I've been doing things I shouldn't be doing. It's been going on for a long time. I've crossed lines I should not have crossed. I feel awful, but I don't think I can stop." I told him most all of the details *trying to dump shame.*

My brother loves me. I know he would never intentionally do anything to hurt me. But he has his own struggles and "shame filter" that everything gets sifted through in his own head and heart. I think he put himself in my shoes and thought through what my predicament might look like if he were me.

He told me, "You know you can NEVER tell your wife that, right? She'll leave you."

There was this moment of sobering silence as I let that concept sink in. "Yeah. I know."

"OK. You've confessed it. God forgives you. I forgive you. Stop doing it and move on."

This is the message of shame. "Keep it a secret. Don't talk about it. Don't tell anyone. When you feel it, just stuff it down there in one of those deep, dark crevices of your heart and keep on acting like you have it all together. Be an imposter. Wear a mask. Put on a show and just SOLDIER ON." At the time, it's probably the exact same thing I would have said to *him* if he had told me HE had been doing those things. Today, knowing what I know and having been through what I've been through, I would tell him something completely different. I NEEDED him to tell me something completely different.

I NEEDED him to tell me something completely different.

This is where men need God's courage, strength, wisdom and hope when speaking with each other. Courage is what is needed to tell a brother you love THE TRUTH. Don't get me wrong - I'm not faulting my bro. He was there for me, he listened, had empathy, forgave me and accepted me in spite of my sin. He'll always do that because I know he loves me and he is still one of my best friends in the world. But I needed something more from him at this moment. I needed him to have the courage to tell me something maybe more like this...

"Brother, I'm not the one you sinned against. You need to consider what it would look like to confess to your wife. She is the one you need to ask for forgiveness. And then you need to get some help if you really can't break the cycle. I'll walk with you through the whole thing. God is bigger than this. He's bigger than your sin, your failure, your marriage. He loves you and He will never leave you. Put your trust in Him and ask Him what He wants you to do in this – REGARDLESS OF WHAT YOU THINK THE OUTCOME WILL BE."

I ended up keeping those secrets for several more years after this conversation took place, still in that prison of shame. A couple of years later, I went on a solo backpacking trip into the High Sierras to camp and fish...and drink, alone. I needed to get away from myself (which is impossible, I know) and just numb the incessant lashing of shame that I was imposing on myself in these addictions. I drank heavily after I got my tent and campsite set up next to the river. Then I passed out in my sleeping bag - oblivion. I woke up about 2:30 or 3:00 in the morning and heard this...one word:

DISLOYAL.

I knew what that meant immediately. I was being completely disloyal to my beautiful bride, to myself and to God. While I thought I was loving her as best I could in spite of my terrible spiritual sickness, the fact was, I was being disloyal and had been in my heart for years.

God's word leads me to believe that shame is *rooted* in disloyalty. The NIV translates the idea of disloyalty as someone that is *"treacherous."* Here's the definition of treacherous:

treach·er·ous ˈtreCH(ə)rəs/ adjective *"Guilty of or involving betrayal or deception. Synonyms: traitorous, disloyal, faithless, unfaithful, duplicitous, deceitful, deceptive, false, double crossing, double-dealing, two-faced, Janus-faced, weaselly, untrustworthy."*

Here's what God's word says about the link between shame and the treacherous...

"No one who hopes in you will ever be put to shame, but shame will come on those who are treacherous without cause."
                                                            - Psalm 25:3

God was telling me that my shame was rooted in my *disloyalty (read: treachery).* I was not putting my hope in God, but in my own power and resources. I had been trying to solve my spiritual problem on my own, the way *I wanted* with NO REGARD to what it was doing to my wife or our marriage. This word – "DISLOYAL" - echoed in my head and heart for many more weeks - God repeating this word of conviction over and over until I was finally exposed several months later. My wife found pornography on my iPad for the third or fourth time and I was just exhausted from fighting, evading, striving, hiding, lying…but I didn't have the courage to come clean right then and there. So I ran…one last-ditch effort to solve my spiritual problem on my own…for a few days at least.

Here's the thing about Jesus. He loves us WAY TOO MUCH to allow us to run very far. He understands addiction, shame, idolatry, disloyalty – it's not the first time someone was disloyal to Him (READ: the apostle Peter, Judas). I couldn't run for long until he caught me. I finally responded to the awful situation I had created for myself by confessing everything to several other godly men and then to my wife. Vulnerability - this is the tool Jesus used to finally set me free. It was like a hack saw He threw in through the iron bars of the spiritual jail cell in which I was held captive.

> *"Therefore confess your sins to each other and pray for each other so that you may be healed. The prayer of a righteous person is powerful and effective."*   - James 5:16

Shame HATES that verse, because the verse is true. It opens prison doors. It frees captive hearts and sets broken men like me on a path of recovery and redemption. What I found out by confessing, by telling the truth, was that I had been LIED to. Shame had told me something totally false. My wife DID NOT leave - she chose to stay and fight...for us. My friends did NOT reject me – they reached out in love to me and helped me walk through many dark days of recovery. I know things could have turned out differently. I could have confessed to my friends and to my wife. They could have turned their backs on me and she could have still left me. Either way, in order to move towards the TRUE man God had created, I had to come clean...regardless of the outcome.

  God is a God of *rescue*. I said this in the introduction, that I was a *captive* that had been *rescued*. God sent His son, Jesus, to set captives, like me, *free*. He knows we cannot fulfill His purposes for us while we are being held captive.

  "I will go before you and level the exalted places, I will break in pieces the doors of bronze and cut through the bars of iron, I will give you the treasures of darkness and the hoards in secret places, that you may know that it is I, the Lord, the God of Israel, who call you by your name."

               - Isaiah 45:2-3

  I love this picture of a relentless rescuer, kicking in doors and cutting through steel to *save me*. But still, I had my own work to do. God opened the prison doors, but I had to get up and run out. That meant I had to do MY PART by being vulnerable and by having the *willingness* to do whatever it took to get well. I DO know one thing for sure though: if I HADN'T confessed, eventually my wife would have left anyway...and rightfully so.

  But that's not what God had planned for me. Jesus wanted me to fight. Was I in or out? Was I willing to use the new spiritual tools he had provided? Was I willing to carry my cross into something that seemed like DEATH to me? Was I willing to trust

HIM over everything else? Was I willing to trust HIM even if it meant that she divorced me? Was I willing to fight for her, for us, for our kids? Did I REALLY TRUST JESUS that if I GAVE UP MY LIFE, he would give it back to me?

"For whoever wishes to save his life will lose it; but whoever loses his life for my sake will find it." - Matthew 16:25

I remember reaching a point where in my heart I was able to say without doubt, *"YES. I'm in, Lord. Let's do this. It feels like this is going to kill me. I trust that if it does, you will raise me from the dead."*
Once I made that decision and started walking forward into it by confessing to my wife and my friends, that's when I heard a new sound. It drowned out the incessant droning of the convicting word, "DISLOYAL," I had been hearing for so long. It was the sound of doors being kicked in and iron bars breaking. The prison guard was gone. The sunlight was shining. Life started getting better. My wife chose to stay with me and our marriage got STRONGER. The power of every long-held secret withered in the blazing light of truth. My heart was filled with courage, strength, peace and serenity and the excitement of an amazing new life and journey ahead.

BULLETPROOF GLASS CHALLENGE:
Honest IN (Being authentic with myself, self-assess) –
- How does this discussion on secrets make you feel and why?
- Do you have any sexual secrets that are making you DISLOYAL to your wife or to God?

Honest UP (Being authentic with God, pray, confess) –
- In regards to your sexual behavior and thoughts, are you putting YOUR will before God's will? If so, how?
- Do you have any sexual behaviors, thoughts or fantasies you need to confess as sin to the Lord?

Honest OUT (Being authentic with others, share, discuss) –
- What things do you need to share or discuss with your trusted friends?
- WILLINGNESS CHECK: Are you truly willing to listen and consider how you expect they will respond…or not?
- Are you able to be courageous in responding to one of your trusted friends and lovingly tell him Godly truth if he were to confess sexual sin to you?

CHAPTER FIVE

WORTHSHIP

The police interrupted my idol worship ceremony one night. I was face down, prostrate in a pool of blood, paying homage to the god of my life and they came to stop me. How dare they?!!

I gave my life to Jesus in 1982. From then on, I called myself a "Christian." Jesus was my Savior, my Higher Power. While I may have called myself by Jesus' name, I resisted being His disciple.

In the meetings of Alcoholics Anonymous, recovering alcoholics are encouraged to find a "god of your own understanding." This leads people to believe that there are MANY gods to choose from, MANY "higher powers," if you will. While so much of the text of the Big Book of *"Alcoholics Anonymous"* is based on biblical scripture (without actual reference to it in most cases), the concept of God has been diluted with this notion that there are many "higher powers." The apostle Paul confirms that men will consider other gods than the one true creator, our Father in heaven, when he says...

"For even if there are so-called gods, whether in heaven or on earth (as indeed there are many "gods" and many "lords"), yet for us there is but one God, the Father, from whom all things came and for whom we live; and there is but one Lord, Jesus Christ, through whom all things came and through whom we live," (1 Cor. 8:5-6, NIV).

This tendency of man contradicts the real heart of God, the Father and his Son, which is for man to worship Him exclusively...

"You shall have no other Gods before me." - Exodus 20:3

and...

"I am the Way, the Truth, and the Life. No man comes to the Father but by me." (Jesus speaking, John 14:6)

God is very clear in scripture that He is the one, true God and that we are to worship Him and Him alone. He is the one, true HIGHEST power.

But then again, the statement that God makes in the Ten Commandments, "You shall have no other Gods before me, seems to assume that there are, in fact, other gods...right?

Indeed, there are.

While I thought I was calling Jesus my Lord and I was committed to worshipping him alone, the TRUTH was that I had MANY other gods in my life that I worshipped, many other higher powers. These were the things or behaviors that I would turn to in search of true *life*. In fact, I had a veritable menu of gods that I would choose from at any given time. As I began to recover from multiple addictions, becoming more and more self-aware, I started understanding that much of my illness was spiritual. When I experienced emotional or spiritual pain in my addictions, I reached for other things to appease this pain.

I read an article once that was discussing what idolatry looks like in the 21st century. The question was posed, "How do you know if you have an idol in your life?" The writer responded with this answer: *"If your doctor told you that you must give up or do without a certain thing or behavior for a month or you would die and it would cause you to immediately experience a sense of panic...that thing or behavior is probably an idol."* When I read that,

I was convicted about several things in my life that I could say that were true about - alcohol, pills, pornography, sex, sugar, my smart phone, etc. I eventually came to understand that I had allowed these things to, in fact, become idols...other gods in my life.

When I began to understand what the concept of "idolatry" might look like in my own life, for some reason I was compelled to look up the word "worship." I had been a "worship" leader and I truly enjoyed worshipping God. I was worried that if I really had idols in my life, what if I had been unknowingly *"worshipping"* them in some way? What does the word "worship" REALLY mean? I thought worship was what we did when we sang songs to God in church or when we knelt down in prayer, right? What I found was something quite different.

The word "worship" is actually derived from an old English word, "worth-ship" or in its original form "worthscipe," which means "to ascribe value or worth to something"...

Origin: ...before 900 AD; (noun) Middle English wors (c) hipe, worthssipe, Old English worthscipe, variant of weorthscipe; see worth-ship; (v.) Middle English, derivative of the noun **Worship** *is an act of religious devotion usually directed towards a deity. The word is derived from the Old English worthscipe, meaning worthiness or worth-ship—to give, at its simplest, worth to something.*

Evelyn Underhill (1946) defines worship thus: "The absolute acknowledgment of all that lies beyond us—the glory that fills heaven and earth. It is the response that conscious beings make to their Creator, to the Eternal Reality from which they came forth; to God, however they may think of Him or recognize Him, and whether He be realized through religion, through nature, through history, through science, art, or human life and character." Worship asserts the reality of its object and defines its meaning by reference to it.[2]

Let me repeat that: *Worship asserts the reality of its object and defines its meaning by reference to it.* In layman's terms, that means if I am referring to a physical or non-physical object through my behavior or contemplation (thought, meditation, fantasy), in the strictest form of this definition, I am asserting that it is, in fact, a real object - *a god.* If I am referring to that object in a disproportionate manner (drinking alcohol daily as a way to relieve spiritual pain), my actions are *defining it's meaning* to me in my life - that I've allowed it to become so important that I would rely on it for this purpose even before I would rely on my true Creator. This, at its base level is an example of idol "worship," putting another god before the one true God - our Father in heaven.

Now, if I am properly "worshipping" God, who is spirit, then my act of worship is definitely a "spiritual" act. This kind of worship happens inside me, in my heart through my desires and emotions and in my mind through my thoughts FIRST. We may respond to what we are experiencing in our hearts and minds through a physical act such as raising our hands, bending our knee, bowing our head, taking communion, giving an offering of money - of course worship has a physical component. But God wants ALL of these elements combined in our worship. He created us as WHOLE people - body, mind and spirit. He doesn't want our robotic, physical, religious actions that are divorced from our hearts and minds.

"I desire mercy, not sacrifice, and acknowledgement of God, not burnt offerings." - Hosea 6:6

Jesus told the woman at the well, "a time is coming and has now come when the true worshippers will worship the Father in the Spirit and in truth, for they are the kind of worshippers the Father seeks. God is spirit, and his worshippers must worship in the Spirit and in truth." – (John 4:23-24)   Jesus is THE authority on worship, so His thoughts are definitive. Worship is definitely a spiritual concept.

Let's take it a step further now. When I am experiencing anger, fear, worry, doubt, anxiety, shame, guilt, or any other kind of what we tend to call "emotional pain," is it not fair to say that I am disturbed in my "spirit?" These emotional feelings have a spiritual impact and are driven by spiritual forces. Conversely, if I am full of joy, love, peace, happiness, contentment, serenity, gratitude...is it just as fair to say that I am "right" in my "spirit" or that my spirit is at peace? As a matter of fact, the bible calls these kinds of positive spiritual forces the "fruit of the Spirit" (Gal. 5:22 NIV), meaning God's Holy Spirit. So when I feel these things, positive or negative, my human and natural response is to turn to my "god" with it, either in *pleading prayer* to relieve the painful, negative feeling or in *thanksgiving and praise* for the celebration of peace and joy as I *assert the reality* of this god in my life. That is how I have a relationship with God, my Higher Power. When I do this, I "assert the reality of its object and define its meaning by reference to it." In other words, I WORSHIP.

My problem was that, for most of my life, instead of turning to Jesus with those feelings, I turned to MANY other "gods." When I felt angry, fearful, worried, doubtful, anxious, ashamed, guilty...many times, even MOST times, I would turn to other "higher powers," things like alcohol, pornography, sex, drugs, food, entertainment...even GOOD things like exercise or a hobby in a disproportionate, unhealthy manner...in order to "numb" these negative feelings and emotions. In times of celebration, I might often do the exact same thing to "heighten" the feelings of joy and thankfulness by *celebrating* with alcohol or some of those other things as well. When I turn to these things to relieve pain or heighten joyful celebration, am I NOT *looking to them*, *allowing* them to have power and influence over me? Am I NOT "asserting the reality of its object and defining its meaning by reference to it?" Am I not, at its simplest, giving WORTH to these things, ascribing VALUE? This is how my delusional thinking worked...the idol factory working overtime.

"...a deluded heart misleads him; he cannot save himself, or say, 'Is not this thing in my right hand a lie?'" (Isaiah 44:20 NIV)

If I AM in fact doing what I just described, I am WORSHIPPING alcohol, pornography, sex, drugs, food, entertainment, music, fishing, exercise...etc. I am trying to solve a spiritual problem with the physical solution of a lesser god, an idol. I have become a virtual IDOL FACTORY, bowing down in worship to all of these other, lesser "gods," allowing them to have power over me INSTEAD of turning to my Creator FIRST. My experience is that this is how the enemy influences most people to create idols and take God, the Father and His Son, the Lord Jesus Christ OUT of their rightful order and authority in our lives. We ascribe a higher value to these other things than we do to God when we turn to them FIRST, before we turn to God to alleviate spiritual pain. *THIS is the essence of idolatry.*

Bowing down, putting my body in a prostrate position is an act of worship in and of itself. It is a physical acknowledgement that the one to whom I am bowing is greater than me, deserving of my respect, service and awe. It is the submission of my own will to the will of the god to whom I am bowing. It is the proper and acceptable position to be in before the God of the universe, for sure. It is putting God in the proper order in our lives, above all other gods, with no other god before Him.

"Who shapes a god and casts an idol which can profit him nothing? He and his kind will be put to shame." (Isaiah 44:10-11)

Renowned psychiatrist Jeffrey Satinover is credited with stating that *"idols ask for more and more while giving less and less until, eventually, they demand everything and give nothing."* That was certainly true of my experience with alcohol as an idol. What is so ironic and darkly humorous about my journey of recovery from alcohol is how I found my way into Alcoholics Anonymous. After a three-day binge that culminated in a mixture of anti-anxiety prescription pills and hard liquor as I tried to escape and numb my painful emotions, I found myself being scraped off the pavement by a police officer. She said someone had called 911 because they had found me lying in a pool of blood, "face down" in the middle of the street, as cars passed me by. I had, in fact, assumed an eerie position of worship to the god of alcohol and drugs. Worshipping these other gods almost killed me - literally.

Today, I am grateful, thankful that I don't have to live like that anymore. Now I get down on my knees willfully, in gratitude, thanksgiving and praise to my ULTIMATE Higher Power. Now when I experience those uncomfortable forces of shame, fear, doubt, etc. I don't turn to those lesser gods of alcohol, pills, sex, pornography or anything else. I don't turn to a physical solution to my spiritual problems. I turn to the one true, triune God - my heavenly Father, my Savior Jesus Christ and the Holy Spirit. They occupy the highest order in my life – God is my true King, Jesus is my Lord, the Prince of Peace, and the Holy Spirit their ambassador. It is here, with a properly ordered understanding of God and my relationship to Him, face down in "worth-ship," that I daily find life, joy and a peace that surpasses understanding - strength for today and bright hope for tomorrow.

BULLETPROOF GLASS CHALLENGE:
Honest IN (Being authentic with myself, self-assess) –
- Are you able to recognize when you experience powerful emotions like anger, fear, regret, resentment, confusion, disappointment? Are you able to call them for what they are and turn properly to God with them or do you have a tendency to stuff, ignore or minimize them or medicate their impact through a substance or negative behavior?
- What is one thing, that if your doctor told you that you had to stop doing for a month or you were going to die, would cause significant panic or worry? This is probably an idol in your life.

Honest UP (Being authentic with God, pray, confess) –
- Ask God to reveal any "delusion" you may have in your heart about idols in your life.
- Read all of Isaiah 44 and ask God to give you wisdom in how to apply this passage to your life.

Honest OUT (Being authentic with others, share, discuss) –
- Is there anything that God brought to mind in reading this post that you should discuss with a trusted friend and/or your "Bulletproof" brothers?

- Ask your "Bulletproof" brothers if they see something in your life that might be an idol, a god you are giving higher order to instead of God the Father.

CHAPTER SIX

VERITAS

"Veritas" – Latin for truth.

Imagine if you believed the TRUE speed limit on the road you were on was 75 mph, so you set your car to cruise at 75. That's when you see the flashing red and blue lights in your rearview mirror and you're kind of surprised. You pull over and the officer comes to your window and he's ANGRY. He informs you that the TRUE speed limit on this stretch of road is actually 25 mph – that's because you just blew through a school zone doing 75 and put the lives of lots of little kids in danger. You're not just getting a ticket – you might even be going to jail. You never saw the signs.

As much as we'd like it to be, truth is NOT subjective. It simply IS. Truth doesn't change just because we are ignorant of it or refuse to believe it. There are real and dangerous consequences to living life in conflict with the truth. Doubt me? Try speeding through a school zone and telling the officer that you THOUGHT the true speed limit was 75 and see how that works out. Wait a minute...on second thought...DON'T.

What IS truth anyway? Don't we all come to a point where we ask ourselves this question? One commentator, Matt Slick of the Christian Apologetics Research Ministry (CARM), makes a worthwhile comment regarding truth....

"If we ever hope to determine if there is such a thing as truth apart from cultural and personal preferences, we must acknowledge that we are then aiming to discover something greater than ourselves, something that transcends culture and individual

inclinations. To do this is to look beyond ourselves and outside of ourselves. In essence, it means we are looking for God. God would be truth, the absolute and true essence of being and reality who is the author of all truth. If you are interested in truth beyond yourself, then you must look to God."[3]

    The world WANTS to make truth about *"cultural and personal preferences,"* but God disagrees. HE alone is the source of truth. Read John 18:37-38. It is the short account of Pontius Pilate's private conversation with Jesus. Or even better, watch this amazing scene come to life in Mel Gibson's *The Passion of the Christ*. This is when Jesus has been brought to Pilate after he has been flogged almost to the point of death and Pilate presents the bloody, beaten Jesus to the angry mob before him, trying to dissuade them from their collective rage. But the mob is relentless and on the verge of riot, wanting Jesus' crucifixion. This is where Pilate wrestles with this very question.

    Pilate just can't come to grips with the situation he is in with this Jesus character. He has never seen anyone like this in his life. He's seen LOTS of criminals, condemned many men to their deaths. If anyone knows what a vile, guilty, despicable criminal looks like, it is Pilate. But that is not what he is seeing here with Jesus. He is hearing the shouts from the angry mob outside to "crucify him!" "Blasphemer!" The Jewish leaders are telling Pilate that Jesus is a criminal, a scoundrel, someone leading a rebellion against Caesar. But Pilate is torn, confused. He finds himself in a back room, alone with Jesus…in the presence of someone so loving, so filled with peace and righteousness that he cannot reconcile what he is seeing with what he is hearing from the angry mob. This is their conversation as recorded in the book of John:

> *"You are a king, then!" said Pilate.*
>
> *Jesus answered, "You say that I am a king. In fact, the reason I was born and came into the world is to testify to the truth (veritas). Everyone on the side of truth listens to me."*
>
> *"What is truth?" retorted Pilate. With this he went out again to the Jews gathered there and said, "I find no basis for a charge against him."*
>
> *- John 18:37-38*

Pilate was onto something, standing in the presence of the very author of truth. He knew something smelled fishy but he couldn't make sense of it. The Pharisees and the mob were trying to impose their own brand of *"personal and cultural preferences"* upon Pilate but he had no STANDARD with which to measure truth. As much as he wanted to believe Jesus, he couldn't.

Why is it that our consciences condemn us when we do something we know to be wrong? For instance, why is it that we can FEEL the spiritual force of GUILT when we lie to someone? Have you ever taken something that is not yours, maybe stolen something from a store or someone's house or locker or from your work? Cheat on a test? Do something shameful in secret? Did you not walk away with a sense of guilt, that you had TRULY done something wrong? That you had violated your TRUE self, done something that is against who you TRULY are? I have...and most of my friends and family that I speak with tell me they have felt this way as well.

Now, I recognize this is not the case with everyone in the world, but it is for the majority of people. Man has an amazing capacity to shut down his heart so that he cannot feel things like guilt, shame or conviction. There are people in the world that have truly shut their hearts off so completely that they can't feel

ANYTHING – I get that. Shutting off your heart, compartmentalizing the things that cause us pain is a tendency common to man. It's a kind of protective spiritual reflex that we develop in order to avoid pain. There is a reason for this and it is the same reason that we have an inherent sense of right and wrong. Why is this?

Because we are made in God's image.

You and I are created in the image of the ONE, TRUE GOD...in His image of TRUTH.

What comes with being made in God's image? Along with having a conscience, feelings, a heart and other important and valuable aspects of God's makeup, we were made to live in TRUTH because GOD IS TRUTH. When we live in conflict with the truth, we are living against the very nature in which we were made- THAT'S WHY IT *FEELS BAD*. It's also the reason we compartmentalize to protect our hearts.

This is the dilemma Pilate finds himself in with Jesus. He realizes he is in the presence of something bigger than himself and the decision to let the Jews crucify Jesus FEELS bad to him. He knows it is wrong...but he doesn't understand WHY. He is looking for God. Jesus knew men would ask this question - "What is truth?" This is why he said early on in his ministry, *"I am the way, the TRUTH and the life. No man comes to the Father but by me." (John 14:6)* Jesus is the truth. He and the Father are one and we are made in their image of truth.

God cannot lie. He cannot break his word. When he says something, he means it. When he makes a promise he keeps it. When he tells us something, he does not manipulate us with his words or try to deceive us in order to get us to do his will. He simply speaks...and it IS truth, forever. Because God gave us free will, he leaves it up to us to decide if we will submit to His truth in us, our "true selves," or rebel and live under our own form of subjective truth, our own *"cultural and personal preferences"*...which is a lie.

THIS is why most of us feel this sense of guilt when we lie, steal, cheat, deceive or cause hurt to someone else – because we are not being TRUE to the way we have been created. We are living out of FALSEHOOD. I believe that all men experience this in a *general* way because we are all made in God's image but we also experience it in a *unique and specific way when we live in a manner that is NOT CONGRUENT with the true man that God originally intended when He created us.* I'll unpack this idea more as we go, but for now, I think it's fair to say that when we live in a way that is diametrically opposed to the way our Creator designed us, the resulting feelings are uncomfortable in the least if not downright crushingly painful.

Living in a manner that is NOT CONGRUENT with the true man that God originally intended when He created us is uncomfortable.

Why? Why in God's great name would we do that? Why would we live in a way that is against our original design? I mean, if God is good and true and all-powerful and all knowing...why would we *want* to live like that? Why would He allow us to live like that?

Because we have been LIED to...and we have BELIEVED it!

We need to sincerely consider this: We have been lied to. We have believed this lie with our entire hearts and it has caused us to live in a way that is completely opposed to the way God designed us. We have accepted this lie as truth all the way to the core of our beings so that it has become foundational to our very lives. You and I (and ALL mankind) have a SERIOUS problem. As a matter of fact, it is THE MOST SERIOUS problem a man or woman can have. And the worst part is that there is absolutely NOTHING we can do to fix it in and of ourselves. To sum it up: WE'RE SCREWED.

Stop right there for a moment and just allow all of that to sink in because this is at the very root of almost EVERY problem we experience in life.

- *We are created in God's image*
- *We have been lied to*
- *We have believed this lie*
- *We now live our lives in falsehood BECAUSE of this lie*

OK, let's unpack these ideas a bit...

Genesis 1:27 says *"So God created man in his own image, in the image of God he created him; male and female he created them."* This means we are made in the "likeness" of God. Want to know what God is like? Don't look at the sky or the stars or the mountains or an animal - look at a man or a woman. We are the only ones made "in His image." Even better, if you REALLY want to know what God is like, look at the *perfect man* – the one without sin – God's own Son, Jesus. Jesus is our example of how to live in TRUTH, true to the way we were originally designed.

So what is the lie we have been told? Back in the Garden of Eden, Satan tells Eve, "You will not surely die. For God knows that when you eat of it, your eyes will be opened, and you will be like God, knowing good and evil." (see Genesis 3:4,5)

So here is THE GREAT LIE: "God cannot be trusted," and a second is like it, "You can be like God." Satan takes direct aim at our TWO MOST IMPORTANT RELATIONSHIPS - both our vertical relationship with God (we don't need God because he cannot be trusted) and our horizontal relationship with mankind (we don't need others, we can do this on our own because we can be like God). This is the two-part lie we have been told since the beginning of time and we have believed it, we've accepted it as truth. Satan WANTS us disconnected from God and from others.

Where is there proof that we have believed these lies? *Sin is the proof.* If we took God at his word, there would be no sin in this world. Every time a person sins, we have asserted our own will over God's, choosing our own version of the truth over the REAL truth. In effect, we make OURSELVES God each and every time we sin. We sin against God (validating the broken vertical relationship with Him) and we sin against our brothers (validating the broken horizontal relationship with mankind). The really sick part about Satan's lie is that it is tainted with just enough truth to get us to believe it. "You will be like God," he tells Eve. And in believing this lie, we assert our own wills over God's and put ourselves in his rightful place; making us in a sense "like God" just like Satan said. Insidious!

Enter Jesus in the New Testament, coming into the scene as a man on a mission to dispel these lies and to set the truth straight. He takes direct aim at this two-part lie when he responds brilliantly to the Pharisee's attempt to trap him in Matthew 22:35-39...

"One of them, an expert in the law, tested him with this question: 'Teacher, which is the greatest commandment in the Law?' Jesus replied: 'Love the Lord your God with all your heart and with all your soul and with all your mind. This is the first and greatest commandment. And the second is like it: Love your neighbor as yourself. All the Law and the Prophets hang on these two commandments.'"

Jesus WANTS man connected to God and to others. He takes apart the two-part lie Satan told Eve in the garden with a two-part quotation from scripture. He refutes the first vertical lie, "God cannot be trusted" with a validation of God's own command to Moses, "Love the Lord your God with all your heart," saying in effect, "God CAN be trusted. He is worthy of ALL our love. He desires *relationship* with us! Look UP to Him to meet your needs."

He refutes the second, horizontal lie, "You can be like God" with "Love your neighbor as yourself" saying in effect, "This isn't about living in isolation, trying to satisfy your desires on your own, by looking inward to your own power and resources. Look *outside* of yourselves to your brothers and sisters – they are your family, God's children. He wants to fulfill his desire for relationship with us THROUGH a relationship of love with each other!" When I read this, I see Jesus' response to the Pharisee's question as a restoration of these two broken relationships: "Love the Lord your God," restores the VERTICAL relationship and "Love your neighbor as yourself," restores the HORIZONTAL relationship. Beautiful, isn't it?

The result of believing this lie is that, because we don't trust God and take him at his word. Because we've learned to rely on our own power and resources, we are left with a vacuum of *desire for God.* In order to fill the vacuum of our hearts NEEDING Him, we <u>make ourselves god</u>. That's the fulfillment of Satan's lie to Eve in the Garden, "You can be like God."

We are created to live in relationship with God – this is His deepest desire; to be IN RELATIONSHIP with us. We are His children, His family. Because we are designed to have relationship with Him, when we shut Him out of our hearts and lives, we are left with an insatiable desire that nothing BUT Him can fill. Living in this conflict of needing God, but NOT having Him is *impossibly uncomfortable*. We simply can't go through life like this without consciously or unconsciously struggling to resolve the desire. This is why our lives become centered around ourselves. You've probably heard someone say, "we are born with a God-shaped hole in all of us." The rightful desire for relationship with our creator IS that hole.

In his beautiful work, *"Renovation of the Heart,"* Dallas Willard makes the following statement about man's dilemma here on earth...

"...the intellect becomes dysfunctional, trying to devise a "truth" that will be compatible with the basic falsehood that man is god..."[4]

This is why Paul laments, "Why do I do what I don't want to do?" in Romans 7. He is putting words to this conflict that we all experience of *not living in congruence* with who God made us to be, our true selves. As we continue to stumble through life like this, frustrated that we cannot succeed in *"trying to devise a truth compatible with the basic falsehood that man is god,"* we become extremely, terribly confused *about who we are in God's eyes.* The only solution to this is to turn back to our Father, who designed us for relationship with Him and to *seek the truth of who we really are* from Him *and be willing to accept it.*

Larry Crabb, noted Christian author, speaker and counselor discusses a helpful concept he calls "the platform of truth" in his book, *"The Marriage Builder."*

"Spiritual truth can be compared to a balance beam, a narrow platform from which we can easily fall off either side. The central truth that serves as the platform...for all Christian relationships - is that in Christ we are at every moment loved and genuinely significant.

Too often Christians fall off this platform of truth into error. When key relationships (marriage, family, friendship) or life events (job, health, prestige) fail to make me feel secure or significant, it may be difficult to hold firmly on to the fact that I remain a worthwhile person."[5]

This was certainly true in my own life. Feelings of insecurity and insignificance DEFINITELY made it difficult for me to hold firmly onto the fact that I am a worthwhile person. That was a major underlying factor driving my own addictions. When we fall off of the "platform of truth," we become confused about our TRUE identity, how God sees us. We experience feelings of insignificance, impotence and incompetence and we begin to see ourselves as abandoned, alone and unworthy of love. This is Satan's lie becoming real and true in our lives and it leads to all sorts of unspiritual, fleshly behavior. Jesus dispels these lies and sets *veritas* straight for the world.

Jesus himself told us that, when the devil speaks, he speaks his native language, for he is a liar and the father of lies. In the next chapter, I'm going to discuss how the enemy capitalizes on our insatiable desire for relationship with God and twists it with more and more lies leaving us awash, in what the Bible calls in the original Greek language, "epithumia" - *deceitful desires.*

BULLETPROOF GLASS CHALLENGE:
Honest IN (Being authentic with myself, self-assess) –
- Can you answer Pontius Pilate's question, "What is truth?"
- Do you really believe that God is absolute truth? If not, why?
- From what sources have you derived the truth that you currently live by? Can they truly be trusted?

Honest UP (Being authentic with God, pray, confess) –
- What do you base your understanding of the truth of God on? Are you getting information from the best, most reliable source? If so, what is it?
- Ask God to show you your "true self." How would you describe that person? How is he or she different than the present you?

Honest OUT (Being authentic with others, share, discuss) –
- Do you need to ask some questions of your trusted friends about what you believe to be true and consider other viewpoints?
- WILLINGNESS CHECK: Are you truly willing to listen and consider how you expect they will respond…or not?
- Do you need to reassess how you "love your neighbor" as yourself? Discuss what this looks like with your "Bulletproof" brothers.

CHAPTER SEVEN

DECEITFUL DESIRES

*"You were taught , with regard to your former way of life, to put off your old self, which is being corrupted by its **deceitful desires**, to be made new in the attitude of your minds, and to put on the new self, created to be like God in true righteousness and holiness. Therefore each of you must put off falsehood and speak truthfully to his neighbor, for we are all members of one body."*
— Ephesians 4: 22-25

One night, which I was spending in a hotel by myself after I had confessed to my wife, the Lord brought this verse to me. I sensed him ask me, *"What are your deceitful desires?"* I sat alone in the hotel room and pondered that question. The desires I had that were deceiving me had been my desire to be validated by women, which I had sought to satisfy through pornography and visits to massage parlors. Another deceitful desire had been to be out of physical and emotional pain, which I satisfied by medicating with alcohol and pills. I had turned to these things for comfort in my life when I was in pain or experiencing shame instead of turning to God for comfort and *seeking the truth about what I was feeling.* These desires were deceitful in that they promised relief but only delivered something that was empty, unfulfilling, temporal...instead of towards Jesus who is fulfilling, eternal and true.

It brought to mind another verse about desire in James:

"...but each one is tempted when by his own evil desire, he is dragged away and enticed. Then after desire has conceived, it gives birth to sin, and sin, when it is full grown, gives birth to death."
                                              - James 1:14-15

One bible commentator expounds on this verse...

"In the words, drawn away by his own lust and enticed (in the original Greek: ὑπο της ιδιας επιϑυμιας εξελκομενος και δελεαζομενος), there is a double metaphor; the first referring to the dragging of a fish out of the water by a hook which it had swallowed, because concealed by a bait; the second, to the enticements of impure women, who draw away the unwary into their snares, and involve them in their ruin. Illicit connections of this kind the writer has clearly in view; and every word that he uses refers to something of this nature..."[6]

When I read that I understood. I had been lured and dragged away like a fish and much of it actually had to do with impure women. Here's the brutal, honest truth about my desire to be out of this kind of discomfort. When I felt the powerful spiritual forces of shame, fear and anxiety which produced feelings of *incompetence, insignificance and impotence,* I was not strong enough in and of myself to withstand their power. I FELT (that's just another term for "believed") that sitting under the influence of those forces would destroy me in a spiritual sense. It FELT like death. Fear, shame, anxiety – these are DREADFUL forces. They can CRUSH a man's spirit, especially when they are constant, relentless and incessant over a long period of time. They are like the power of water on a rock over time – it just wears you down, reshapes you, no matter how strong you think you are. This was my experience with these forces. They FREAKIN' HURT! To me, sitting in fear, anxiety and shame was like being on fire...which only sent me running to find something to quench the flames. My desire to be out of pain was brought to a fever pitch by powerful, dark spiritual forces that *I could not control.*

I love this quote by Dennis Dirks, Dean of Talbot University from 1992 - 2012, from a chapel sermon...

"When the hour becomes dark, and our fears intense and the challenges immense, ...we must resolutely resist the tantalizing temptation to find confidence in our abilities, and to trust the tangible, and to lust for security. A rightly-ordered mind sees human enemies or obstacles as but heavenly tools driving us toward the divine sanctuary. Our hope is trusting a gracious Lord as our only true help and deliverance."

When I was under the influence of fear or shame, I did exactly what Dirks warned *not* to do - I put my hope in my own abilities, trusted the tangible, lusted for security. I thought I could solve these spiritual problems on my own. In reality, being under the influence of something I couldn't control was the essence of *powerlessness,* the cornerstone of the First Step in recovery from addiction. It's a state of being that is common to man, not just those struggling with addiction. When we find ourselves doing something we *don't want to do,* like the apostle Paul struggled with (Romans 7), we're experiencing *powerlessness.* I think it's important here to explain the cycle of addiction that is so often brought on by our own *powerlessness.* It goes like this:

EMOTIONAL TRIGGER: We experience feelings of incompetence, insignificance or impotence brought on by the spiritual forces of shame, anxiety, fear, etc.

CRAVING: These feelings produce emotional and spiritual discomfort, causing us to crave RELIEF.

PRE-OCCUPATION: Our minds start working overtime to create a strategy to relieve or satisfy the craving.

ACTING OUT: We engage in the chosen (usually negative) behavior, bad habit or substance usage in order to satisfy the craving.

GUILT/REMORSE: We experience guilt and remorse which leads to MORE feelings of incompetence, insignificance or impotence and the cycle starts all over again.

I'm not aware of ANY negative pattern, bad habit or addiction that doesn't follow this model in almost every way. In this cycle, the BEHAVIOR or SUBSTANCE *is not* the driving force. The driving force is INTERNAL and has to do with the EMOTIONAL and SPIRITUAL forces brought on by *the false way we think about ourselves*. The perpetuation of this cycle depends on us believing wrong things about who and what we are, how valuable we are. So what is so *deceitful* about these kinds of desires to be out of pain and discomfort? We are DECEIVED through these powerful spiritual forces in TWO IMPORTANT and DISTINCT ways:

> 1. We are deceived by the feelings of incompetence (I'm not smart enough), insignificance (I'm not valuable enough) and impotence (I'm not strong enough). These are all lies working to convince us that we truly ARE these things.

These are lies about our IDENTITY.

> 2. We are deceived that we can satisfy our craving BY OUR OWN POWER in reaching for whatever negative behavior or substance that our self-devised strategy tells us will work.

This is a TWO-PRONGED lie from the enemy. Here's the TRUTH:

> 1. God would not send His Son to shed His blood and die for someone He viewed as incompetent, insignificant or impotent. God did not CREATE US in this manner. If He had, he would not have proclaimed us "very good" upon completion of His work. His word has MUCH to say in the face of these lies. For more on how God views us, see Chapter 26, "In Jesus, I Am."

> 2. Reaching for a behavior or substance to satisfy a craving WORKS...until it DOESN'T work. We are trying solve a spiritual problem with a physical solution and it doesn't work. These things simply don't possess the power necessary to solve these kinds of problems in a lasting way. They are temporal. Their effectiveness dissipates over time.

The way that God views us is radically different from the lie that we are incompetent, insignificant and impotent. To the contrary, we are of the HIGHEST value to our Creator. We are *valued, accepted, secure, significant and free.* This is God's TRUTH about WHO we truly are to Him.

Haven't you ever felt like you just don't measure up or you just don't have enough? Ever thought to yourself "If I just had more skills then I could succeed?" or "If I could just make more money then everything would be OK?" or "I need to drive a better car?" "If I could just lose some weight?" "If I could just get in better shape?" "If I could just get a better job?" "If we could just get that nicer house?" "If I could just have more sex?" "If I could just get that promotion?" We all have different life situations, jobs, circles of friends and family structures. But one thing we ALL have in common is that we live in a CULTURE OF SCARCITY where good enough never is *(thank you Brene' Brown for pointing this out in "Daring Greatly"[7]).* Our culture leaves ALL OF US, at one time or another, wanting more and feeling less than.

This kind of culture leaves men like me believing these lies of INCOMPETENCE, INSIGNIFICANCE AND IMPOTENCE:

- *Do I really know what I'm doing? Am I smart enough to pull this off? That's INCOMPETENCE.*
- *Does all of this that I'm doing really MATTER? Am I really all that valuable to others, my family, to God? That's INSIGNIFICANCE.*
- *Do I really have what it takes? Am I strong enough to handle this on my own? That's IMPOTENCE.*

These are the spiritual messages that the world forces upon us in our culture today and they are ALL lies about our identity, our true selves.

The effect of EVERY behavior or substance that a man or woman can use to try and alleviate the discomfort of fear, anxiety, shame and any other spiritual force is TEMPORAL – it works for a while...but it does not last AND then comes the guilt, shame and negative consequences. Like I said earlier, this is because we are trying to solve a SPIRITUAL problem with a PHYSICAL solution and it DOESN'T WORK.

You can't solve a SPIRITUAL problem with a PHYSICAL solution.

A spiritual problem must be solved with a spiritual solution. Physical solutions to spiritual problems work...but only for a while and then with many negative consequences. The ONLY thing that will bring lasting relief and will break the cycle of negative patterns, bad habits or addiction *permanently* is *found in Jesus.*

"Everyone who drinks of this water will thirst again; but whoever drinks of the water that I will give him shall never thirst; but the water that I will give him will become in him a well of water springing up to eternal life." – John 4:13-14

That thirst Jesus is referring to, that is the CRAVING for relief from the spiritual forces of this world that constantly wage war against us. Think of all the experiences you have every day that leave you feeling a sense of worry, doubt, fear, anxiety, shame, discontentment...I could go ON and ON and ON. The world *imposes* these feelings upon us, FORCES them down our throats and we are compelled to deal with them in one way or another. So the question then becomes, **who will I turn to in order to satisfy my craving for RELIEF from these forces?** Will I turn to my own devices? Will I believe the lie of my own deceitful desires? Or will I turn to the source of life, the fountain of living water? This is a moment-by-moment process of living in *dependence on Jesus* that He calls us into. Working the 12 Steps of recovery, a step-by-step journey to sanctification, was the path God took me on to learn this lesson.

But before I started my journey to recovery, I had to learn *the hard way* that turning to my own devices, trying to light my own path, satisfy my deceitful desires on my own only brought misery. It was a futile way to live. Living life like that simply doesn't work and only brings more pain and serves to keep us in the cycle of addiction – which is TORMENT. Maybe this kind of torment is what Isaiah had in mind when he prophesied God's words thousands of year ago...

"But now, all you who light fires and provide yourselves with flaming torches, go, walk in the light of your fires and of the torches you have set ablaze. This is what you shall receive from my hand: You will lie down in torment." - Isaiah 50:11

BULLETPROOF GLASS CHALLENGE:
Honest IN (Being authentic with myself, self-assess) –
- What are your own "deceitful desires?" Write them out in a journal or notepad.
- What kinds of things draw you away and entice you?

Honest UP (Being authentic with God, pray, confess) –
- Ask God to reveal the lies you believe about yourself that are contradictory to what His word says about you.

- Ask God to reveal the ways in which you seek to resolve your own "cravings" with your own strategies, methods or devices.
- Ask God to reveal what the next right thing is that you need to do in order to move closer to Him based on what you've learned.

Honest OUT (Being authentic with others, share, discuss) –
- Have you been deceived by your own desires in a way that you should discuss with a close, trusted friend?
- WILLINGNESS CHECK: Are you truly willing to listen and consider how you expect they will respond...or not?
- Ask your trusted friend if they think there is any action you should be taking to avoid this kind of behavior in the future.

CHAPTER EIGHT

THE MAGPIE

> *"Praise the Lord, my soul, and forget not all his benefits – who forgives all your sins and heals all your diseases, who redeems your life from the pit and crowns you with love and compassion, who satisfies your desires with good things…"*
> - Psalm 103:2 – 5

When I was in fifth grade, I had a teacher named Mr. Constantine. He was a stubby, red-headed man with a thick mustache. The other teachers called him the "Old Red Fox" and he taught shop and science. He also happened to be the "D" hall teacher. "D" hall was short for "detention," but in our eyes it stood for "damnation" and was synonymous with "Hell"…which made Mr. Constantine *the Devil*.

I can't remember what my crime was that sent me to hell on this particular occasion (seems I experienced a few trips to hell and back as a fifth grader as I can recall). It was probably something like running in the hall or being late to come in from recess or chewing gum in class – me coloring outside of the boundaries as I was prone to do. Whatever it had been, I was sentenced to a brief stay with Satan in Hell.

I don't remember all of the times I went to Hell ("D" hall), but this one stands out to me. For whatever reason, on this particular day, I had gained the focused attention of Satan and he wanted to make me pay, so he ordered me, "Mr. Wilcox, go up to the blackboard." I got up from my chair and stood at the blackboard in front of 8 or 9 of my fellow hell-mates. "Mr. Wilcox, do you know what a magpie is?" I stood there glossy eyed, sweating, feeling like if I didn't get this right I was going to spend eternity there with the Devil.

"Uh...isn't that like...a crow?" I muttered.

"Yes, Mr. Wilcox. A magpie is like a crow. And you know what, Mr. Wilcox? YOU are a magpie," Satan stated with such authority over me, the powerless fifth grader.

"Uh...I'm...a magpie?" I didn't understand.

"I want you to write on the blackboard, 'I am a magpie' one-hundred times."

And so I did.

I told this story to my wife and she replied shockingly, "Oh my gosh! That really happened? That's AWFUL!" Yes, it really happened. My fifth grade teacher labeled me a magpie and humiliated me in front of my classmates. This was but one of several *public shamings* that I had suffered as a kid.

My mid-life crisis was serious. Flash forward 35 years or so and I find myself married to the most wonderful, beautiful woman in the world (truly, my best friend), four beautiful daughters, a good job, a good church, great friends, a house in the suburbs, some money in the bank – everything looked great on the outside. But on the inside and in my secret, personal life, I was drowning in addictions, fear, anxiety and shame...and virtually no one knew. Sure, there were signs and the tensions were mounting in my marriage due to my excessive drinking habits and bouts with pornography, but those were just the symptoms of a deeper disease and even other, much worse behaviors. Inside, I believed awful things about myself. On the outside, I was working 24/7 to keep up the façade that all was good, but on the inside I believed I was bad: *a magpie*.

Things finally came crashing down for me in my late 40's and I was forced to deal with my addictive behaviors or suffer losing everything - my wife, my family, my business, my health...even my life. I sought out help for the addictions and found a place that definitely got me headed in the right direction and probably saved my life. It started me on a path of emotional and spiritual health. It was during this time that I met a very influential doctor that worked in the recovery program that I was going through and in one of his lectures, I had my moment of clarity about what I believed about myself.

The doctor was lecturing about "self-talk" and how our behaviors are products of our beliefs about ourselves. He was discussing how our self-talk reveals our true beliefs and asking us to share what our own "self-talk" sounded like. In the middle of all of this, I asked him...

"So what do I do if, for my entire life, my self-talk has been bad? Inside, I believe I'm a piece of crap." I asked.

"A piece of crap? Do you really believe that you're bad?" the doctor responded.

"Well, no, but some of my behaviors would prove differently. I don't know." I was spiritually and emotionally sick and totally confused.

"Let me ask you a question. Where do you think you came from?" the good doctor asked me.

"I believe I was created, by God."

"You really believe that?"

"Yes, I do. Absolutely."

"What do you believe God thinks of you?"

"I believe he loves me."

"Really? What makes you think that?"

"He sent his Son to die for me. I believe his love for me is that great."

This was all just head-knowledge for me, a product of years of church attendance and Bible reading. I believed it in my head, but it certainly wasn't translating into my heart, my life. I was parroting back to the doctor what I heard in hundreds of sermons over the years. Now I was feeling like the doctor was challenging my faith right there in front of the 15 or 20 other patients in the lecture. What was really going on was the he was about to give me a serious lesson in values clarification.

"OK then. So here's my question; if you really believe that God created you and that he loves you SO MUCH that he would send his only Son to die for you...(now yelling) WHO THE HELL DO YOU THINK YOU ARE THAT YOU CAN TELL GOD HE CREATED A PIECE OF CRAP?!!"

The room was silent. God's spirit welled up inside of me and confirmed that he DOES love me and that I am NOT bad. I held back tears and from that moment on, I understood at the deepest level that my behaviors do not define me anymore. It was a moment of clarity like no other. My suspicion is that the doctor had seen many people like me whose problem is that we are not being true to who we really believe we are. We've been brainwashed to live as *inauthentic* people.

We've been brainwashed to live as inauthentic people.

These are two, powerful, yet opposing exchanges about my identity that both affected me deeply. Now, I'm not blaming my behaviors on teachers like Mr. Constantine or my parents or anyone else. *I'm the one* that made the decisions that led me to my crisis and I take full responsibility for my actions and behaviors. But the magpie event definitely had an impact on how I thought of myself. I believe we have an enemy that is hell-bent on a "steal, kill and destroy" mission (John 10:10) and no, the *enemy* is not you, Mr. Constantine. My identity was brutally attacked by the enemy for years and years through many different similar circumstances. But these false beliefs (read: lies) were literally killing me and the only way I was going to be redeemed was by knowing God's truth about what he thinks of me at the deepest level of my heart. It's easy to blame the bad things that happen to us (even the negative consequences of our addictions) on God, but He is NOT our enemy.

"For I know the plans I have for you," declares the LORD, "plans to prosper you and not to harm you, plans to give you hope and a future."

-Jeremiah 29:11

God is FOR us. He is NOT against us. He has plans to prosper us and not to harm us, plans for a future and a hope. These bad things that happened to me aren't God's fault. They are the result of a vicious enemy force set against me that God had been working to *rescue me* from all the way along. God literally had to bring me to a life and death crisis to get me to understand this.

Several months into my recovery, my wife, Celeste, had to take a personality test for her work – a Meiers-Briggs MBTI test. It's designed to *"make the theory of psychological types described by C.G. Jung understandable and useful in people's lives. The essence of the theory is that much seemingly random variation in the behavior is actually quite orderly and consistent, being due to basic differences in the ways individuals prefer to use their perception and judgment."*[8]

She thought the test was interesting and said that, once you determine your personality type, they have a chart that associates that type with a specific type of animal. Her personality type was determine your personality type, they have a chart that associates that personality type with an animal. Her personality type was associated with a green mouse. She wanted me to take it and see what my personality type was. I agreed, and one night over dinner, she started grilling me with all the questions on the test (maybe 40 or more). An hour or so later, we drove down to pick up one of our daughters from a dance lesson. As we were waiting in the parking lot, sitting there in the car together, she started grading the test to find out my results. I grabbed the page from her that had the chart of all of the different personality types (there are 16 of them) and started looking through all of them. I told her, "I bet I can tell you which one of these I am just by reading this chart." Before she was finished with her calculations, I told her, "I'm an 'ENFP'." According to Meiers-Briggs, the ENFP *(Extraverted iNtuitive Feeling Perceiving)* personality type is described as...

ENFP - *(Extraversion, Intuition, Feeling, Perception)* *Warmly enthusiastic and imaginative. Sees life as full of possibilities. Makes connections between events and information very quickly, and confidently proceeds based on the patterns they see. Wants a lot of affirmation from others, and readily gives appreciation and support. Spontaneous and flexible, often relies on their ability to improvise and their verbal fluency."*

Her calculations confirmed, according to the test, that I was in fact an "ENFP" personality type. We both agreed that adequately described my personality. So I asked her, if you're a green mouse, what are the other animals that I can be associated with? Which animal am I?

She pulled out another page and on it were the four animals with which the personality types are associated: a green mouse, a white buffalo, a bear and a golden eagle. *"Which one is an ENFP?"* I asked inquisitively.

"You're the golden eagle."

I liked that. It was a declaration of *who I am* - a golden eagle. That was something I could definitely identify with. I immediately did some research and found that the golden eagle is one of the largest of the birds of prey, a "raptor," capable of taking down animals as large as 150 pounds...even wolves. They are massive birds with wingspans that can surpass nine feet. They are hunters, graceful, swift, beautiful and regal. They are associated with courage, wisdom, strength and royalty.

As I was doing my research about the bird, I came across an amazing photo of a massive golden eagle taking down a wolf. I was so fascinated by this image because it shows the eagle's great strength and courage as well as its impressive size in relation to the wolf it is taking down, but more importantly because of the bird that is fleeing on the right hand side of the image. There, scurrying for its life towards the edge of the image's frame is a frightened, black bird with small white wing markings...

A magpie.

I began this chapter with a quote from Psalm 103:2-5, but I intentionally only quoted the *first half* of verse 5. In its entirety, it reads like this:

*"Praise the Lord, my soul, and forget not all his benefits – who forgives all your sins and heals all your diseases, who redeems your life from the pit and crowns you with love and compassion, who satisfies your desires with good things **so that your youth is renewed like the eagle's.**"*

- Psalm 103:2 – 5

So the truth is, both the Meiers-Briggs personality test and my Father in heaven are telling me that I am an eagle. It took 47 years and a mid-life crisis for me to finally break the lies I had believed about myself and see myself clearly through God's eyes. God truly does work in mysterious ways. My life is completely different now. I am no longer in the grips of addiction, but I'm living a successful life of recovery. Life is centered around my relationship with the Lord, my wife, my kids and helping others. My marriage has never been better. Work is good. My kids are awesome. I am forgiven and redeemed. Jesus is my Lord. My youth is in the process of being renewed...*like the eagle's.*

A magpie was probably a pretty good symbol of the kind of person I had become...

Magpies are scavengers, takers. They survive off of road-kill, nuts and rotting fruit. Truth is, a magpie was probably a pretty good symbol of the kind of person I had become before my journey to recovery. Today, I am learning to be a giver, a protector, a leader, a loyal friend, husband and father - qualities much better symbolized by the golden eagle.

So for me, this lesson from the Lord was about understanding how God sees me, untangling a former viewpoint gained from a childhood experience with a foolish man and learning that I receive my value from God, my Creator, rather than from what others think or say of me. Misled people like Mr. Constantine don't get to determine *my value or worth*. God does, because He is my Creator. Mr. Constantine, you were wrong, sorry to say. I'm not a magpie. I'm a golden eagle…so you can go write that on *your* blackboard a 100 times.

I also came across another image as I was researching eagles. It's an image of an "old red fox" tangling with a HUGE Golden eagle.

Wonder how *that* worked out?

See these images at: www.brokentobulletproof.com/the-magpie

BULLETPROOF GLASS CHALLENGE:
Honest IN (Being authentic with myself, self-assess) –
- How does this discussion on your identity and the way you view yourself make you feel and why?
- What does your own self-talk sound like? Is it negative? Is it positive? Is it proud or self-deprecating?
- Would you say you have a "right" view of yourself in relation to God?

Honest UP (Being authentic with God, pray, confess) –
- PRAY THIS: Lord, do you see me right now as proud or properly understanding who you made me?

- Is your heart in agreement with the scriptures that describe who you are to you, God? If so, are you living in congruity with that belief?

Honest OUT (Being authentic with others, share, discuss) –
- Share with your "Bulletproof" brothers what your own self-talk sounds like.
- WILLINGNESS CHECK: Are you truly willing to listen and consider how you expect they will respond...or not?
- Do you need to confess negative self-talk or an improper view of myself to your brothers and hear their response?

CHAPTER NINE

THE DIAMOND

I am a diamond.

I know that sounds like a completely PROUD statement, but I've come to understand that it actually takes tremendous HUMILITY to be able to say it in truth. I'm not trying to boast in saying that, so stick with me here. I don't believe this about myself because it's something my dad said to me...although many times he did. I don't believe it because my mom did either. Although, so often, her love and care for me communicated this very fact. I don't believe it because I have accomplished great things or because people have given me praise even though sometimes that has been true also. I don't believe it because I like what I see in the mirror - I used to, but the fact is I'm getting old now, gray is showing up, fleckish in my hair and beard and I'm definitely rounder than I'd like. Nah, don't necessarily like what I see in the mirror these days...and that's ok.

I don't believe I'm a diamond because my wife says I'm awesome, which she actually does more and more now that I'm finally allowing God to make a true man out of me. I don't believe it because my kids adore me even though I know for a fact that they do. I don't believe I'm a diamond because I'm extraordinarily wealthy...although I'm sure I am in the top 5% wealthiest people in the world just by the fact that I'm a middle-class American.

No, none of those reasons are why I believe...today, finally...that I AM a diamond. But I haven't always believed it. For the longest time, I believed I wasn't worth crap.

There's two feet of topsoil and a little bit of bedrock,
*   limestone in between.*
Fossilized dinosaur and a little patch of crude oil
A thousand feet of granite underneath...
And then there's me.
                              -Brad Paisley, "Two Feet of Topsoil"

That's what I used to feel like and believe about myself. I believed I was so far down, I couldn't go any farther. I was hearing lies from a dirty, false, lying spirit of self-loathing and I've believed it for much of my life. I was too far gone, a lost cause, in a place too dark for anyone to ever find me. The way I felt, if Mr. Constantine hadn't called me a magpie, he probably would have called me a lump of coal.

Oh sure, there used to be a time when I was pretty high on myself...for all the WRONG reasons. It probably started when I was a teenager and I thought I knew everything...literally (like MOST teenagers think, right?). I thought I was really something because of my talent or my athletic ability or my good looks or my intelligence or my sense of humor. I believed the lie that "I'm awesome and in control." *Pride* (a wrong understanding of my relationship to God) can make one believe some really outrageous things about one's self...and I actually believed THOSE things about myself for all the WRONG reasons...for a long time.

I mean, let's be honest here. When it comes right down to it, our success in life is really rooted in what we believe and much of it has to do with what we believe about OURSELVES. Do we believe the truth or a lie about who we really are? Do we have a general misunderstanding of how God views us or do we have a RIGHT understanding of who we are in relation to Him? I know I didn't. I've believed lies about myself for the most part and for most of my life. And my life began to show it. I got to a point where my life was crumbling around me in every way...relationally (my marriage was a disaster), financially (I lost pretty much everything and had to start over at zero), health-wise (I had to have a brutal surgery on my neck, got addicted to pain meds and gained about 30 lbs.), spiritually (bankrupt here too, couldn't hear God's voice at all). What a nasty, black freakin' lump of coal my heart had become!

It takes hitting rock bottom to finally buy into and understand the TRUTH about one's self. SUDDEN REALIZATION: Wait a minute - I thought I was AWESOME??? What the heck happened?!!!!

When I first became a Christ follower back in high school, people at church used to say to me, "God doesn't care what you look like on the outside. He cares about your heart." Well, that sounded real nice and everything and since I felt pretty good about how I looked on the outside ANYWAY at that time, I thought, "Sure, God loves me. I mean, what's not to love? Right? What does my heart even have to DO with any of it?" I was selfish and self-centered from very early on, desperately needing the grace of Jesus and his work of sanctification in my life.

I was selfish and self-centered from very early on, desperately needing the grace of Jesus and his work of sanctification in my life.

That kind of thinking got me through most of my life, until I reached my 40's and I started having to look at my heart and really see what was in there. I mean, how bad could it be?

Well...it was bad. REALLY bad. Yeah, I know. Shocker.

Once I prayed. I knew not what I said.
Show me myself, O Lord, alas, I did not dread
The hideous sight, that now I shudder to behold
Because I knew not self aright.

And I was lead, in answer to my prayer
As step-by-step to find my wretched heart laid bare!
Then I prayed, "Stay! O Lord, I cannot bear the sight"
Because I knew not self aright.

-Phil Keaggy, "Once I Prayed"

Once God gave me a really good look at what was in there...I wanted to vomit. It was like peering into a deep cavern of dead bones. It took me 47 years of life to really, truly come to the very end of myself. For me to FULLY realize that my heart is an absolute train-wreck, a nuclear-contaminated wasteland, an empty, condemned shell.

> *"The heart is deceitful above all things, and desperately wicked: who can know it?"*
>
> *- Jeremiah 17:9*

Without going into the dirty details, the end of myself - you know, "ROCK BOTTOM" - looked like this for me: addiction, unfaithfulness, dishonesty, pain, shame and self-hatred.

That's what I saw when the light was shined into my heart. What does one DO with all of that? Where can one go to escape it? It is the result of living a life of complete and utter selfishness.

Ugh.

Why do I do the things I don't want to do? What a wretched man I am! Who will rescue me from this body of death?

I can SO relate to the apostle Paul's struggle in Romans 7. This is where the lies take complete hold of a man. When you really come to grips with these things in your heart and you acknowledge that they are there and they have caused you to do terrible things that you hate and that you are ashamed of, things that hurt others and hurt yourself too. When you finally grasp the depth of that depravity...you come to understand that you have believed the lie: *I am no good.*

This is the lies of incompetence, insignificance and impotence all rolled into one. I said it earlier, but this is the message of SHAME and it's just not true. It's NOT! It is a dirty lie about our identity from the pit of hell - the greatest of lies probably. It is the flip-side of the "I'm awesome and in control" lie...the other end of the spectrum from pride. This is why the book of James speaks about both ends of this spectrum of false beliefs about ourselves:

"The brother in humble circumstances ought to take pride in his high position. But the one who is rich should take pride in his low position, because he will pass away like a wildflower."

- James 1:9, 10

James (the half-brother of Jesus) is trying to get us to see ourselves PROPERLY in relation to God, the way God sees us. See ourselves truthfully. If our heart of hearts were REALLY no good – and I'm talking about our TRUE hearts, the one God gave to us originally before it was decimated by sin...if we really were of no value, worthless, wretched to the core...Jesus would not have had to die for us. He knows the enemy will lead some men to think too much of themselves, others too little. Both ends of this spectrum put us out of fellowship with God. I've lived life to both of these extremes and neither of them work!

So who WILL rescue me from this body of death?

Jesus will. Jesus does. Jesus HAS.

Jesus is THE truth (remember, "I am the way, the TRUTH and the life"?). And no matter how the enemy (READ: the devil, Satan) wants to spin this lie, sugar coat it...the truth is that God LOVES me. Whether the devil wants to inflate my ego with PRIDE or beat me into an addictive submission with SHAME, God STILL LOVES ME. He loves me IN SPITE of what I've done. Am I going to let others, this world, our culture, my possessions or achievements define me or am I going to accept my Creator's definition of me?

My actions (accomplishments, failures) don't define me. What others (even those closest to me) say or think of me doesn't define me. What the enemy says about me doesn't define me. The size (or lack thereof) of my bank account doesn't define me. My possessions don't define me. There is one and only ONE thing that defines me and that is what GOD the Father - the one who CREATED me - thinks of me. And here is what He says about that:

His love is not conditional on me achieving a certain status or being good.

"But God demonstrates his own love for us in this: while we were still sinners, Christ died for us."   *- Romans 5:8*

I am his son, a member of his family.

"Yet to all who received him, to those who believe in his name he gave the right to become children of God - children born

not of natural descent, nor of human decision or a father's will, but born of God." - John 1:12-13

I am redeemed and forgiven.

"In him we have redemption through his blood, the forgiveness of sins, in accordance with the riches of God's grace."
- Ephesians 1:7
"For he has rescued us from the dominion of darkness and brought us out into the kingdom of his Son he loves, in whom we have redemption, the forgiveness of sins."   - Colossians 1:13-14

I am a new creation.

"Therefore, if anyone is in Christ, he is a new creation, the old has gone, the new has come!" - I Corinthians 5:17

I am more than a conqueror.

"No, in all these things we are MORE than conquerors in him who loved us." - Romans 8:37

I am a citizen of heaven.

"Consequently, you are no longer foreigners and aliens, but fellow citizens with God's people and members of God's household." - Ephesians 2:19

THAT is what God says about me. That is what he thinks of me...and that is what He says about YOU. I choose NOT to believe the lies of the past any more but instead, I choose to believe *these* things. He ought to know - HE created me! My heavenly Father, my Creator - HE is the higher authority that determines my value - no one else does. Others can comment, spread opinions, speculate...but in the end, God is the ONLY one that gets to determine my value. Who am I to say something to the contrary? Who do I think I am?

> *"But who are you, a human being, to talk back to God? 'Shall what is formed say to the one who formed it, 'Why did you make me like this?'"*
>
> *- Romans 9:20*

Brothers, *this* is the essence of spiritual battles. The enemy almost always attacks our IDENTITY. That really is the question, isn't it? Who DO I truly *believe* that I am?
And not only did God say these things...he backed them all up by signing them in blood. Jesus loves you and me with such unimaginable intensity and passion that *He died for us!*

> *I got treasure up in heaven, I got dirt all over me*
> *I have only scratched the surface of the man I'm meant to be*
> *I got something down inside of me that only You can see*
> *Help me dig a little deeper now and*
> > *Set that diamond free.*
>
> *- Brandon Heath, "Diamond"*

So now that I've put things in context, let's go back to that seemingly PROUD statement I made at the beginning of this chapter about being a diamond. Humility *"does not in any way deny our own self worth. Rather, it affirms the inherent worth of all persons."*[9] Humility is a proper understanding of our relation to God and others. Pride is when we perceive ourselves as being more important than others or even of God; an *improper* understanding of our relation to God and others. It took a lot of pain, shame, destruction...and then redemption for me to fully and properly understand my relation to God...and my value.

So I've decided to stop looking at myself the way *I see myself* or the way others see me and start looking at myself PROPERLY, in humility – a right understanding of my relation to God.

"When I was a child, I talked like a child, I thought like a child, I reasoned like a child. When I became a man, I put the ways of childhood behind me."

- I Corinthians 13:11

I am God's son. I have true, important value here on earth and eternal value in heaven. He has given me great power and responsibility as his son and I am responsible to steward that power and responsibility well. I am worthy of His love and blessings *because He created me.*

So I am making a shift...from my FALSE self, the one that believed all of the lies...over to my TRUE self, the one that is keenly aware of my eternal worth and value. That's why I can say this in true humility, fully understanding my relation to my Father in heaven: *I AM a diamond.* Not of my own making, but because my Creator...no, because my FATHER *says I am.*

BULLETPROOF GLASS CHALLENGE:

Honest IN (Being authentic with myself, self-assess) –
- How does this discussion on how you see yourself make you feel and why?
- How would you describe how you see yourself?
- Do you see yourself somewhere along the spectrum of PRIDE/SHAME or do you honestly see yourself as a diamond – someone with eternal worth and value?

Honest UP (Being authentic with God, pray, confess) –
- Ask God if, in regards to your self-worth and thoughts about yourself, you might be seeing yourself wrongly.
- PRAY THIS: Is there something I need to claim from this chapter specifically as truth from you to me, Lord?

Honest OUT (Being authentic with others, share, discuss) –
- What things do you need to share or discuss about how you think about yourself with your Bulletproof brothers?
- WILLINGNESS CHECK: Are you truly willing to allow them to challenge the way you feel about yourself...or not?
- Do you have the courage to ask your brothers to give you an honest assessment of how THEY see you?

CHAPTER TEN

THE SHAMED

Like the magpie incident I shared earlier, I can remember several experiences as a young boy, even from as far back as 4 or 5 years old that involved me feeling embarrassment and shame. Some of these involved me exploring the development of my sexuality, learning to go to the bathroom properly, learning to stop wetting the bed, learning who it was ok to be naked around and who it wasn't, etc. – the kinds of things all little boys and girls go through as they grow up. Other experiences involved me simply being a little boy and getting in trouble: throwing rocks at things, getting lost, hurting myself by taking unnecessary risks. I'm sure I was a *handful* for my mom and dad - their first experience with an active, rambunctious little boy.

It's not helpful to try and figure out the "whys" of those times I experienced shame as a child. I think most little kids end up experiencing shame in one way or another. Each of us translate it differently based on our surroundings, the adults we are around, our parents, our teachers and how they all interact with us – this is the "nurture" part of growing up. I had a great childhood and parents that cared for me well, disciplined me, kept me safe and loved me a ton. Regardless of how I interpreted my surroundings as a kid, somehow along the way, I learned to *feel ashamed* when I did things others did not approve of and I carried this practice into adulthood.

I've mentioned how much I learned about the subject of shame a few years ago when my sister-in-law forwarded me the links to the Ted Talks by Brene' Brown - one on shame and the other on vulnerability. You can view both of her talks on the media page of my website:

www.brokentobulletproof.com/media

As a professional "shame" researcher, Brene' Brown spent much of her career interviewing, researching and learning about the subject of shame and its impact on our society. I've mentioned earlier that she defines shame as "the fear of disconnection." That rang true with me. I definitely had experienced the fear that I may lose important relationships if others knew who I TRULY was or what I had actually done. Shame asks the question, *"Is there something about me that makes me unworthy of connection?"* The message of shame is simple...yet brutal.

>*"I'm not good enough."*
>*"I'm not smart enough."*
>*"I'm not beautiful enough."*
>*"I'm not strong enough."*
>*"I'm not brave enough."*

These messages are completely contrary to what God says about us, contrary to our TRUE selves and are the primary drivers of the feelings of insignificance, incompetence and impotence that are the common emotional triggers of the addictive cycle discussed earlier.

Shame has no resting place in the heart of the true man that God created in me and you

Shame is in direct conflict with the TRUE MAN that God created us to be. God did not create us to live in shame. Remember in the Garden of Eden, Adam and Eve were created and were "naked and unashamed" from the very beginning. It simply has no resting place in the heart of the true man that God created in me and you.

According to Brene' Brown, another interesting aspect of shame is, the *less* you talk about it, the *more* of it you have. Shame *hates* vulnerability. Think about it – shame works to destroy community or "connection." If people feel unworthy of being accepted by others, they stay away. This is how the isolation of addiction is created. It's really a vicious spiritual force. So what is the difference between someone that feels "unworthy" and someone that feels "worthy?" Brene' Brown's research indicated that people who believe they are worthy have a strong sense of love and belonging. These people have the courage (Brown calls it "wholeheartedness") to be imperfect, the compassion to be kind to themselves first and then kind to others and finally they have connection as a result of authenticity. They FULLY embrace the practice of being vulnerable. These kind of people believe that what makes them *vulnerable* is the exact thing that makes them *beautiful*. Vulnerability is the capability or willingness to be hurt in an effort to express love – Brown calls this attribute "shame resiliency." People that don't believe they are worthy have a weak or non-existent sense of love and belonging which makes them weak or deficient in shame resilience.

Not only did Brown's research show that *vulnerability is actually the antidote to shame,* but also that it's really the birthplace of joy, creativity, belonging, and love. Vulnerability allows others to see us for exactly who we are, without pretense. I'll discuss this further in Chapter 23 when I talk more about living life like a clear sheet of *bulletproof glass*. Because being vulnerable leaves us open to being wounded, we avoid it or numb it through negative patterns, bad habits or even worse, serious addictions. This was DEFINITELY how I dealt with shame. I did not have the spiritual capacity to withstand much shame at all, especially from those closest to me or ones whose opinions I held in high esteem. The deeper I got into addiction, the more shame I felt and the more I chose to numb those feelings which only served to increase the grip of addiction even more. It's an insidious, vicious cycle.

The problem with trying to numb shame (or fear or any other negative spiritual force) is that you cannot SELECTIVELY numb the impact of these kinds of painful spiritual forces and feelings without also numbing the joy, gratitude, happiness and all of the positive spiritual forces and emotions we experience in life. That just leaves us even more miserable, thirsting for purpose and meaning.

I didn't understand how deeply shame had affected me until I was in my 40's. It was like a terrible sunburn. Almost any rough interaction with others would inflame it in me. My poor wife was on the receiving end of MANY of my angry outbursts as a reaction to the shame I wasn't even aware I had. Robert D. Caldwell, M. Div. states this about shame...

"Shame is the inner experience of being 'not wanted.' It is feeling worthless, rejected, cast-out. Guilt is believing that one has done something bad; shame is believing that one IS bad. Shame is believing that one is not loved because one is not lovable. Shame always carries with it the sense that there is nothing one can do to

purge its burdensome and toxic presence. Shame cannot be remedied, it must be somehow endured, absorbed, gilded, minimized or denied. Shame is so painful, so debilitating that persons develop a thousand coping strategies, conscious and unconscious, numbing and destructive, to avoid its tortures. Shame is the worst possible thing that can happen, because shame, in its profoundest meaning, conveys that one is not fit to live in one's own community."[10]

Wow. That's EXACTLY how I experienced shame – *"so painful, so debilitating."* It created a tremendous sense of *unworthiness* in me.

Shame was a progressive force in my life. No matter what tactic or strategy I used to try and minimize shame, it only seemed to increase the next time, further driving me into addiction. By the time I hit rock bottom, almost any negative force I experienced in life was translated into shame. I remember having a dream where I woke up with the sense that God was telling me I had a *"shame translation filter"* so that everything I heard was being interpreted as a message of shame. I later came to understand that this was simply a byproduct of my own selfishness and self-centeredness. When I'm constantly looking INWARD, evaluating myself by the opinions or supposed opinions of others, I come up empty and typically experience shame. God makes a promise to those that have experienced shame...

"I trust in you; do not let me be put to shame, nor let my enemies triumph over me. No one who hopes in you will ever be put to shame, but shame will come on those who are treacherous without cause."   - Psalm 25:3

Thank God he brought me to a place where I really had no other option than to be vulnerable and to come clean with my secret life of addiction to my wife, family and friends. Actually, there *was* another option – to run from reality and commit fully to a life apart from God into a life of sin and addiction - but I knew that would end badly, most likely in jail, great injury or worse...death.

My story of *Broken to Bulletproof* and the message of *Bulletproof Glass* is really about being set free from SHAME. The freedom I found in FINALLY being transparent was so fulfilling, brought so much relief and life that it's really hard for me to describe. Being transparent truly was the antidote to the shame I was under. Learning to be vulnerable in the face of shame was a crucial part of me moving towards fulfilling the role of the true man God has created me to be. This is what the apostle James was getting at when he wrote,

> "Confess your sins to one another that you may be healed."
> - James 5:16

True to this verse, I experienced healing *through the process of being vulnerable and transparent* with others.

I've played guitar, sang in a band, led worship and written songs for most of my life. I love music and I use it to express what I'm struggling with, what I'm feeling inside. I was a music major in college and had a dream of being a rock star for a long time, but that didn't quite work out. Not long after I finally confessed to my wife, family and friends, I wrote a song about my experience of being vulnerable, showing others my true self and finding new life through being transparent. It's called "Tattoo." You can download a recording of it for free from my website if you'd like.

TATTOO - Words and music by Tony Wilcox

Free audio download at www.brokentobulletproof.com/tattoo

It didn't need to be on the outside
It never was meant for show
Nobody even needed to see it
When they run into me, they'll know

Thought about using a marker
Just in case I changed my mind
But that would just defeat the purpose
Cause this was coming down from the Divine

CHORUS:
This tattoo is written on my heart
This tattoo is written on my soul
It was paid for by the blood of redemption
This tattoo...it's just the way I roll

I could have done it up in blood and needles
Could've inked it down in black and blue
Could've gone to see that old guy named "Elvis" down at the shop where they do tattoos

People, well they can say what they want to
Spread their shame, believe their lies
They mock me and beat me and try to burn off my skin
But they CAN'T erase the message written deep inside

CHORUS

BRIDGE
I'm forgiven. I'm redeemed (yes, I am).
I'm accepted.   I'm loved. I am free!

Now I've finally found my freedom
By telling the truth at last
You can see right through to my new tattoo
It's behind...man, it's behind...

This clear sheet of...*bulletproof glass*

© 2014 Tony D. Wilcox

    I think I have felt and still sometimes feel the most shame when I am confronted with the fact of how badly I hurt my beautiful wife because of the things I've done as a result of my addictions and selfish choices. In the process of our healing together, we've endured MANY painful, difficult discussions about what I did, how it hurt her, how it made her feel, how it devalued her own sense of self-worth, making her feel unloved, ugly and alone. These are deep waters to navigate. It takes *great* willingness and courage on both of our parts, but it is a sacred journey into deep intimacy with each other.

It takes great willingness and courage on both of our parts, but it is a sacred journey into deep intimacy with each other.

This is how I've allowed my wife to fully know me and she has allowed me to fully know her. We don't sweep these tough issues (or any issue for that matter) under the proverbial rug anymore. We dig in and talk about it like loving, respectable adults. Coming face-to-face with these realities and taking responsibility for them was something I could not accomplish without the Lord's supernatural strength and healing and the 12 Steps of recovery. The shame I would feel from entering into those conversations would be unbearable – the exact thing I feared before I finally came clean. It would feel like the fiery darts of the enemy, hollow-point bullets piercing my heart and soul, ripping the life from me.

But that wasn't the Lord's promise to me. His promise was, *"As long as you keep telling the truth, you will be like a clear sheet of bulletproof glass."* He has been true to that promise. Through the *process* of being vulnerable and transparent, He developed in me a resilience to shame that truly is *bulletproof*...and just one more of His myriad blessings upon me to be eternally grateful for.

BULLETPROOF GLASS CHALLENGE:

Honest IN (Being authentic with myself, self-assess) –
- How does this discussion on shame make you feel and why?
- What things have you done in the past that cause you to sense the spiritual force of shame when you consider them?
- When do you feel the spiritual force of shame?
- Who are you afraid of being "disconnected" from when you feel shame most of the time?
- Do you really believe that if they knew you the way you truly are, with all your flaws and shortcomings, that they would reject you?

Honest UP (Being authentic with God, pray, confess) –
- Is God using shame to point you towards repentance of a secret sin? If so, are you willing to confess (agree that it is sin) to Him and seek forgiveness?
- Are you putting your hope in the Lord and receiving your value from Him alone or do you rely on the approval of others to have a sense of worthiness?
- What does God's word say about the subject of shame?

Honest OUT (Being authentic with others, share, discuss) –
- What do you need to be vulnerable with your Bulletproof brothers about in order to defeat shame in your life? (Remember James 5:16)
- What do you need to hear from your trusted friends in response to the shame you may be experiencing?
- Discuss what it means to be "shame resilient," to live life behind "a clear sheet of bulletproof glass" and gauge your own shame resilience.

CHAPTER ELEVEN

CARRYING MY CROSS

Then he said to them all: "Whoever wants to be my disciple must deny themselves and take up their cross daily and follow me."
- Luke 9:23

If someone had asked me a few years ago what this verse meant, I would have said something like "It's talking about giving our daily struggles to Jesus. We have to pray daily for him to help us with the trials in our lives." While that may be true in a shallow, superficial sort of way, the Lord has revealed something much deeper to me in this verse through my recovery. This one small sentence holds SO many rich layers of deep truth if we will dig a little deeper. At first glance, this verse can be brushed away because it might be hard to understand on the surface. It sounds like a cute little cliché, a quotable quote...and that's about it. But let's explore it more.

Take a look with me at the trial leading up to Jesus' crucifixion. The Jewish leaders are grilling Jesus ABOUT WHO HE IS. Read the account of Jesus' trial in John 18 and 19 as well as Matthew 26 which I've included below...

Then the high priest stood up and said to Jesus, "Are you not going to answer? What is this testimony that these men are bringing against you?" But Jesus remained silent.
The high priest said to him, "I charge you under oath by the living God: Tell us if you are the Messiah, the Son of God."

"You have said so," Jesus replied. "But I say to all of you: From now on you will see the Son of Man sitting at the right hand of the Mighty One and coming on the clouds of heaven."

Then the high priest tore his clothes and said, "He has spoken blasphemy! Why do we need any more witnesses? Look, now you have heard the blasphemy. What do you think?"

- Matthew 26:62-66

The Jewish leaders want the TRUTH about *who Jesus is*. The problem is, they want it to be THEIR truth, not THE truth *(recall my quote from Dallas Willard on page 59)*. If he really IS who He claims, it would change everything for everyone. They are so committed to their own truth that they are not willing to look at the possibility that they are wrong. This is a dangerous spiritual attitude for mortal men to hold. During this time, Peter is being faced with a similar situation as he waits outside for Jesus…

Now Peter was sitting out in the courtyard, and a servant girl came to him. "You also were with Jesus of Galilee," she said.

But he denied it before them all. "I don't know what you're talking about," he said. Then he went out to the gateway, where another servant girl saw him and said to the people there, "This fellow was with Jesus of Nazareth."

He denied it again, with an oath: "I don't know the man!"

After a little while, those standing there went up to Peter and said, "Surely you are one of them; your accent gives you away."

Then he began to call down curses, and he swore to them, "I don't know the man!"

> *Immediately a rooster crowed. Then Peter remembered the word Jesus had spoken: "Before the rooster crows, you will disown me three times." And he went outside and wept bitterly.*
> *- Matthew 26:69-75*

The locals questioning Peter want to know the same thing – *who are you*, Peter? Are you one of his followers? Show us your TRUE self, Peter. Because of FEAR, Peter is unwilling to be true to himself. Both of these exchanges are getting to the heart of how we present ourselves to others, if we let our true selves be seen or not – *this is the test of vulnerability.* Fig leaves, layers of self-protection, masks...call it what you will, but we ALL do it to one degree or another *in an effort to evade spiritual pain.* We are all tempted to present to the world a FALSE self, one that is safe...so we think. I'll discuss how I wore different "masks" to present a false self to the world around me in greater detail in the next chapter.

When Jesus said what he did in Luke 9:23 about taking up the cross, he said it because he knew that EVERY man in history is going to face this very same question:

"Who are you?"

We will face it again and again and again in our lifetimes and then ultimately, we will face it one final time when we stand before God on the Day of Judgment. I came to a point in my own life where I was forced to answer this question for myself when I finally confessed to my wife, family and friends about my secret life. When it comes right down to it, after I stripped away all the layers of self-protection, the pride, fear, shame, bitterness, guilt...I had to ask myself, "WHO AM I? What is the TRUTH about who I am?"

More on this in a minute. But first, back to Jesus' trial. You see, the Pharisees were asking Jesus to *tell the truth – "are you the Son of God or not?"* At this point, there was only one way Jesus could avoid being crucified – *he would have to lie about His TRUE identity.*

There was only one way Jesus could avoid being crucified – he would have to lie about His TRUE identity.

Jesus would have to deny his TRUE self and *present himself as someone else if he wanted to avoid being crucified.* Doesn't this sound familiar?

Peter was facing the exact same situation. He was afraid that if he were true to himself and said "Yes, I AM a follower of Christ," that he too might be crucified along with Jesus. But he caved. He caved to his fear of pain, fear of death and he LIED, THREE TIMES mind you, and told them that he was NOT a follower of Christ when in fact he was. He COVERED himself with a lie *to avoid death*……just like Adam and Eve covered themselves with fig leaves to hide from the Father back in Eden. Instead of being transparent, truthful and trusting in God's power to deliver him from the situation (like Jesus was doing), Peter hid behind a lie and showed himself to be someone other than his true self TO AVOID PAIN.

This is the spiritual strategy called "appeasement" – *giving in to a dangerous power to avoid pain.* We discussed it earlier in Chapter 1 - Jabbok. In Peter's case, he gave in to the dangerous power of *fear*. Jesus on the other hand DID NOT. He bravely told the Pharisees the TRUTH about who He is, an act of vulnerability that moved him forward *towards the crucifixion.*

The False Self vs. True Self

So what does all of this have to do with "carrying my cross?" What's my point? Being crucified, carrying my cross is about being TRUE to myself - *acting in congruence with the TRUE man that God originally intended when He created me.* Think about it — Jesus knew if he told the truth, he would be walking literally into the greatest pain he could experience. If he presented his TRUE SELF, he would die. And so he did. And in so doing, he put to death his NATURAL SELF (His physical body) so that he might experience the miracle of God and be resurrected as His TRUE SELF, His eternal, perfect, spiritual body. If you want to experience the miracle of God's resurrection, you have to DIE first.

If you want to experience the miracle of God's resurrection, you have to DIE first.

Jesus was unique in that He was sinless. His NATURAL/FLESHLY SELF and SPIRITUAL SELF were always in congruence because He knew no sin. That's not how it is for us, however. Each of us has these two "selves" also, but ours are in conflict with each other - they are NOT congruent because we are sinful. Scripture is clear on this division in the way that man is created *(see I Corinthians 2:14 and 15:44 for two examples).* The "spiritual" man is my "TRUE SELF," the man God intended for me to be when He originally designed me – a man capable and willing to live by God's Spirit and not by my own flesh. The "CARNAL MAN or FALSE SELF" is me in my physical body, living life according to *my own* fleshly desires yet wearing a mask to make it look like something I am not. My "FALSE SELF" is set against my "TRUE SELF" or "spiritual man." They are opposed to each other, which keeps us from doing what we want, living as our TRUE SELF. God's word confirms this as well...

> *"For the flesh desires what is contrary to the Spirit, and the Spirit what is contrary to the flesh. They are in conflict with each other, so that you are not to do whatever you want."*
> *— Galatians 5:17*

Jesus knows that we will only experience *true life* by exchanging our FALSE SELF for our TRUE SELF. He knows that we must allow our FALSE SELF to be crucified and DIE so that God can perform the miracle of resurrection to our TRUE SELF. This "exchange" is the process of spiritual formation which the Bible calls "sanctification." When we make the decision to follow Jesus, to become His disciple, He wants us to know that it is an invitation into the *death* of our FALSE SELF. He wants us to learn how to live in a manner in which we are constantly, daily *willing* to pursue the TRUE SELF and allow the FALSE SELF to be crucified. This is what He is getting at when He says, *"Whoever wants to be my disciple must deny themselves and take up their cross daily and follow me."*

I recently started doing an exercise with some of the men that I work with that is designed to give us a clear view of both our FALSE SELF and our TRUE SELF, the man God originally intended when He created us. It includes two sheets, each with a large circle on it. The circle on the first page represents the carnal man, our FALSE SELF. In this circle, we write all of the behaviors that we perform in our lives that are "of the flesh." Actions we know aren't good, aren't true, are contrary to God's word and blatantly immoral...even behaviors that simply produce a sense of guilt. These are behaviors that are contrary to our TRUE SELF.

Then, on the next sheet, we describe our TRUE SELF. On this side we write down the behaviors and actions that we believe we would perform or WANT to perform which would rightly represent God's standard, things that are congruent with His word AND the unique ways in which He designed us. This exercise displays a stark contrast between our FALSE SELF and our TRUE SELF. Without the power of Jesus in our lives, we are *incapable* of living in a way that fulfills the TRUE SELF. We need God's power to do this – apart from Him, we can do nothing.

Here's an example. Early on in my sobriety (I had just passed my first 30 days without alcohol), God gave me a moment of clarity I won't forget. My wife and I were separated and I was staying at a friend's house because my drinking had caused such division in our marriage. We had both just attended a recovery meeting together one evening and then we got into an argument out in the parking lot before I headed off to my friend's house for the night. I didn't like the things she was saying to me. I was angry, my thoughts were spinning and my sobriety was in danger. This was exactly the kind of emotional trigger that I had used as an excuse to drink for years and years. I did not possess the spiritual tools I needed to take responsibility for my part in our relationship or process conflict in a healthy way and it was showing.

Earlier that morning, I had been in an AA meeting. As I sat there listening to others tell their stories of how alcohol had decimated their lives and what they were doing to get sober, my thoughts drifted. I had picked up a chip that day for achieving 30 days of sobriety and I was holding it in my hand, examining it, reading the inscription. On one side is inscribed the phrase, *"To thine own self be true."* That phrase struck me and I remember contemplating its meaning. I didn't understand.

On the way home after our argument, I remember thinking to myself, "I need a drink. I don't care what happens. She's not going to talk to me like that!" This is typical alcoholic thinking, selfish and self-centered. I remembered this little convenience store on the way home where I had been stopping for coffee each morning. They sell little single shots of liquor in small plastic bags at the checkout stand. I thought, "I can stop by there and buy a couple of those little bags, slip them into my backpack, and drink them before I go to bed. My roommate will never know. My wife will never know. I just won't tell my sponsor. *Nobody will ever know.*"

That's when the moment of clarity came. My TRUE self screamed out at me inside and said, "I'll KNOW!" It hit me like a bolt of lightning. I remember pulling over to the side of the road, breaking into tears and thinking, "What the hell is wrong with me? I've got to quit lying to myself like this!" And then that phrase I had read on my 30 day chip that morning came back to me, *"To thine own self be true"* and I suddenly understood. I confessed to God that I couldn't do this on my own and cried out for His help. I called my sponsor and told him *everything* that had happened, how I was feeling about it and what I was thinking. He offered some wise, sober counsel and helped me through the struggle. For me, this was a pivotal moment in my healing by denying my *natural self* and being true to my *true self,* bringing these two conflicted selves one step closer to reconciliation.

Going to the cross for Jesus was an act of obedience, an act of worship. He gave honor to his heavenly father by doing His will, even though he had to walk into tremendous pain, even death, to do it. THIS is what Jesus is getting at in Luke 9:23. When he says a man "must deny himself" he means we must deny our current, fleshly "self" – the self that was born into and is steeped in sin and wants to avoid pain and seeks pleasure. He means we must be willing to show others our "TRUE SELF," the one that God sees when He looks at us because of Jesus' sacrifice. If we are Christ's, God sees us as *sinless* when he looks upon us – this is our TRUE self – the authentic man that God had in mind when He created us. We ALL struggle with finding our TRUE selves. Peter struggled with it and lost. Jesus struggled with it as well...and was victorious for our sakes.

What would be Death to You?

So what does "carrying my cross" look like in everyday life? How do I know how the Lord is asking me to pick up my cross and what situation is He asking me to carry it into? A close friend and brother in the Lord taught me that if I ask myself the question, *"What would feel like death to me?"* in a particular situation, I can start to see the sacrifice God is inviting me into more clearly.

For instance, sometimes the things my wife says to me about the past might cause me great pain in the form of regret, shame or sorrow...spiritual forces I would rather avoid. This is an example of when I am presented with a choice between my TRUE SELF...or my FALSE SELF. My TRUE SELF is a man that wants to honor God by being obedient to His word, specifically in this case, *"Husbands, love your wives as Christ loves the church."* I know if I continue on in the conversation, I will encounter more of this pain and it may even get more intense, but it is what God is calling me into. Jesus didn't love the church by *walking out on her.* My wife needs me to listen to her, she DESERVES for me to listen to her, to hear past her angry words and to hear her heart.

So what "feels like death" to me in this situation? Listening to my wife's angry, hurtful words and feeling the sting of the shame, remorse and guilt that will come from it. If I choose to act in accordance with my FALSE SELF by giving way to anger and responding bitterly and harshly or by deflecting or manipulating the conversation or by simply walking out (hiding), I am choosing NOT to carry my cross into this situation. I am denying my TRUE SELF, choosing NOT to be the man God designed me to be – a man that loves his wife as Christ loves the church. Carrying my cross into this situation means sitting still, patiently listening to my wife's broken heart and showing empathy for her pain instead of saying *"Screw you! I'm not going to let you talk to me like that!"* and walking out (like I USED to do).

When I find myself in a situation where I experience the strong spiritual forces of fear, anxiety or shame, I know God is directing me to pick up my cross. As I sit in the discomfort of those painful emotions, I hear God's voice, asking me, "Who are you, Tony? Aren't you one of HIS followers?" I can lie, present a false self to my friends, my wife and the world and act like everything is cool, stuff my emotions and then reach for the closest thing I can get my hands on to relieve the spiritual discomfort: alcohol, a pill, porn, food, a movie – anything to numb it and find relief. That's exactly what I used to do when I lived FALSELY.

Now I have learned to "die" so that I can truly experience life. I can confess who I truly am – a man who does not have the spiritual power to make fear or anxiety or shame go away on my own. I need the power of my Savior and so I turn to Him instead and ask for help. I ask Him directly in prayer (reaching UP, vertically) and I ask Him by calling one of my Godly friends that He lives in also (reaching OUT, horizontally). Together, they help me kneel down and take hold of that splintery, bloody wood, heave it over my shoulder and they hold me up as I trudge forward into the spiritual forces set against me, into the spiritual death where the miracle of *resurrection* awaits. It takes a while. I must be patient. I must wait in the darkness of the tomb in the presence of the fear, the anxiety and the shame. And Jesus waits there with me. And when it is time, he bids me "RISE." That's when the stone rolls away.

Death is the only state in which a man cannot take credit for the miracle God is about to do.

Once we can see this with spiritual eyes, understand what He is calling us into and are willing to enter into it...willing to "pick up our cross," we will experience the miracle of *resurrection*. Remember when Jesus said, "You shall know the TRUTH and the TRUTH will set you free" and "if a man wants to gain his life, he must lose it?" These are all statements having to do with this spiritual sacrifice He calls us into – the place where miracles happen and God does his most amazing work. "Carrying our cross" is all about TRUTH. It is about being true to who we really are in the spiritual condition that we are in – HELPLESS, POWERLESS...DEAD. The exact place God needs us to be so that He can do what He does best – BRING LIFE!

BULLETPROOF GLASS CHALLENGE:

Honest IN (Being authentic with myself, self-assess) –
- What strategies do you tend to use to avoid "dying" to yourself or to avoid presenting your true self to others?
- What feels like "death" to you – something you're deathly afraid of doing (in regards to your relationships with others)?

Honest UP (Being authentic with God, pray, confess) –
- Can you think of a time when you denied Jesus or the Father like Peter did and appeased fear by lying and presenting a false self to others?
- Ask God to reveal the ways in which He wants you to "die to yourself" so that He can perform a miracle of resurrection and new life.

Honest OUT (Being authentic with others, share, discuss) –
- Discuss with your "Bulletproof" brothers what it looks like to "carry your cross" in daily life.
- Are you presenting a "false self" to your friends in some way? If so, confess it to them and show them your true self, trusting God with the outcome.
- You can download and work through the FALSE SELF vs. TRUE SELF EXERCISE on my website at:

http://www.brokentobulletproof.com/true-self

CHAPTER TWELVE

THE MASK
How I hid my True Self

It's a covering for all or part of the face, worn as a disguise. When worn effectively, a mask hides the true self and leads others to believe that you are in fact someone other than who you really are. For me, I needed it to hide my secret life.

I wore the mask that made others think I had it all together. The clothes I wore, the watch on my wrist, the cars I drove, the neighborhood I lived in, the kind of house I owned, the way I carried myself, the way I talked and the things I said were ALL part of an elaborate scheme to make others think I had it all together. I wanted you to WANT TO BE ME, admire me, like me, maybe even *envy* me if I'm brutally honest. In general, I wore a mask because I wanted to be accepted.

I wrote earlier about Brene' Brown's definition of shame; "the fear of disconnection." Shame says, "You're not good enough. If others knew who you REALLY are, they would reject you." This is really what was at the heart of why I wore my mask, because of *shame*. Regardless of how nice I made it look on the outside, how smart, articulate, funny or talented I made others think I was…inside I was dying. I believed that if you really knew me, you'd hate me. If you really knew the things I've done, the ways in which I've tried to fulfill my secret desires that I couldn't control, you'd be repulsed. I believed this lie to the core of my being. I believed it of my friends, my boss, my pastors, my extended family, my kids and my wife. I was FULLY committed to wearing the mask. I HAD to wear the mask. It was a matter of life and death for me. As far as I was concerned, if I took off my mask, I would die.

And so I became a master of keeping it in place.

John Eldredge, in his quintessential best-seller, *Wild at Heart*, puts it like this:

"We are hiding, every last one of us. Well aware that we, too, are not what we were intended to be, desperately afraid of exposure, terrified of being seen for what we are and are not, we have run off into the bushes. We hide in our office, at the gym, behind the newspaper and mostly behind our personality. Most of what you encounter when you meet a man is a façade, an elaborate fig leaf, a brilliant disguise." (Wild at Heart, page 52)

So very true.

I was talking with my wife recently about how, when I was in college, my roommates and I used to shame one of the guys that lived with us because we had found a Victoria's Secret catalog hidden under the sink in his bathroom. Well, we ALL knew what *THAT* was about and so the shaming began. It was all sophomoric joking and picking on our friend in and around the apartment. "Wonder where Kevin is?" One of us would say when he was not in the room. "I think he's on a date with Victoria." Or even worse, when he WAS in the room, someone would crassly poke at him, "Have you seen Victoria lately, Kev?" One day, someone had decided to take matters into their own hands (no pun intended) and took the catalog and threw it in the dumpster outside the apartment. Somehow, almost as if by magic, a few days later it reappeared under the sink – God only knows how! The shaming intensified.

But here's the rub (ok – pun intended that time), my wife asked me, "I don't understand how you guys could shame him like you did when all of the rest of you were doing the exact same thing.

You'd make fun of him to me years later about how he used to hide that catalog and yet you were doing things WAY worse than that, right? I don't get it." I responded, now able to tell the truth, "It's one of the ways I used to keep the mask in place. It's a way of manipulating what I wanted others to think of me – that I have it all together. It is part of the façade and it can only be kept in place by lies, deceit and manipulation." I don't have to live like that anymore, thank God.

There are many different types of masks people will wear in trying to hide the true self. Here are a few of the more common ones...

- *I've got it all together mask – designed to achieve acceptance, admiration*
- *I'm a victim mask – designed to solicit pity or concern*
- *I'm a badass mask – designed to keep others intrigued, but at a safe distance*
- *I'm better than you mask – designed to solicit worship of me, assert power over others*
- *I'm smarter than you mask – designed to solicit the*
- *intellectual attention of others (this is a subtle variation of "I'm better than you")*
- *I'm wealthier than you mask – designed to keep others at a distance*
- *I'm cooler than you mask – designed to selectively attract other cool people only and keep the "uncool" at a distance*
- *I'm more religious than you mask – designed to win the comparison games people play in church*

Remember these are all empty façades. There is little or no substance behind them most of the time. There are MANY more types of masks people can wear, all probably as different as each individual. Jesus commonly used a harsh term during his ministry that had to do with mask wearing, usually directed at the Pharisees: *"hypocrite."* It is a word used to describe actors in ancient Rome at the time. A hypocrite was someone playing a role in a drama or comedy. These actors would hold a mask in front of their face as they delivered their lines to portray their character in the play. Hypocrite literally means "mask wearer" or "actor." Wearing a mask to project a false persona is nothing new.

There are also myriad *strategies* that we use to keep the mask firmly in place. There are both internal strategies – the way we think, the way we manage emotion, our self-talk – and there are external strategies – our clothes, jewelry, car, house, hair style, the way we talk, the activities we participate in, etc. Combine all of these things and you have a complex and unique projection to the world of a false self. Another word for it is our "persona" or "personality."

For me, for the longest time I wore a Rolex Submariner watch. Now don't miss my point here – there is *nothing* wrong with wearing a Rolex (I loved that watch!). But it was the REASON I wore the watch that I eventually had a problem with. More than the simple fact that the watch was a fine timepiece, more than the fact that it was a good investment and held its value…I wore it because of *what people would think of me when they saw me wearing it.* That was the cold, hard truth. It was purely part of my persona. I wanted people to believe I was successful, I had it all together, I had life figured out. THAT's the biggest reason I wore that watch. After I got sober, I sold it. Part of my recovery was to stop projecting a lie about myself. It was but one elaborate piece of the strategy to keep my mask firmly in place.

One way you can tell when someone is adjusting their mask is when they can't stop talking about themselves. Next time you're at a party or crowded function and you experience that person who can't help themselves and they just talk, talk, talk about their life, their kids, their job, their problems, their health, their vacation, their Rolex watch and blah, blah, blah...this is pure mask-adjusting going on. They are working hard to project the persona they want you to see. The truth is people like this are dying inside. They are extremely insecure and they want someone to validate them, to prove to them without a doubt that they are in fact ENOUGH just the way they are. These kinds of people typically are feeling insignificant and carrying the weight of deep shame in their hearts...like I was.

Here's one of the biggest problems with wearing a mask: when we don't express our true selves and show real feelings, we are prevented from experiencing real intimacy in relationships. Mask wearing simply won't allow us to develop deep, meaningful relationships because they are all built on a false perception.

The church is full of mask-wearers like I used to be. You'd think church would be the one place where I don't have to wear my mask, but sadly that is not the case in most churches today. While there are exceptions, my experience is that many, even most churches lose sight of their understanding and love for Jesus and fall into a pit of "religiousity." Being "religious" is easier and less painful than being *real* about our struggles. That's why Jesus called the act of following Him a "narrow road." It's not for the faint of heart.

Religion is completely different from having an intimate relationship with God through his Son, Jesus. Religion puts a misplaced emphasis on the way we act, the way we appear, what we do, how we perform. It creates an atmosphere of fear and shame when one's *feelings and emotions* conflict with the religious requirements. Vocalized or unsaid expectations from religion with a message like "you should never be angry" or "if you have a bad habit you need to just stop it" are problematic when people actually

DO get angry on occasion or are caught in an uncontrollable negative pattern or addiction. This conflict leads to serious feelings of resentment, frustration and shame. Religion over-emphasizes "works" and underemphasizes "faith", "hope" and "love" or our experiences with God. Our churches need to be a place where broken people come together to celebrate Jesus' redemption of our brokenness.

Our churches need to be a place where broken people come together to celebrate Jesus' redemption of our brokenness.

We ALL suffer from the same spiritual malady the apostle Paul suffered from when he laments in Romans 7:15, *"I do not understand what I do. For what I want to do I do not do, but what I hate I do"*. This is why we experience feelings, emotions we simply cannot control that are in direct opposition to our true selves. Therefore, we wear a mask to project the appearance that we are compliant with the religious requirements – it keeps us safe from the religious police. So here, in my opinion, is the *bigger* problem with masks, especially in the church environment: *they serve to keep the lid sealed on a pressure cooker of hidden hurt, anger and resentment.*

Masks serve to keep the lid sealed on a pressure cooker of hidden hurt, anger and resentment.

This is why *transparency* is critical. These kinds of feelings, emotions and desires are common to man and they need to be explored, inventoried and turned over to God, our only hope (this is *exactly* what a 12 Step program accomplishes). Jesus is always faithful, safe and overflowing with grace when we bring these things to Him. We need the safe haven of an empathetic community to explore these feelings, free of shame and judgment. Religion, however, works against transparency. Religion sends a message (often unspoken) that "you don't measure up" and "you need to go fix yourself" and only offers a checklist of liturgical acts to solve the problem. "Read more scripture. Are you having a quiet time? You should get in a small group. Did you sign up for the men's retreat? We need help in the nursery and Jesus wants you to serve others." It's a completely unsafe place to be REAL. When a conflicted or hurting person is dying inside from these awful emotions and desires swirling about and we turn to the church for help and all we get is instruction to "DO" something different, it puts the burden and responsibility on ME to fix myself. Ugh. Trying to *fix myself* was my problem all along.

Steps 1 & 2 of the 12 Steps of recovery are...

STEP 1: We admitted we were powerless over our addiction and that our lives had become unmanageable.

STEP 2: Came to believe that only a power greater than ourselves could restore us to sanity.

The 12 Steps rightly puts the responsibility on our Creator to fix what our human efforts have made a complete mess of.

King David was familiar with mask wearers. While he himself was fiercely committed to being the *true* man God had created him to be, he had come across others that weren't.

> "Do not drag me away with the wicked, with those who do evil, who speak cordially with their neighbors but harbor malice in their hearts."
>
> - Psalm 28:3

These kinds of people talk and act one way to your face but you know they don't *truly feel that way in their heart* because their actions outside of those conversations prove differently. These kinds of people don't *live* in a way that is congruent with what they *truly believe.* We've all seen these kinds of mask wearers and with some it's just painfully obvious. Move away from the church and you'll still find mask wearers. At work it's usually easy to see the huge gap between the true leaders and team-players and the "shapeshifters" that mysteriously seem to become what others want them to be on cue. We can't take them at face value because we don't know which face they're actually wearing. Is this your "real-person" face or the "game" face? Everybody acts and reacts differently towards people like this depending on which mask they are wearing. This is hugely frustrating for those that value "worthiness" that are hoping to build any kind of real, substantive relationships with those around them. Conversely, we can offer those that want to live authentically something invaluable: our trust, and we receive theirs back in return. This is how true community is built, true intimacy between friends, family, neighbors, co-workers. This is how my men's group has been built over time, my relationships with my true "Bulletproof" brothers. Wearing a mask confounds and thwarts the building of real community which typically leaves the mask-wearer lonely, disappointed and confused.

Constantly propping up a persona like this is exhausting. It takes a lot of energy, strategizing and manipulating to keep a mask in place. For me, this process was so exhausting that it only fed my need to medicate. It also generated a serious sense of anxiety, fear and paranoia – I could be exposed and found out at any moment. Add to all this exhaustion, anxiety, fear and paranoia the steady pressure of knowing deep inside that I really am just a fraud, a poser... and at some point it just becomes unbearable. This is an awful, crushing and debilitating way to live. It literally sucks the life out of a soul. Regardless of the motivation, almost everyone on earth wears a mask at one time or another. *Except one.*

Jesus.

Jesus was the antithesis of a mask-wearer. He was His own true self every moment of his life here on earth. He didn't need to self-promote or draw attention to himself – he was a magnet. People followed Him to see something they had never seen – *authenticity.* His true self exuded love, truth and grace like no one else. Jesus was the REAL DEAL. When he was sad, he cried (when his friend Lazarus died). If he was angry, he showed it (expelling the money-changers from the temple). If he was worried, he told his friends and asked them to pray for him (asking the disciples to pray in the Garden of Gethsemene). He didn't have to pretend that He was something that he wasn't. He was so committed to being his best, true self that he was willing to die for it (see Luke 22: 66-71). At any time, Jesus could have put on a mask and pretended to be something that he wasn't and he could have avoided death. Jesus was the most REAL and TRUE human being the world has ever seen.

I have a sign in my office with a simple phrase in Latin; *"Esse quam videri."* It means "To be rather than to appear" (thank you John Eldredge for introducing me to this phrase in *Wild at Heart*).

I'm not a tattoo guy, but if I ever got one, I'd have the cross of Christ etched with that phrase on my skin. I'm dismantling the framework that held my mask in place. I don't want to be defined by my watch or my car or my $1500 suit, my bank account, my house, my job, my words or my writing any longer. I want others to see me for who I truly am – someone who could not fix himself. I am a broken, unrighteous man redeemed and restored *only* by the grace of my Heavenly Father and the death and resurrection of the only one that never had to wear a mask.

BULLETPROOF GLASS CHALLENGE:

Honest IN (Being authentic with myself, self-assess) –
- What kind of mask do you wear? What is it that you desire for others to think of you and more importantly, WHY? (Having trouble with this question? Start by describing your own "persona.")
- What strategies do you use to keep your mask in place?
- How does the "false self" that you are projecting with your mask differ from your TRUE self, the person God created you to be?

Honest UP (Being authentic with God, pray, confess) –
- Ask God to reveal to you the truth about WHY you wear your mask or rely on your "persona." Ask Him to show you steps you should take to dismantle the strategies and framework you use to keep it in place.
- Is there something that you can relate to in this chapter that brings you a level of guilt in your heart? Confess this to God and ask Him to reveal how He wants you to deal with it.

Honest OUT (Being authentic with others, share, discuss) –
- Tell a trusted friend (or friends) about what God has revealed to you about the mask you wear. Ask them to confirm or refute your feelings about it.
- Ask the person or persons who know you BEST (your men's group, wife, best friend, parents) if they think you sometimes pretend to be someone who you really aren't. This is a daring question that requires courage. If you sense fear here, this is definitely an area you should pray diligently about. Ask God for the courage to open this discussion with someone you trust.

CHAPTER THIRTEEN

THE JAILERS
The Prison of Resentment and the Torturers Who Run It

There's a chilling scene in the 2013 movie "Zero Dark Thirty" that made the hair on the back of my neck stand up the first time I saw it. U.S. forces have captured a key terrorist operative and he is incarcerated in a makeshift jail cell in Pakistan. A cold-as-steel CIA agent (played deftly by Jason Clarke) is in charge of the prisoner's interrogation. His mission: to obtain information on the whereabouts of Osama bin Laden. He sits on the outside of the cell, looking in at his captive, calm and stone-faced he says, *"Can I be honest with you? I have bad news. I'm not your friend. I'm not going to help you. I'm going to break you. Any questions?"*

You can only imagine how that interrogation went.

This scene is about the assertion of one man's will over another, the understanding of who is in authority. The CIA agent (the jailer) is there to *change the prisoner's mind*. The stubborn prisoner has *refused* to give the jailer what he wants. The higher authority (in this case, the U.S. government) has given power to the jailer to inflict punishment, torment and torture upon the prisoner *until his will is broken* and he changes his thinking...until he stops *refusing* the jailers authority.

In this world, we have physical jails where we send criminals that have committed crimes against others – these people aren't capable of behaving properly in relation to the rest of the world in one specific way or another. The goal of a jail sentence is to bring about "rehabilitation" – a changed and healthy way of thinking about the rest of the world, at least in most cases. These criminals need this kind of punishment to "break them" mentally and emotionally as to put their minds back in proper order so they can function in society.

Frighteningly, there is also a *spiritual* prison like this. It is a place where men find themselves when they think wrongly about forgiveness and its purpose is to accomplish the very same thing. It has a force of equally brutal guards or "jailers" that inflict *spiritual* torment instead of physical torment. Jesus infers that these jailers are there for one reason; to torture their captive until he has paid his debt in full. I should know... I have been there.

Then Peter came to Jesus and asked, "Lord, how many times shall I forgive my brother or sister who sins against me? Up to seven times?"

Jesus answered, "I tell you, not seven times, but seventy-seven times.

Therefore, the kingdom of heaven is like a king who wanted to settle accounts with his servants. As he began the settlement, a man who owed him ten thousand bags of gold was brought to him. Since he was not able to pay, the master ordered that he and his wife and his children and all that he had be sold to repay the debt.

At this the servant fell on his knees before him. 'Be patient with me,' he begged, 'and I will pay back everything.' The servant's master took pity on him, canceled the debt and let him go.

But when that servant went out, he found one of his fellow servants who owed him a hundred silver coins. He grabbed him and began to choke him. 'Pay back what you owe me!' he demanded.

His fellow servant fell to his knees and begged him, 'Be patient with me, and I will pay it back.'

But he refused. Instead, he went off and had the man thrown into prison until he could pay the debt. When the other servants saw what had happened, they were outraged and went and told their master everything that had happened.

Then the master called the servant in. 'You wicked servant,' he said, 'I canceled all that debt of yours because you begged me to. Shouldn't you have had mercy on your fellow servant just as I had on you?' In anger his master handed him over to the jailers to be tortured, until he should pay back all he owed.

This is how my heavenly Father will treat each of you unless you forgive your brother or sister from your heart."

This is the story of the Unmerciful Servant found in Matthew 18:21-35. The Unmerciful Servant doesn't properly understand his role in the King's kingdom and he doesn't properly understand the King's heart. In his disordered thinking, he believes *he* is more important than the other servant who owed him money (selfishness, self-centeredness). He wrongly believes he has the right to exact his own justice upon him. In so doing, he refuses to consider the great debt of which the King had just forgiven him. His thinking is out of order and it must be restored for the King's kingdom to run properly.

The word Jesus uses when he says *"unless you forgive your brother"* is the Greek word "ἀφῆτε" or "aphēte."

It means *"to let go, give up, a debt, by not demanding it."*[11] It is a releasing of the right to set things straight into the hands of God. This is biblical forgiveness, to release the payment of a debt.

The day I finally allowed myself to be vulnerable and transparent by confessing my hidden, secret sins to my friends, one of them spoke a tremendous truth from the Lord to me. He said, "Bro, you're being held captive and tortured by *the jailers*. You have resentment in your heart and THAT'S what God wants you to deal with. These things you've been doing (pornography, sexual sin, deception, drunkenness, prescription pill abuse) are just symptoms of the deeper problem which is in your heart and has to do with resentment, unforgiveness. These things you can't stop doing are the jailers who are torturing you to bring about repentance. God is allowing the jailers to break you so that you're willing to submit to His authority."

He then read me the parable of the Unmerciful Servant (Matthew 18:21-35). It was as if the large, iron bell of my heart had been rung. The truth of this story in my own life echoed deep within me. At the time, I didn't fully understand the details involved – I just knew there was truth to be explored here because, in a spiritual sense, I had definitely been in jail and my jailers had been harsh, bringing about devastation and negative consequences in my life, marriage, family, career, finances, health. Resentment and unforgiveness was the jail. My addictions were the jailers.

There is a particular phrase in this story that jumps out at me..."But he refused."

The Unmerciful Servant is doing this. He is making a spiritual determination in his heart that is the opposite of forgiveness and he *demands payment.* Instead of releasing the debt, he stubbornly refuses and holds onto his right for repayment. The text uses the words "οὐκ ἤθελεν" or "ouk ēthelen," which means "would not," and in this text is translated *"but he refused."*

I was doing this. I was *refusing to release* long-held resentments against others, against God, but mainly against MYSELF. I was *refusing* to fully embrace the Lord's forgiveness of the awful things I had done. I was refusing to give up my sinful lifestyle and submit my life to God. *"Refusing"* - this is a spiritual determination made in a man's heart. The Unmerciful Servant *refused* to *do the right thing, which in this case was* to have mercy on his fellow servant. Through his actions, he was saying to the other man that owed him money, *"Nope. I'm not going to do it. I'm not going to have mercy on you. You can beg and cry and plead all you want, but I'm going to EXACT VENGEANCE upon you. I'm going to do things MY way and have my vengeance right here and now. You owe me. Pay up!"*

It is in simple acts of spiritual defiance like this that we harden and shut off our hearts to God and rebel against him every day. We *refuse* to let go of all kinds of things in our lives that God wants to work a miracle with if we would just *release* them into His hands, which is *also* a spiritual determination. "God, I will give this thing over to You to do what YOU want to do with it in my life. I will let YOU administer justice. I trust You to do that." When we *refuse*, we assert our own will above God's and, in effect, make *ourselves god*, taking our Heavenly Father's place of judgment. At the most basic level, this is actually the sin of idolatry, a direct breaking of the second commandment, "You shall have no gods before me."

Because God loves his children so intensely, He goes to the greatest of lengths to NOT allow us to continue in bondage to "the jailers" forever. His justice allows us to go to jail, but when we are there, we are separated from Him. He desires to be near us, not apart from us. This is about proximity for God. It is about family – we're his *kids*. This is much more about us being "with" Him than it is His need for justice. When we fail to understand this, we miss God's heart for us. Can you imagine how a loving Father must feel when one of His kids is in jail, especially while knowing it really is the best thing for them? His heart must break!

Yes, God is a God of justice. But He is also GOOD and He is a God of grace. He wants his children SET FREE from this kind of bondage. He understands the power of idols like alcohol, pornography, sex, pills and countless other things in our lives and how we can become imprisoned by them. He allows these *jailers* to inflict their punishment so that we will HIT ROCK BOTTOM, cry out to Him and beg Him for an appeal to our case. He knows that His love for His children and His GRACE is greater than His need for justice – ALWAYS.

It took me well over a year of wrestling and resisting and trying in my own strength to break free from my addictions, attitudes, habits (the jailers), to fully understand the significance of my friend pointing out the truth of this parable in my life. Freedom came when I was *literally* arrested and put in jail. No, really - SO ironic. You've already read about that event in Chapter 5 (Worthship).

While I only spent one night in jail, even after I had been released physically, my heart and mind were still imprisoned and being tortured by my own "jailers."

The *spiritual* jail cell door opened for me when I finally addressed the resentments I had in my own heart, which included forgiving *myself and many other people, institutions and principles with whom I had been angry.* I was not able to do this on my own. I needed the help of some trustworthy friends (a safe community of the church body and my men's group) and a man who patiently guided me through the 12 steps of recovery. In this process, I made a "searching and fearless moral inventory" (4th step) which included everyone I had a resentment towards (unforgiveness). I was able to talk through each of these situations and relationships, examine what had happened and why I still held resentment (5th step). Then I *became willing* (that's the opposite of refusing) to have God remove these shortcomings and I humbly asked Him to do so (6th and 7th steps). These are spiritual steps that require the help of someone who has taken them before and understands how to move through them effectively.

Steps 8 and 9 allowed me to take responsibility for my part in each of these relationships and to make amends with the people I held resentment against. It was through this process that my spiritual jail sentence was completed. The jailers stopped their

torturing. The cell door was opened and I took the final steps into spiritual freedom. Steps 10, 11 and 12 are how I continue to walk in transparency now, being of service to others each day.

Jail is a hard place to be, I know. Our jailers are harsh and they can come in many forms - usually the things we turn to in place of God when we are in spiritual pain. Yet God's goal with this process of spiritual torment is to bring about "rehabilitation" – right thinking about our relationship to Him and his children. It is a painful act of love that God allows in our lives to bring stubborn hearts back to him. I know this may sound crazy to some, but I'm THANKFUL for the jailers. I would not know Jesus like I do today without their painful punishment. This is how Jesus taught me to make *proper* spiritual determinations in my heart – to *release* people, processes and institutions that have harmed me into God's hands instead of *refusing* His will and insisting on my own brand of retribution.

On the other side of the 12 steps, as I live OUTSIDE the jail cell today, away from the jailers, my only regret is that someone had not taken me through these steps earlier in life - BEFORE I had allowed my addictions to spiral out of control. I could have received so much benefit from this process as a young man. These steps bring life, serenity, freedom, hope...and I am so thankful for those things today in my life. Now, by God's grace, I am FREE on the OUTSIDE of the spiritual jail cell and able to live a restored life of gratitude, peace and joy.

BULLETPROOF GLASS CHALLENGE:

Honest IN (Being authentic with myself, self-assess) –
- What would you say are "*the jailers*" in your own life?

- How long has your jail sentence been? For how long would you say you have been suffering their punishment?

Honest UP (Being authentic with God, pray, confess) –
- Ask God to reveal any resentment or unforgiveness that is the cause of a spiritual incarceration like is described in this chapter. Who do you need to forgive?
- Ask God for the willingness to pursue forgiveness and making amends. What things are holding you back from doing this?
- Is there something God is asking you to do or to give up that you are "refusing" in your heart to do?

Honest OUT (Being authentic with others, share, discuss) –
- Discuss with your "Bulletproof" brothers the different people or institutions that you need to forgive and make amends.
- Ask them to help you formulate what it would look like to move forward in this process.
- WILLINGNESS CHECK: Are you truly willing to listen, consider and pray about their input? Are you willing to move forward in the process of making amends? If not, why?

CHAPTER FOURTEEN

THE BRAVE ONE
Crushed

I wasn't paying attention. The truth was that I was solely focused on my own problems. I didn't look behind me when I backed out of the driveway in my GMC Yukon 4x4. It was the nightmare nobody ever wants to experience. I KNEW I had ran over something because I felt the tire go over it...but what? I slammed the truck into drive, pulled forward back over whatever it was again and jumped out to go see what I had hit. Probably one of the kid's scooters or toys. But it wasn't. It was the absolute worst thing I could imagine.

I had backed over my wife.

There she lay, sprawled out on the concrete driveway, blood everywhere, her body badly mangled, broken beyond any repair. She was gasping for air, struggling to breathe. A look of sheer terror in her eyes as she looked up at me, standing over her. I was shell-shocked. I didn't know what to do! She was laying there helpless, dying, bleeding out, suffering with mortal wounds that could never be repaired by any doctor. "No! No! No! Babe!!!!! OH DEAR GOD! What have I done????!!!!"

This was the recurring nightmare/vision I had for about a year or more after I confessed my betrayal and secret life of addiction to my wife. Thank God this didn't really happen – at least not in a physical sense, but it was very real and just as horrifying to us both in a spiritual sense. It was as if I had mangled her spiritually and emotionally in a way that was just beyond repair. I had the same helpless feeling I described above, only spiritually. I was completely powerless to help heal the tremendous, bone-jarring spiritual damage I had inflicted upon her. She was heart-broken and I had done it to her. Even worse, there was ABSOLUTELY NOTHING I could do to put her heart back together.

Why would a woman stay with a man who had crushed every dream, hope and semblance of order she had in her world? What would motivate a woman to put up with, endure everything that would come with the decision to NOT walk away - spiritual and emotional pain, uncertainty, shame, regret, grief, moments of despair - when she had EVERY right to leave?

brāv/ adjective: brave; 1. ready to face and endure danger or pain; showing courage.

My wife would tell you that truth and justice are the two most important values for her. She tends to see things mostly in black and white. She also thrives on order. She struggles when things are out of order – at home, at her office, in our finances. I think truth and justice are part of that desire for order in her life. She wants things to be set straight when they are wrong. She would say she is a rule follower. She sees things in black and white...at least she used to. Everything changed when I confessed my betrayal to her.

She is a fighter too. While she doesn't seek out conflict, she is definitely not someone to back down from a fight...with ANYONE. I've seen her point her finger in the face of another man three times her size that was in an out of control rage and tell him, "In the name of Jesus, you back down right now and get behind me, Satan!"

True story. And guess what? He did! But that's a whole other tale for another book.

These are the things that attracted me to Celeste when we first met. Her name might have meant "heavenly", but to me she was "feisty." Her pet name for me was "Tone" and my friends and I called her "Cesty" for short. Once I got to know her better, instead of calling her "Cesty" I would often call hero "Zesty" instead. Her inner strength and courage was like a drug for me when we first met – and I was hooked. To me, her strength DEMANDED that I be a better man than I was. I felt like I was going to have to up my game to keep this girl. Sadly however, as our marriage progressed along with the shame and guilt of my secret life, I found myself more and more blaming our struggles on her and her attitude. I was too spiritually sick to be able to take responsibility for my own awful, hidden actions, so I blamed her for most of the problems we had. Not long ago, I read a phrase that I can now relate to:

"A strong man can handle a strong woman. A weak man will just say 'she has an attitude'."

That was me. When I was personally failing as miserably as I was, not taking responsibility for my own actions, blaming her and her attitude was the only card I thought I had to play.

The day I confessed to her was the hardest day of our lives. twenty-two years of marriage, four beautiful daughters, a gorgeous home tucked away on a cute cul-de-sac, a great career, wonderful friendships...it ALL hung in the balance. We both drove away from the meeting in tears. To me, it was all over. That's when the vision of me backing over her in the truck started. I had crushed her heart and was awaiting her wrath, her swift justice...and I deserved every bit of it. I expected divorce papers to pop out of the CD player in the dash of my truck as I drove back to the hotel where I was staying.

Instead, this is what I received – a text message on my phone that read:

"I have never been more proud of you as a man than I am right now. Thank you for having the courage to give me the truth."

I was stunned. These words came from the heart I had just crushed to a pulp. This is what God's grace looks life in real life. This is Jesus in my wife. THIS is love.

The bible says, in John 1:14 that Jesus was "full of grace and truth." There is a tension in that statement. It is a tension that Jesus walked the earth with and was completely comfortable with throughout his ministry. It is the tension that says, in the same breath, "Yes, you are a sinner" and "No, I do not condemn you." It is the tension suspending the drama of the crucifixion when the thief next to Jesus says, "We are getting what we deserve!" Without denying the thief's claim, Jesus replies, "Today, you will be with me in paradise." The same tension surrounded the scene of the woman caught in adultery. Jesus forgives her and acknowledges her sin in the very same moment..."Where are your accusers? Neither do I accuse you. Go and sin no more." (my paraphrases – see Luke 23 & John 8).

Truth and grace. I was not expecting this from my wife. I was expecting her justice, what I deserved – rejection, a divorce, alimony, child support along with bitterness, anger and shame heaped upon me. What I got was forgiveness.

Later, when I would ask her why she chose to stay, she would say, "God told me to. I heard him say 'do not turn this broken man away.'" She really had no idea what she was getting into by staying with me. She was just being obedient because she trusts God. Not to mention that she loves me with all of her crushed and broken heart. She could have stayed and got a man who continued to act out, get drunk, be unfaithful, embarrass her, put the truck in reverse and run over her again and again and again. She chose, in spite of that very real possibility (I was a very spiritually and emotionally unhealthy person), to stay and FIGHT for our marriage, for our family and for us.

Our recovery has not been an easy road. We have had many, many painful talks, shed oceans of tears together, said hurtful things, failed each other, failed God. And, at the same time, it has been wonderful, amazing and beautiful...more so than we could have ever imagined. While we certainly did not enjoy the pain in our story, neither of us would have chosen a different path. Isn't that crazy? This is the mysterious tension of truth and grace.

"The Spirit of the Lord is on me, because he has anointed me to preach good news to the poor. He has sent me to heal the brokenhearted, to proclaim release to the captives, recovering of sight to the blind, to deliver those who are crushed.

– Luke 4:18 (WEB)

Most nights now, before we drift off to sleep, I lay my hand upon her chest and I BEG the Lord to restore the heart that I have crushed. I am painfully aware of my own powerlessness to heal all of the damage I have caused. This is where God must do what I cannot and Jesus' words from John 15 echo in my mind..."Apart from me, you can do nothing." My wife is the brave one. She is the bravest woman in the world as far as I am concerned. She trusted

God with a broken heart and stayed with a broken man and FOUGHT for our marriage. How could I not fight alongside her also?

One evening, a couple of years into my recovery, my best friend invited us up to his house one Saturday night for a barbecue. Our two oldest daughters were away at college, but we brought our two younger daughters with us. We drove up the long driveway to my friend's beautiful home in the mountains and parked. He greeted us at the bottom of the driveway and we walked the rest of the way up the hill together, talking small talk about our week, laughing with each other. I was carrying a bowl of salad that Celeste had made and she and the girls walked behind us. He opened the door to his home and I stepped into a darkened room, wondering where the rest of his family was.

Suddenly, the lights came on to reveal over 50 of my very dearest friends and family, shouting "SURPRISE!" at the top of their lungs. I was speechless. Why were they all here? It was a dream-like moment...ethereal and surreal. These were the faces of the people I love the most and that love me. My two oldest daughters from college were there, my brother and his wife from out of town, the guys in my men's group, friends from church – everyone TOTALLY out of context. My birthday was over a month ago, right? Why were they all here? I was totally confused. Tears flooded my eyes when I finally realized what was happening. This was for me.

My wife had put together a surprise party to celebrate the two year mark of sobriety from my addictions and God's restoration of our lives together. It was the most wonderful party I have ever been to in my life. My very best friends and family coming together to honor what God had done in our lives. It was an experience I will NEVER forget. I wish I could relive that party every day. I kept thinking to myself, "this MUST be what heaven will be like someday." *(Read my wife's thoughts about this event on her blog:*

www.celestewilcox.com/a-time-to-celebrate-a-letter-to-my-husband)

The evening included a special song that my good friend Bill and my oldest daughter Tori performed together and a tear-filled letter to me that my wife read out loud to us all. She finished off the celebration by giving me a beautiful, custom-made two-year token to commemorate my sobriety. I keep it inside of my wallet at all times. The whole thing was, in a word – unforgettable.

This is how God works. He takes the things we have broken and restores them. He takes the shattered pieces that should be swept up and thrown in the trash heap and he makes a breath-taking mosaic from them. He takes the ashes from the fire of failure and pain...and makes something amazing and beautiful.

So to my wife, the Brave One, I honor you in return. I am grateful beyond words for your love, commitment, loyalty to me. You're strength has truly made me a better man than I ever hoped to be – still not EVERYTHING you deserve, but we're working on that, right? Tomorrow is a new day. We will hold hands tightly and walk into what God has for us together, letting Him change us even more. Thank you for fighting with me, for me, for us. I love you more today than I ever have...but not as much as I will tomorrow!

I couldn't help but think of the song below as I wrote this chapter because it describes our relationship and commitment to each other now so perfectly.

Love is not a Fight – Warren Barfield[12]

> Love is not a place
> To come and go as we please
> It's a house we enter in
> Then commit to never leave

So lock the door behind you
Throw away the key
We'll work it out together
Let it bring us to our knees

>**CHORUS**
>Love is a shelter in a raging storm
>Love is peace in the middle of a war
>And if we try to leave
>May God send angels to guard the door
>No, love is not a fight
>But it's something worth fighting for

To some love is a word
That they can fall into
But when they're falling out
Keeping that word is hard to do

>**CHORUS**
>Love is a shelter in a raging storm
>Love is peace in the middle of a war
>And if we try to leave
>May God send angels to guard the door
>No, love is not a fight
>But it's something worth fighting for

Love will come to save us
If we'll only call
He will ask nothing from us
But demand we give our all

CHORUS
Love is a shelter in a raging storm
Love is peace in the middle of a war
And if we try to leave
May God send angels to guard the door
No, love is not a fight
But it's something worth fighting for

Yes, I will fight for you
Would you fight for me?
It's worth fighting for

BULLETPROOF GLASS CHALLENGE:

Honest IN (Being authentic with myself, self-assess) –

- Am I willing to honestly look at how my selfish actions hurt others?
- Am I able to take responsibility for those things and consider what it would look like to make amends?

Honest UP (Being authentic with God, pray, confess) –

- Ask God to bring to mind any and all selfish actions you've committed that have hurt others and ask Him for forgiveness.
- Pray this: "God, please show me what I need to do to mend these broken relationships and bring about reconciliation. Give me courage to do my part to make things right."

Honest OUT (Being authentic with others, share, discuss) –
- Discuss, in detail, what God reveals to you about your own selfishness with your trusted friends.
- Ask your bulletproof brothers what they think would be involved in making amends and repairing the relationships.
- WILLINGNESS CHECK: Remember, God is in your friends and will speak through them into your life and situation. Are you willing to truly listen, consider and pray about how they respond? If not, why?

CHAPTER FIFTEEN

FUR, TEETH & KNIVES

The two large English Bulldogs ran fast through the open gate out of their yard across the street towards us. I expected they were coming to put my dog, Gunner through the sniff test and make a new friend. We've had lots of dogs do that to us when Gunner and I are out walking. Normally, a dog would run up to Gunny and they do this little circular dance and after things pass the sniff test, they play.

That's not what went down this time. These dogs wanted blood.

But first, a little background. I've lived for a long time with six females in my house. My wife, my four daughters and a devilish miniature Yorkshire terrier named Cocoa – (yes, I am guilty of calling this dog the "devil dog"). I am WAY outnumbered and up until just last year I was the sole source of testosterone in our family. I don't know what caused me to make the decision, but at some point I began feeling at such a disadvantage to all the women in the house that I decided I needed some backup. It was time for me to buy a "man dog."

About the time I started thinking and talking about my "man dog" idea with Celeste, we noticed a Facebook post from one of our friends that they had a litter of pups for sale. The dogs were super cute and of a breed we had never heard of called "Black Mouth Cur." We did some research and found out these dogs are bird dogs, hounds and they are known for their loyalty and friendliness. When I read that, I knew I wanted one. Their name comes because of the distinctive black shading around their nose and mouth area. The word "Cur" simply means "mongrel" or "mutt." We also discovered that one of the most famous Black Mouth Curs was the fictional dog in the book "Old Yeller" by Fred Gipson, written way back in 1956. When Disney made a movie out of the story years later, they used a yellow lab to play the character of Old Yeller, but in the original book, Yeller was a Black Mouth Cur.

So one day my wife and I went over and picked one of the last male pups left in the litter. We took him home and the whole family tossed around potential names. My third oldest daughter, Mattea, suggested we name him after the town of "Gunnison," Colorado where we go on family vacation almost every year together. I loved it, so he was formally named "Gunnison," but we all started calling him Gunny right from the very start.

I started taking Gunny to work with me every day for the next year and we became fast friends. I worked in an office alone at the time and he would sit at my feet or sleep by the door most of the time. In the rare times when I'd have a visitor or if the UPS or FedEx man would drop off a package, Gunny would get so excited to meet a new friend that he'd usually roll over onto his back and pee on himself…literally. One day, four girls that worked for one of my clients stopped by my office to pick up some materials that I had created for them to take to an event. They saw Gunny staring with his puppy dog eyes at them through the front door and asked if he could come out so they could see him. I agreed and opened the door. Gunny jumped all over the girls and was so excited that he peed all over their feet! Nice. Still, I loved having him at my office, a fun, loyal companion to hang out with. Gunny is the best.

As much as I had predetermined that Gunner's official role in my life was to be my new "man dog," the reality was that I probably more looked to him as a "therapy" dog. He was just what I needed as I was entering my second year of sobriety and continuing to recover from addiction. I installed a special wire separator in the back of my Jeep so he could ride back there and not be tempted to jump over the seat and up into the front. If it were up to him, Gunny would ride with his head out the driver's side window as he sat on my lap and I drove.

At home, Gunny couldn't have been more fun. He's got tons of energy, a lovable, playful personality and a super loud but harmless bark. He sleeps on a big giant circular pad I call his "pie." "Get on your pie, Gunner!" That's his signal to settle down when he's getting too rambunctious and he almost always obeys. Gunny likes to talk too. He can darn near say "I love you" in his moany dog language. It's pretty hilarious. We also love to sing songs together. I'll start singing out loud, "Ohhhhh the Gunny!!" and he'll usually join in and begin howling along. Another thing Gunny does that cracks us all up is that he insists on being in the middle of any physical affection between family members. When I hug Celeste or give her a kiss, Gunny runs and jumps up on us and starts barking. He can't stand to be left out of any physical touch that is occuring. If we're sitting down in a chair reading or talking, he'll come and place his body against our legs and lean against us just to have the physical connection. That's why we also call him "the leaner." "Uh oh. Here comes the leaner!" In addition to adding to the "male" factor in our household, Gunny is just a ton of fun in general. He's always up for an adventure and loves to go hiking on the trails with my wife and me.

About six months before we bought Gunner, I had read a blog post by a guy that works for John Eldredge's ministry, Ransomed Heart (John and his team at Ransomed Heart have had a strong, positive impact on my life and marriage). The blogger's name is Morgan Snyder. I had met him briefly at one of the Ransomed Heart men's conferences I had attended. I had been following his blog for a while – great spiritual writing focused on men called "Become Good Soil." He had written a post called,

"*Castration – the Case for Carrying a Knife."*
(*www.becomegoodsoil.com/castration-a-case-for-carrying-a-knife*).

The article was about true manhood versus false manhood and he used the act of carrying a knife as the literary vehicle for making his point. I thought it was funny as hell and it really got me thinking about my own sense of manhood. After I read it, I was inspired and went out and bought a nice folding knife. I've worn it in almost every situation since then and it has come in handy many times. But never more necessary than on the Sunday morning that Gunny and I were out for a walk.

I had just bought him one of those choker collars with the metal spines that kind of pinch in on the neck if the dog pulls too hard and we were trying it out. Gunny had been a bit wild on the leash and I was working with him to get him to settle down a bit. We had gone about two miles or so and were headed back home, probably still about a mile out. That's when the bulldogs showed up.

I've been around a few bulldogs in my life and every one of them was pretty laid back and friendly, so that's what I expected this time. The ones I had been around in the past just slobbered and farted a lot, so my impression was that they were fairly harmless. When these two came running out of the yard across the street, I expected they were just coming to introduce themselves and then play. Gunny saw them coming and I think he expected the same thing too. But instead, they both took one sniff of Gunny and then attacked – FAST and HARD.

...they both took one sniff of Gunny and then attacked – FAST and HARD.

The attack took us both totally by surprise. It was an ambush. The bigger one jumped on top of Gunny, took a giant mouthful of his fur and flesh into his jaws, clamped down and then pulled Gunny over onto his side and held him down. The other one just started biting and ripping, biting and ripping, taking advantage of Gunny's vulnerable position on his back, feet up in the air. Gunny howled and was in no position to fight back. Adrenaline rushed.

I started yelling at the top of my lungs at the dogs "Get off him! Get off him! HEY!!!" I pulled as hard as I could on the leash trying to get Gunny up off the ground but the tines of the choker collar just dug into his neck and made him howl even more. That wasn't working at all, so I started kicking the big bulldog on top as hard as I could with the tip of my shoe, right into his ribs. I'm a pretty big guy – 6'2", 250-ish. I ride a bike and I've got pretty big legs but this dog didn't even flinch when I kicked. I kicked him seven or eight times as hard as I could and he didn't react at all. It was like kicking a giant, wet sand bag. I screamed louder, looking up and down the street to see if someone was hearing this and would come to help, but no one was in view. I decided we needed to run and I was going to have to just pull on that choker and drag Gunner out of the fray. Surely if we could get just put a little distance between us and them we could out run these fat, vicious beasts. "Come on Gunny! RUN!" I screamed at the top of my lungs, took off running and yanked on the leash. The bulldogs clamped down, Gunny rolled over and my feet got tangled in the leash. I fell hard on my shoulder, scraping off a layer of flesh from my elbow and back. I looked up and the smaller bulldog sees an opportunity, let go of Gunny and comes at ME! I jumped up just before he could get his teeth into me, but he took several swipes at my ankles with his huge jowls. I looked up and down the street again and yelled for help. "HELP! SOMEBODY HELP US!" I was out of options and no one was coming for help.

These dogs were going to kill Gunner.

These dogs were going to kill Gunner.

That's when I noticed my knife on the ground. It had fallen out of my pocket when I fell. What I did at that next moment was purely instinctual. I didn't have time to think through consequences or consider the dangers - I knew if I didn't act fast, Gunny was going to die. I reached down and grabbed my knife, flicked it open and drove it deep into the side of the big bulldog TWO TIMES as he was still holding Gunner on the ground. I expected that would hurt him enough that he would let go and Gunny and I could run...but it didn't. The adrenaline must have been flowing so hard in this dog that he never even felt the slice of my knife. I pulled it out and waited for a second to see if he would respond to the pain and let go, but he didn't. The other one jumped on Gunny again and started biting him all over. His paws, his groin, his ears – where ever he could get his teeth into my dog amidst the violent thrashing. Gunner was completely helpless – just a pup less than a year old, crying out in pain and getting eaten alive. I had no choice. No one was coming to our aid. I was going to have to kill one or both of these dogs to save Gunner.

My reaction visceral, instinctual. I was protecting one of my own. I stabbed the big dog three or four more times in the ribs, driving my knife all the way to the hilt each time. All I wanted him to do was let go of Gunny, but he wouldn't. Finally after the fourth jab, the dog realized he was hurt and let go. He shook his huge body in reaction to the pain, looked up at me and then turned and waddled away back towards the yard where they had come from, leaving a trickle-trail of blood in his wake. The smaller one stopped biting as well and followed the alpha male away. Gunny was in shock, lying on his side, bleeding in the middle of the street and still, no one came to help us. He tried to stand up, but couldn't, so I lifted him to his feet. "Come on buddy. Let's get out of here." I tried to get him to jog with me and he did his best, but he was hurt. We both dripped blood as we limped along the last mile back home, looking over our shoulders the whole way...filled with fear.

When Gunny and I walked into the house and my wife saw us, she was shocked. "What the heck happened?!!" I was still so hyped up on my own adrenaline and out of breath that I had a hard time telling her the story. I assessed both of our wounds. I was bruised and had two large abrasions on my arm and shoulder, both bleeding. Gunny had a couple of large "rip" wounds where a layer of flesh had just been stripped away leaving bright pink, bleeding skin. He also had puncture wounds literally all over, maybe fifty or so. We both got in the shower, got the blood washed off of us and I made sure Gunny didn't need serious medical help. He didn't have any wounds that were going to be life threatening, but he was definitely torn up, sore and scared. More than anything, both of us were just shook up emotionally. It was by far the most violent thing either of us had ever experienced.

Putting spiritual concepts into words can be difficult. It has always helped me when writers, pastors or teachers use analogies, metaphors or even better, examples from popular culture like scenes from movies or words from a song to make a spiritual point. I find spiritual concepts much easier to grasp and understand when they are put into those kinds of contexts. I think that's why Jesus used parables so often when He taught. To me, my experience with these dogs is a parable in and of itself which taught me a lot.

I don't want to over-spiritualize, but I did learn two important lessons from this frightening event. First, it reminded me of how similarly the enemy can attack us – fast and hard. These attacks often come out of nowhere and without warning, just like the dogs did.

"Your enemy the devil prowls around like a roaring lion, seeking whom he can devour." - I Peter 5:8

"Resist the devil, and he will flee from you." - James 4:7

Our enemy hates us. John 10:10 tells us that the devil's primary mission is to "steal, kill and destroy." Just like I was prepared in having my knife with me (although I never could have imagined having to use it in the way I did), the spiritual equivalent would be being prepared to fight the enemy whenever he attacks. Not only must we be prepared, we must be willing to resist and to do the dirty work of spiritual battle. Using a knife like that was hard (really, it was awful), but it was necessary. It's spiritual equivalent would be doing the spiritual things that I might not want to do when I'm under attack: reaching out for help from a friend, asking someone to pray for me, praying specifically against the enemy in the name of Jesus, confessing sin to a friend, taking responsibility in the way I've wronged or hurt someone, making amends, risking embarrassment, etc. These are spiritually hard things to do – taking out the knife and defending our own.

The other lesson I learned is that emotional injuries are real and need to be cared for. Both Gunner and I suffered after the attack. I had nightmares (literally) for several nights afterwards causing me to lose sleep. I'd have these horrifying visions of me driving that knife into the dog that would flash across my mind in the middle of the day while I was working. I carried this heavy sadness for over a week – grieving that I had killed someone's pet. It was an opportunity for me to seek out help from some of my friends and a pastor at church to talk through the event and for prayer which helped me reconcile the strong emotions and guilt I was feeling.

After things had calmed down, my wife said this to me: "You know, two years ago if this had happened, you'd be drinking to numb it and would already have a lawyer lined up to sue those people. You're a different man today." That was a true statement and it was good to hear her say. God working in my life through the 12 Steps had given me a new set of spiritual tools to deal with difficult life circumstances like this.

Gunner struggled for several months afterwards as well. He became skittish for a while around other dogs, expecting them to jump him and attack when they came around. For several months he wouldn't let me walk him up that section of road where the dogs had attacked. He'd freak out when we went on a walk and someone's sprinkler system went off suddenly – just weird stuff like that. We both had a bit of PTSD – post traumatic stabbing of dog.

Just as a follow-up, I called the Sherriff that day and reported the attack. They put me in touch with the officer that had gone out to the house – turns out the dog's owners had called 911 when the big bulldog arrived home with his wounds. I gave the officer my side of the story, scared that I was going to be in trouble for stabbing the dog and thinking no one had seen the event to corroborate my story. He said that two other people had actually called 911 also and had seen the whole thing. They told the exact same story as what I had told him. He said I had a right to press charges against the dog's owner if I wanted. I told him I had not interest in pressing charges but was more concerned about the safety of the people in the area. What if it had been my little girl walking with me or an elderly woman? I just didn't want anyone else to get hurt in the future.

When I asked him what happened to the dog I had stabbed, he told me that the owner had taken him to the vet but the vet had to put him down because he was not going to survive the wounds. He also told me he was headed back to the owner's house with Animal Control to pick up the other dog and they were going to put that one down as well. Turns out this was the THIRD time the police had been called about these dogs attacking someone. They had been terrorizing that neighborhood for a long time, he said.

Gunny and I have both recovered from our wounds. While I would never want to go through something like that again, I'm so thankful we both survived without serious injury. It could have been much worse for both of us. He is by far the best dog we've ever owned and a full-fledged member of our family. We got Gunny at a time in our lives when we all needed to heal, to laugh, and to take life a little less seriously. He is so loyal, lovable and friendly to everyone and every other dog we meet. He trusts me as his master and knows I've got his back always. I am so grateful for Gunny! The Lord uses him to teach me lessons of love, loyalty and kindness every day.

BULLETPROOF GLASS CHALLENGE:

Honest IN (Being authentic with myself, self-assess) –
- Can you recall your own traumatic experience like the dog attack?
- How would you describe a *spiritual* equivalent of that kind of traumatic event that you've experienced in your own life?

Honest UP (Being authentic with God, pray, confess) –
- How would God empower you to act or react in this kind of spiritual situation?
- Are you comfortable and experienced in "fighting" with spiritual warfare tactics and strategies?
- Pray and ask God for help in this area if needed.

Honest OUT (Being authentic with others, share, discuss) –
- Are you willing to reach out to a trusted friend or pastor for prayer/encouragement/wisdom when you face a difficult circumstance like this or does pride keep you from letting someone else in?
- Have you recently experienced something like this that you can share with your trusted friends in order to hear God's response to your own need? If so, share it…and listen.

CHAPTER SIXTEEN

WAR
Fight Club

I have a .50 caliber bullet that I keep in my Jeep. It's a HUGE round of machine-gun ammunition, designed for destruction for sure. No, it's not for personal protection – I don't own a gun capable of firing it and this one is a "dummy" round anyway; no gunpowder inside.

It's a symbol, a reminder for me that I am at war.

It's really not my intention to sound all weird and spooky when I talk about spiritual warfare. There have been volumes written about the subject, some good, most just flat bizarre. Before, when I was deep into my addictions, living a very self-centered and selfish life, I didn't really have a sense that I was in a spiritual battle. For sure there were dark days, suspicious occurrences and certainly a sense of fear, shame and confusion that surrounded me, but the thought of being at war was just not really on the radar. I realize now that's because I had chosen NOT to fight. If there was a real spiritual battle going on around me at the time, I was AWOL.

The further I get into recovery, the clearer becomes my understanding of the spiritual world, what is going on in it and how it works in general. The Big Book of Alcoholics Anonymous hints at this kind of newfound spiritual awareness that is common to those seeking God in recovery...

"We have found much of heaven and have been rocketed into a fourth dimension of existence of which we had not even dreamed."   *- Alcoholics Anonymous, page 25*

There is one verse in particular about spiritual warfare in the Bible that is quoted often because it sounds so mysterious and intriguing, but it is nonetheless terrifyingly true. Here is what God's word says about the spiritual war in which we are engaged:

"For our struggle is not against flesh and blood, but against the rulers, against the authorities, against the powers of this dark world and against the spiritual forces of evil in the heavenly realms."
- Ephesians 6:12

This verse used to remind me of Halloween. Spiritual forces of evil? Seriously? Something in me would read this and I would give it a big eye-roll and just brush it off as myth, a part of the Bible that I just wasn't going to understand, something I should just overlook and move on. It's been said, "The greatest lie of the devil is to convince one that he doesn't exist." I wouldn't say that back then I didn't believe the devil existed, but I definitely didn't take him or his forces very seriously. Today, I see things quite differently...thus the bullet. It reminds me that I have a constant choice to make in my own spirit – to fight against a very real enemy that is opposing me.

Or, of course, there is always surrender.

Hollywood has made much of the devil. I was exposed to Hollywood's version of the enemy as a very young boy when I watched old black and white horror movies on TV (think late 60's, early 70s). You know, stuff like the old Frankenstein, Dracula and Werewolf movies, Vincent Price stuff, etc. I think a defining moment for me was when I was spending the night with a couple that was babysitting my brother and me when we were maybe 12 and 10. They had rented "The Exorcist" and allowed us to watch it.

Bad idea.

This proved to be the start of a very unhealthy interest in the horror genre for me. My brother and I were attracted to almost any horror movie after that and we watched so many of them; A Nightmare on Elm Street, Friday the 13th, Halloween, Alien, Jaws, etc. What I thought was simply harmless fun eventually turned into an unhealthy striving after the rush of adrenaline generated by being in the presence of the spiritual force of evil called "fear." A steady dose of fear desensitized me to the spiritual pain and power of other spiritual forces like violence, murder, terror, hatred, anger, vengeance and more. These are all common themes in horror.

Horror movies are really just modern day parables about the enemy and how men have submitted to his power. These are simply twisted, upside-down, evil reproductions of Jesus' teachings of life, love and goodness. Horror movies teach about death, fear, pain and hatred. In a way, horror movies make a fictional character out of evil which allows us to easily dismiss its very real presence in the world today. It's just a MOVIE! Right?

Here's what I learned by watching horror movies, and I didn't fully understand this until I learned about the origins of the word "worship" which I discussed earlier in Chapter 5 (Worthship). Here is the definition again...

Origin: ...before 900 AD; (noun) Middle English wors (c) hipe, worthssipe, Old English worthscipe, variant of weorthscipe; see worth-ship; (v.) Middle English, derivative of the noun Worship is an act of religious devotion usually directed towards a deity. The word is derived from the Old English worthscipe, meaning worthiness or worth-ship—to give, at its simplest, worth to something.[13]

When I watch a horror movie, I am proving and acknowledging its value by "giving" my attention to it and thus affirming its value. I am "giving" my personal time to it. I "give" my money in the form of a ticket purchase. Giving attention, time and money are ALL ACTS OF WORSHIP. In doing so I am, in essence, "worshipping" horror and the evil spiritual forces these movies espouse - I am ascribing value to horror, fear and a host of other dark forces. View a horror movie once or twice, now or then and it may not be all that harmful (although I'd now argue that, depending on the content, it is probably contrary to Paul's mandate of Philippians 4:8, "whatever is good, whatever is lovely, etc."). Do it often and over a course of years like I did and I can tell you from experience, it produces a profound, negative spiritual impact that hardens our hearts towards a good, pure and loving God.

...it produces a profound, negative spiritual impact that hardens our hearts towards a good, pure and loving God.

By worshipping horror, I granted a host of enemy forces permission into my life and authority over my spirit and the domain of life God had put under my control. This was an underlying source of my own spiritual sickness.

Where does fear come from? Paul, the same man that penned the verses above, also wrote in his letter to Timothy, "God does not give us a spirit of fear, but of power and love and self-control." - II Timothy 1:7. An overwhelming sense of fear doesn't come from God - it comes from the devil. In and of itself, what good comes of fear? Of course God uses fear for good all the time.

He uses it to alert us to danger and to move us in the opposite direction towards safety – I understand that. But fear in and of itself is just pure evil. Think ISIS, Hannibal Lecter, and abortion clinics. Fear is but one of the devil's numerous tools. You can add to fear anxiety, worry, resentment, rage, violence, death, despair, shame...and there are many more (I'll list them in a moment). Watching horror movies puts our spirits awash in these negative forces. THESE are the "spiritual forces of evil in the heavenly realms" that Paul is talking about. And you know what? We can't control ANY of them on our own. So why would we want to marinate our hearts and minds in them?

I can attest to the power of these forces in my own life and they have had a devastating effect. Bowing to them came in many different forms for me, outside of watching horror. Let's take fear as an example - I want to explain how it worked in my life. I experienced probably the most significant amounts of fear that I ever have when my personal financial world was collapsing around 2009. I want to use that time for me as a real-life example.

When I would sit down to pay personal or business expenses and there was not enough money in the bank or in the coming cash flow of the future to pay them, when all of my lines of credit and credit cards were maxed, when I couldn't afford to pay the lease payments on company equipment that I would use to generate income, when I lacked the funds to pay our car and our house payments – I experienced a significant amount of fear and shame. Fear of what would happen when I failed to make the payments – collections, judgments, repossession, foreclosure, etc. Shame of what friends, colleagues, and customers would think of me and my inability to support my family or sustain my business. Mix fear and shame with the spiritual force of "pride" which tells me I can handle all of this on my own (I'm smart enough to figure this out, right?), which in turn convinces me NOT to discuss what I'm going through openly with really anyone...and you have a deadly, secretive pressure cooker of spiritual and emotional power that demands to be relieved.

I'm sure almost everyone can relate to the discomfort of the forces I'm describing. Being in fear and shame FEELS bad to anyone that has an awareness of the state of their own heart. To me, it felt like being ON FIRE. I hated it. I believe this is a small sense of what hell really must be like. There was no PHYSICAL pain – this was all just unbearable spiritual and emotional pain. I did not have the spiritual capacity to withstand that kind of fear and shame. I did not possess the power to sustain these forces on my own. I simply didn't possess a way to even manage them, much less conquer them. They were so powerful and demanding that it felt like I HAD to take action to alleviate the discomfort they were causing. The best way I can describe it is that it was like I had been set on fire and I was running around in a panic trying to find the nearest pool of water to jump into. The nearest pools I could find were a bottle of alcohol, pornography, pills, sex. These things ALWAYS would put the fires out...for a while. After the numbing effects of these substances and behaviors would wear off, the flames would flare back up and I'd be off and running again looking for another pool. This is just another example of what the cycle of addiction looked like in real life for me.

Here on the other side of addiction, I can look back on this experience, this cycle I was caught in and see something different. God has opened my eyes to what is really going on and through working my process of recovery, He has given me a "simple set of spiritual tools" that allows me to deal properly with these spiritual forces. I had to learn the hard way that this is, in fact, the fighting of a brutal spiritual war just like Paul said.

And a spiritual war must be fought with spiritual weapons. The verse I quoted earlier from Ephesians 6:12 is packed right in the center of Paul's treatise on spiritual warfare and "putting on the full armor of God." This is the spiritual armor that most of us are aware of; the helmet of salvation, the breastplate of righteousness, the belt of truth, the sword of the spirit and the shoes of the gospel of peace. There are volumes available about the full armor of God and I don't have enough room here to give it the attention it deserves.

One of my spiritual gifts is the gift of "discernment." I think this gift has been strengthened and my spiritual senses heightened through my experience with addiction and recovery from it. Most of the time, I have an extremely keen self-awareness and a sense of different spiritual forces impacting me in my own life, which makes it fairly easy to notice in others or around situations. I walk away from many encounters with someone I've met with and I'll have an overwhelming sense of that person "experiencing a lot of fear" or "he seems like he's struggling with pride" or "I can tell that person is experiencing a ton different of shame." This isn't something I use to judge others. It's both a blessing and a curse to be able to recognize shame, anxiety, grief, sadness, despair and a host of other spiritual forces in myself and other people. It's a blessing in that it gives me great insight into how to pray effectively for others and encourage them towards a godly response to their situation. It's a curse in that I often walk away from an interaction feeling a great weight of sadness and frustration in seeing what is going on with someone and yet feeling helpless to rescue them.

My wife also has the spiritual gift of discernment. This can be tricky for both of us because we can often discern wrongly – we're NOT mind readers or psychics, so I don't want it to sound like we have some kind of mystical power, because we don't. But we do often sense things that are difficult to explain, hard to get our minds around, things that compel us to pray for more wisdom and godly insight into a situation. Again, I don't want to over-spiritualize what I'm about to explain and I absolutely do not believe that there's a demon under every bush. But what I will say is that I am convinced that we DO have an enemy and the he is alive and well in our world. Our enemy is a spirit and the Bible tells us much about him. He commands other evil spiritual forces that are set against us. He has significant power over us as the Prince of this world and can affect us in many harmful ways, much like I've described. While I have spent a good amount of time studying spiritual warfare and I have a pretty solid understanding of it, I am by no means an expert. I'm not an exorcist or a demon-hunter. But I DO now possess enough basic knowledge about how to deal effectively with a very real and dangerous spiritual enemy.

My wife and I have experienced several times when our physical world has visibly clashed with the spirit world. Just like God's Holy Spirit can come upon people and affect their actions (read Acts chapter 2), I have experienced these enemy forces "manifest" themselves in different ways in the physical world as well. I don't believe by any means that the things I've seen are unique and I don't believe this is how the enemy typically or even commonly manifests – I just know what I've seen and discerned and experienced – stuff that is extremely REAL and yet difficult to explain.

Here's an example. One night, my youngest daughter came into our room in the middle of the night (this was at a time when I was still struggling with alcohol, sex and pornography addictions). She woke my wife up, crying, asking if she could sleep in our room. She had a really high fever and was sweating profusely so we let her lie down on a large love seat we had in the bedroom and we laid back down in bed ourselves. Within a few minutes my daughter started crying, moaning loudly, yet unintelligibly. My wife got up and went to console her. I was dead tired and the whole thing was irritating to me – I showed very little empathy for my daughter, but was more concerned about my own sleep (remember, I was an addict consumed by my own selfishness and self-centeredness).

She had been complaining that she was seeing things – "They're all over the bed! Make them go away! They're scaring me!" My wife assumed she was just hallucinating because she had a very high fever, maybe 103°, so she put her in a cool bath and got the fever down. When she laid her back down on the loveseat, she started getting REALLY agitated and scared. She was clawing at my wife, crying uncontrollably. This wasn't normal behavior at all for my daughter. My wife prayed for her – I could hear her praying against whatever was there bothering my daughter. Then I heard my daughter say loudly, "Make them go away, mommy! Make them go!" So I sat up and looked over at her and she was pointing up at the ceiling above our bed - nothing there but the ceiling fan which was off. My wife asked her, "What is it baby? What do you want me to make go away? What do you see?" My daughter replied, "They're coming out of the bed! Don't you see them? They're coming up out of the bed! There's so many of them! Make them go away!" My daughter was completely terrified at this point and obviously seeing something she believed was real.

My wife turned to me and said, "You need to get over here right now and pray for your daughter and make this stop!" I could sense fear and anger in my wife's voice and DEFINITELY FEAR in my daughter. This wasn't a request, it was a demand. I jumped up and complied. I laid my hands on my daughter and simply prayed that whatever she was seeing had no rights over her and I commanded them to get out of our room immediately, in the name of Jesus. The result was almost instant. Within less than a minute she was sound asleep on the love seat and her fever did not return.

The next morning at the breakfast table we asked her if she remembered what had happened and she said, yes, she did. "What was it you were seeing coming out of the bed?" my wife asked her.

"There were all these things with wings flying up out of the bed by daddy and going up into the roof. There were tons of them." She paused and then said, "Can I have some more cereal?" I had a nagging feeling that those "things" were there because of me and the secret sin I was hiding. I had given the enemy permission to come into our home through my sinful behavior and he was having a field day with my family. My wife had prayed similar prayers of spiritual warfare over my daughter but with no result. Since I am the spiritual authority of our home and of my family, the spirits had to respond to my command under the ultimate authority of Jesus...and they did. Trust me, that's NOT because I am some kind of amazing prayer warrior - it's because this is simply how spiritual authority works. God has granted ALL spiritual authority in the entire universe to His one and only Son, Jesus. Jesus has granted His followers the authority over these spirits as well (see Mark 3:15 and Matthew 10:8) - all other spirits must assume their proper place of power according to HIS will...period.

Now when I encounter and recognize the powerful spiritual forces like fear or shame or confusion, I simply pray against them and let the enemy know that I am putting them under the authority of Jesus and that I am revoking any privileges they've been given. I often will call one of my close friends in my men's group to pray this with me if I sense the force is particularly strong or if there is a lot of spiritual chaos going on. They'll pray with me on the phone and things are usually back in order within a few hours if not sooner.

Look, this is not magic or some kind of secret formula. There are numerous examples of demons being cast out of people in the Bible – by Jesus, by his disciples, by the apostle Paul and others, so it's nothing new. This is simply one way to claim the authority issued to us by Jesus over the spiritual forces we encounter. All we have to do is be willing to pray and claim the authority that Jesus has given us.

"I have given you authority to trample on snakes and scorpions and to overcome all the power of the enemy; nothing will harm you."   *- Luke 10:19*

The Bible also seems to indicate that many demonic spirits can represent specific spiritual forces. Consider when Jesus commanded a "deaf and mute" spirit to "come out of him and never enter him again" (Mark 9:25). This appears to be a spirit devoted solely to keeping a person from communicating; hearing OR speaking. I would call this a spirit of "impairment." Again in Matthew 12:22, Jesus is presented with a demon possessed man who was blind and mute and Jesus healed him so that he could both talk and see (Matthew 12:22). The book of Acts speaks of a woman that had a "spirit of divination" that was harassing the apostle Paul (Acts 16:16). I believe this is a spirit whose sole purpose is to promote "witchcraft." King Saul was sent an evil spirit by God (I Samuel 16:14) that "terrorized" or "tormented" him. I'd call this a spirit of "torment." Malachi 3:11 speaks of "the devourer," a spiritual force that gnaws away at a person or nation's resources and assets – a "devouring" spirit.

It is passages like these along with the confirmation of my own personal experience that leads me to believe that there are demonic entities whose sole existence is to promote specific spiritual forces like fear, shame, doubt, confusion, distraction, etc. I believe they focus their efforts on increasing these kinds of negative emotions to the point that we are held captive by them, specifically influencing us to discharge our God-given power of "causation" in ways that are contrary to God's will. The Bible clearly states that demons are fallen angels, eternal beings, no doubt granted the gift of free will just as we have been. What would keep a determined, rebellious, eternal being from fully committing and marshalling all of its God-given resources to promoting a specific type of evil? I think nothing.

Look, I am not a "demonologist." Like I've already said, I do not believe there is a demon under every bush or behind every painful or difficult circumstance. I DO however believe that these spiritual forces are REAL, they are set AGAINST the purposes of God and they require specific, strategic warfare tactics to defeat…ALL and ONLY in the name of Jesus and subject to the truth of God's word. Because I had lived my life pursuing my own selfish, evil desires, I had made way for many enemy forces to enter into my domain. Just because I am saved by Christ does not mean I don't have an enemy or that he has stopped pursuing me with evil intent. I NEED a Savior, a higher authority, that gives me the power and authority to banish his evil forces from my domain when they come slithering back in.

If you're not familiar with spiritual warfare, I'd encourage you to use your own language when you pray against the enemy. I've included a prayer below that you can use as a pattern or inspiration for your own prayer if you think it is helpful. This is the type of prayer I often say when I discern there is a specific spiritual presence or force working against me or my family or at times when things just don't "seem" right in my own spirit or in my household. AGAIN – I MUST EMPHASIZE: this is NOT a formula or some kind of magic spell. This is simply a recitation and acknowledgement of God's truth in the face of spiritual forces that are set against us. It is simply a prayer that assists us in rightly ordering the way we relate to these spiritual forces in our hearts and minds in accordance with God's word (see specifically Paul's treatise on spiritual warfare in Ephesians 6). It is how I have learned to pray and I've found it effective, so I want to share it for you to consider as you grow in your own personal relationship with Christ.

Example of a Prayer used in Spiritual Warfare:

"Lord Jesus, I am experiencing dark, spiritual forces that are opposing me and making life difficult, painful and confusing for me and my family. I am your son, Lord, and I submit to your authority. I claim your spiritual authority over my life, my family and everything you've given me in my domain. I come against these enemy forces now in your name, Lord Jesus. I specifically bind and render powerless the forces of _____, _____, and _____, that are present here along with any other enemy forces set against us. These forces have no rights to me, (my wife, my children by name). I revoke any rights or privileges they may have been given and I break any vows or agreements that have been made with these forces now in the name of Jesus (Sometimes I may speak directly to these forces in the name of Jesus just as He and His disciples did many times in scripture). Shame (or fear or doubt, etc.), you have no rights over our hearts, minds, spirits or bodies. You have no rights to anything in my domain or to anything under my authority. You have no rights to any of my possessions including our home, cars, electronics, computers, phones, appliances, pets, finances, jobs, bank accounts, expenses or income or anything else in my domain. I command all of you now, in the name of Jesus, to take your servants, works and effects and go immediately to the throne of Christ for judgment and you may not return. I command this by the power and authority of the Lord Jesus Christ. You must submit to him and it's in His name that I pray. Amen."

Below is a list of common spiritual forces that has been helpful in allowing me to recognize, name and pray against their specific effects in different situations. It is by no means exhaustive, but will hopefully broaden your view of the different ways that spiritual forces may oppose you in your day-to-day life. As you read through the list, consider how you might have experienced these forces in the past and what their spiritual impact was on you at the time.

Common Negative/Evil Spiritual Forces:

EMOTIONAL
Fear, anger, pride, resignation, shame, confusion, doubt, worry, anxiety, distraction, frustration, ambivalence, cowardice, foreboding joy, aloneness, self-pity, self-loathing, discontentment, discouragement, vanity

PHYSICAL
Drunkenness, gluttony, laziness, indulgence, dissipation, violence, murder, death, suicide, self-mutilation, self-harm

FINANCIAL
Greed, thievery, wastefulness, devouring spirit, destruction, gambling

SEXUAL
Lust, sexual immorality, adultery, pornography, whoredom, prostitution, fornication, nudism, voyeurism, masturbation, sadism, masochism

SOCIAL
Deceit, envy, resentment (unforgiveness), unfaithfulness, disloyalty, hatred, dishonesty, jealousy, vengeance, mistrust, murder, selfishness, isolation, desolation, hatred, rage, justice

OTHER
Idolatry, witchcraft, sabotage, sorcery, accusation

On that .50 caliber ammo shell that I keep in my Jeep, I've written the words, "Bulletproof Strong" and the scripture reference, "Romans 13:12", which reads...

"The night is nearly over and the day is almost here, so let us put aside the deeds of darkness and put on the armor of light."

That verse means a lot to me. It is the verse God brought to me during that very darkest of times in my life which I described earlier in Chapter 3 (Broken to Bulletproof). I had lived my life for SO MANY YEARS in darkness; lying, hiding, manipulating others to conceal my own "deeds of darkness" that I was too ashamed to put out in the light. I have a choice to put these deeds aside and to actively resist, in Jesus name, power and authority, the forces that are pushing me towards the darkness.

And why else would I need to put on armor but for the fact that I am at war? To me, the image of bulletproof glass came to be symbolic of the term "armor of light." It was God's reminder to me to LIVE WITH TRANSPARENCY – in TRUTH. As long as I keep telling the truth, I am protected by spiritual bulletproof glass. Truth is the FIRST piece of spiritual armor that Paul mentions in Ephesians 6 – "stand firm, having girded your loins with truth..." (Ephesians 6:14). It is symbolism for living a life of honesty...with myself, God and others. It's a constant choice I have to make: stay in the light by not keeping secrets...or...cover myself in a cloak of darkness by lying, hiding and manipulating those around me, presenting my FALSE self to the world. The .50 caliber bullet reminds me that the enemy always has me in his crosshairs and to fight this battle. It is my responsibility to keep telling the truth, stay transparent and stay in the light, regardless of how others are reacting or responding around me.

By putting on the armor of light, living transparently, others are able to see the miracle of God's power as I allow it to meet my own brokenness. This is fleshed out in my own life when I reach out to my wife, a friend or the guys in my men's group and say, "Hey, I'm not doing well. I'm struggling with this. Will you pray for me about it?" It is fleshed out when I'm willing to listen to God speak through THEM into my life. Being honest about my own sin, my character defects, my weaknesses and struggles...MATTERS. It matters to my wife, my kids, my friends, co-workers...the world. Regaining the trust I have broken, making amends to those I've hurt MATTERS. Being vulnerable and letting others see my own brokenness allows them to know me intimately, makes me a safe person in their lives that they can trust and opens up new opportunities for me to be used by God in the lives of others.

War is messy. Blood, guts, tears...they get spilled. People die. People get wounded. But in the spiritual realm, this looks quite different than in the physical.

FEAR keeps people like me from doing what God wants in everyday situations; "I'm afraid that if I tell my wife what I've done, she'll be disappointed in me so I'm just not going to tell her THAT."

SHAME keeps us from telling someone we trust what's REALLY going on in our hearts; "I'm feeling really ashamed of something I did. I wish I could talk to them about it but I'm afraid they'll reject me."

RESENTMENT keeps us from being at peace with God and others; "I'll never forgive her for what she did. She's such a &*$%#! I'm going to avoid her the next time I see her at church."

HATRED drives us to pick up an old transgression and weaponize it against someone we love; "Yeah, well YOU'RE the one that ran up the credit card and got us in this mess!"

VENGEANCE compels me to put myself in God's place and administer justice that I don't have the right to; "I don't have to let her talk to me like that. Next time she does that, I'm going to make her pay."

We face these forces and others like them every day. For me, engaging with these forces is a constant battle of owning up to my own shortcomings, failures, slip-ups, character defects and being honest with myself God and others about it, reminding myself that I am under a Higher Authority, and then commanding these forces set against me to submit to the authority of Jesus in my life and domain.

Shame, resentment, fear, hatred, vengeance. These are the "spiritual forces of evil," just to name a few. There are many more, indeed, and they can't be resisted in my own flesh. Spiritual problems like these require a spiritual solution that I don't have the ability to produce on my own. I need God and HIS power to overcome these forces in my life - through PRAYER and through being TRANSPARENT IN COMMUNITY with other believers. The .50 caliber round reminds me of this fight. It reminds me to stay engaged. Stay alert. Be ready to fight...by surrendering to my Lord's will...every moment, every heartbeat, every breath. This IS NOT a fight in which I have to BE STRONG and FIGHT OFF TEMPTATION so that I don't sin. On my own, I'm powerless over sin. But there is one who has ALL power and authority over these forces – Jesus.

In the movie, Braveheart, William Wallace rallied his rag-tag army of Scottish highlanders assembled at the battle of Sterling and said,

"...I see a whole army of my countrymen here in defiance of tyranny. You have come to fight as free men, and free men you are. What would you do without freedom? Will you fight?"

It's the same question I'm constantly presented with: Will I fight? Or am I going to run for the cover of my own selfish desires? Am I going to defect from under the authority and protection of God to pursue my own way? Who's side am I on anyway? So in these sometimes dark days, when there is much to be said about guns and violence and war, this is how Jesus speaks to me - in the simple imagery of a .50 caliber bullet (the flaming arrows of the enemy) and bulletproof glass (God's armor of light), reminding me to stay TRANSPARENT...and always be ready to FIGHT.

BULLETPROOF GLASS CHALLENGE:

Honest IN (Being authentic with myself, self-assess) –
- Are you able to recognize when you experience the "spiritual forces of evil" – forces such as anger, fear, regret, resentment, confusion, disappointment?
- How have you experienced some of these negative spiritual forces mentioned above and what impact have they had on you?
- Do you have an effective strategy to deal with these kinds of forces or do you frequently find yourself "ambushed" by the enemy with them?

Honest UP (Being authentic with God, pray, confess) –
- Do you acknowledge the spiritual battle discussed in this chapter or is it something you feel unaware of or deny outright? Explain your position on the subject.

- Ask God to help you form a solid spiritual strategy to fight the spiritual war you are engaged in.

Honest OUT (Being authentic with others, share, discuss) –
- Share your thoughts about spiritual warfare with your "Bulletproof" brothers and ask them for their experience with it.
- Discuss forming a strategy to work together to fight spiritually. Are you able to call each other in times of spiritual attack and ask for prayer and are you all willing to meet the request by praying prayers of spiritual warfare over each other?

CHAPTER SEVENTEEN

OUT OF ORDER
SORRY – Take the Stairs

When the planes hit the World Trade Centers on the fateful day of September 11, 2001, one of the first things that stopped working properly in those buildings were the elevators. Either the shafts themselves were damaged or the power was interrupted by the impact and explosions of the aircraft. Either way, this sent literally hundreds of people into the stairwells, and forced them all to make a slow, deadly march downward towards safety. It also forced fire personnel and first responders into the same stairwells trying to move upward in the buildings to help others. For some, the descent was more than 100 stories in a traffic jam of panicked crowds, and as we know, so many never made it out.

When an elevator is out of order, like in the Word Trade Centers, no one is getting to the top or the bottom unless they take the stairs. Similarly, if a toilet is out of order, things can get smelly and messy pretty quick. If a judge screams at you in a court of law, "you're out of order!" you're probably in big trouble. If your car is out of order, you're walking. When things are out of order, it affects life on many different levels, causes extra work, requires additional cleanup and can even create a dangerous and deadly situation. Order is good. Being "out of order" is bad.

In my work with other alcoholics and addicts, I find myself frequently in the company of men and women in their own life and death struggle with addiction. The minds of the sickest of these brothers and sisters have been so warped by substances and behaviors that they struggle even to put two logical sentences together most of the time. These are often the folks you see talking to themselves on the street corners and out in front of the liquor stores asking for spare change. Alcohol, drugs and years of addictive behaviors have knocked their thinking completely "out of order." My heart breaks for these people and usually their only chance for recovery is if they still have the capacity to be honest with themselves and the willingness to seek help. Sadly, so many of these people suffer the same fate as those in the World Trade Centers and simply aren't able to make it out alive.

When I first got into the business of sales, I found myself looking to others that were successful, prosperous and experienced in the business of selling for instruction. You don't have to look long through the book store or search long on the internet to find help in this area from any number of "master" sellers. I remember being particularly attracted to one particular sales and motivational guru (who will remain unnamed, but it is certainly someone you have heard of). I was enamored by this person's "larger-than-life" presentation of himself and his methods. I read his books, listened to his tapes (do they still make tapes?) and even attended a couple of his conferences.

If I were going to summarize what I learned from this man about how to be successful, it would be three-fold:

- *Model the methods, habits and actions of others that were successful at what I want to do to achieve my goals*
- *Learn how to "focus the power of self" to achieve my goals*
- *Learn how to master my emotional state (read: positive thinking) to achieve my goals*

So basically, the message I got was, in order to fulfill my goals, desires, dreams, I needed to copy others and become the "best version of me" that was possible. Sounds like a great plan, right?

This message is commonplace and prolific today in our culture. If I'm falling short in any particular area of life then certainly a "better version of me" will get me where I want to go. Don't make enough money? No problem – just work smarter and do what the masters do and you'll achieve your goals. Struggling with weight loss? No problem – learn how to control your eating better – (you can do it!) problem solved. Depressed? We've got the solution – master your emotional state by thinking positively and your life will change. Everything you need to live a better life lies within. SO many men are taught by their fathers AND our culture to pursue manhood through this line of thinking.

I, unfortunately, had to learn the hard way that all of this is a complete, gigantic, steaming pile of horse dung and I learned by diving headlong right into it. It was through fully committing to this kind of life strategy that my own thinking became out of order. The main problem with this self-powered life-strategy is that it is COMPLETELY OPPOSITE and DIAMETRICALLY OPPOSED to what God's word says...

There is a way that seems right to a man, but in the end it leads to death. - Proverbs 14:12

Whoever tries to keep their life will lose it, and whoever loses their life will preserve it. – Luke 17:33

No branch can bear fruit by itself; it must remain in the vine. Neither can you bear fruit unless you remain in me. – John 15:4

Apart from me, you can do nothing. – John 15:5

Need I continue? God's word says I must be dependent on HIM and not on ME. Here is my experience: life centered around the way of this world; securing myself, promoting myself, improving myself, indulging myself - produced the exact opposite of what that way promised.

But why?

Because, by following the advice and direction of worldly counsel, I allowed my desires, my thoughts, my hopes and dreams to become out of order. This was the "way that seemed right" to me. Thank God I was able to hit a "rock bottom" that didn't physically cause my death...but I certainly was headed that way.

When it came to the way I lived, the way I made decisions, took action, behaved, here's the way my heart was ordered:

- *Me first*
- *My idols second (the things in this world that gave me pleasure and appeased pain)*
- *God third*
- *Others last*

Everything was centered around my own personal benefit. This was the basic order of things, but I would swap the order of numbers one and two periodically if I felt it would benefit me. As much as I'd like to say differently, the reality of my life was that I gave very little consideration to what God wanted of me. Oh, I made sure it looked like I was giving God proper consideration (that was part of the mask I wore – see Chapter 12). I had to keep up my persona, my reputation, my character – that's why I would go to men's groups, lead Bible studies, lead worship at church. Yet in my heart, the reality was that my allegiance was pledged first and foremost to myself and to getting what I wanted, when I wanted, the way I wanted. If doing what God wanted seemed like it would produce what I wanted, then I did it and gave God the credit. If it DIDN'T seem like it would produce positive results for ME, I took matters into my own hands...and usually hid my behavior from others.

...my allegiance was pledged first and foremost to myself and to getting what I wanted, when I wanted, the way I wanted.

The problem with this kind of thinking, and most of the western world thinks like this to one degree or another, is that it leads to all sorts of hurtful, painful behaviors, actions, habits and addictions. It leads to thinking, desires, hopes and dreams that are simply "out of order" from the way God intended them to be. Addicts and alcoholics like myself simply take this kind of thinking to the extreme. We were not designed to live on our own power! When we live like this, extra effort has to be taken (like taking the stairs), things get messy (like the toilet that doesn't work right) and trouble abounds (like the judge who yells at us for contempt of court). Out of order thinking comes when we seek to MEET OUR OWN DESIRES in ways that are contrary to GOD'S DESIRES or that oppose the nature in which He created us.

Here are some examples of how my own out-of-order thinking resulted in pain, discomfort, messes and trouble...

- *My desire for success was chased through hours upon hours of hard work at the expense of my marriage and family and progressed into a lifestyle of "striving." Every success, bonus and promotion only resulted in an increase in this desire, perpetuating a destructive negative pattern.*
- *My desire to be free from physical pain (I have nagging low back and neck injuries which both required surgery and still produce varying levels of pain) resulted in me reaching for enormous amounts of alcohol and pills to relieve the pain which progressed into harmful addictions.*
- *My desire to avoid shame led me to lie about these struggles and develop a strategy to keep the behaviors hidden.*
- *My desire to REWARD myself for successes or hard work resulted in over-indulgence and dependency on alcohol (I worked hard this week. Let's go out for drinks!).*
- *My desire to be validated as a man resulted in an addiction to pornography.*
- *My desire to NOT be controlled or hurt by women resulted in selfish choices to act out sexually in inappropriate, harmful ways.*

I thought I had the best answers when it came to fulfilling my own desires. I mean, who is better suited to figure things out for my own life than ME? This kind of thinking is the essence of the sin of "pride" – thinking of myself more highly than I ought, thinking that MY way is better than God's way. Pride is "disordered" thinking, misunderstood authority in our lives. Pride elevates our own will, desires and thoughts ABOVE God's, leaving Him out of the process of life. He is given little to no input or consideration into the things we do, say or think. It's just SO foolish. It involves a refusal to listen to God through His word and/or through His people that He puts in our lives. Pride puts "self" in the place of God and makes an idol out of "self." Here's what God's word says about the sin of pride (same verse, three different references):

> "God opposes the proud and gives grace to the humble."
> - 1 Peter 5:5, James 4:6 and Proverbs 3:34

Want to set the course of your life directly against the God of the universe? Be <u>proud</u> and see how it works out for you. I can tell you from experience: IT WORKS OUT BAD. The sin of pride is simply "disordered" thinking in regards to the hierarchy of spiritual authority in one's life. Pride may not completely leave God out of one's life, but it definitely puts God in the back seat. Out-of-order thinking like this gave me license to do "what I want, when I want, the way I want" and is simply a selfish and self-centered way to live.

The converse of the sin of pride is the spiritual virtue of humility. Humility is not self-abasement. It is not thinking of oneself as lower than we should. It isn't characterized by self-loathing, a lack of confidence or negative self-talk. Humility is the state of having a proper understanding of our relationship to God.

Humility is the state of having a proper understanding of our relationship to God.

People I've met that truly possess humility are typically extremely self-confident. This is because they know and understand who they are *rightly* in the eyes of God. They understand their tremendous value to God. We are of such value that we were bought with the precious blood of His one and only

Son. We are of more importance to God than ANY of his creations and of the highest value in the universe. We are his sons and daughters, His family! Living a life of humility simply means that we have a very firm understanding of this fact.

My wife and I work now with others that have *serious* addictions to different things and behaviors – from substances like alcohol, marijuana, cocaine, meth, heroin and prescription painkillers to behaviors like pornography, sex, gambling, co-dependency and others. We often encounter some of the most spiritually healthy people you can imagine as we try to help people like this find freedom and become the true person God designed them to be. Without a doubt, *almost ALL of them* (myself included when I was in the grips of addiction) have a deep level of disordered thinking and a wrong view of their value and significance to a loving God. Our broken, sinful state here on earth leads *all* of us to disordered thinking at one level or another. Addiction only compounds the disorder.

A properly ordered heart considers the hierarchy of authority in life like this:

> *God first*
> *Others second*
> *Self third*
> *Other idols (gods)*

Notice that I listed "other idols" in fourth place of this hierarchy of authority, in accordance with God's word ("You shall have no other gods before me"). God (and the apostle Paul) acknowledge that there are in fact other "gods" in our world. But God our Father, the Lord Jesus Christ and the Holy Spirit (the

Trinity) are the creators of ALL things which makes them worthy of the highest authority.

"For by Him all things were created, both in the heavens and on earth, visible and invisible, whether thrones or dominions or rulers or authorities-- all things have been created through Him and for Him. He is before all things, and in Him all things hold together."
- Colossians 1:16-17

God did not command us to "have no other gods" in the Ten Commandments, but to "have no other god before me." When I refer to "other gods," I'm referring to other things in this world that have the potential to control us or to assert power over us in some way (i.e., the "idols" in our lives). God recognizes that these things exist in the world, but commands us not to serve them (Genesis 20:3-6) because they are FALSE GODS. God the Father will not suffer us serving or worshiping other gods - He is a jealous God. There are MANY other verses that testify to this as well (Deuteronomy 5:9, Joshua 23:7, etc.). Other gods do not exist in this world to be served by us because we serve the one true God, our heavenly Father and His Son, the Lord Jesus and the Holy Spirit – the Trinity.

These things we refer to as "false gods" may, however, serve us under the proper hierarchy of authority. Again, please understand that when I use the term "god" (small "g"), I am simply referring to something that has inherent spiritual power, but that man should NOT be submitted to. Alcohol is an example of a false god in some people's lives (it was in mine), but it is something that was created to serve man well if used properly and is not elevated to a place of authority. Money is the same. Power, anger, sex, possessions, food the same. In our sinful state, we have the capacity to make an idol out of just about anything. These kinds of things all have the inherent spiritual power associated with them to serve as another god with us in submission to their forces if we think of them in an out-of-order manner.

"All things are lawful for me, but not all things are profitable. All things are lawful for me, but I will not be mastered by anything. Food is for the stomach and the stomach is for food, but God will do away with both of them. Yet the body is not for immorality, but for the Lord, and the Lord is for the body."

– I Corinthians 6:12-13

Paul is speaking about the proper order of these kinds of things in our lives. He is not saying not to eat or not to have sex – God made these things for our enjoyment, to be UNDER our authority when we are properly under His authority.

There are so many men I've worked with, trying to help them break free from addiction, that I've watched literally almost kill themselves with multiple relapses. They try to get well and want to stop drinking (or using pills or acting out sexually), but they lack the willingness to do something different. They are stuck in the insanity of trying to break their addiction their own way, according to their own terms. I lost count of the number of times I realized I hadn't heard from a guy in a few days and I know they've gone off the rails. So I call, several times and no answer. The pattern is always the same. They've gone off grid, isolated, not showing up for a recovery meeting or for work and no one has seen them. I hear from them a week or so later when they finally call and ask for help...one more time. One of them woke up in an inebriated stupor in a field with one shoe, his wallet and phone stolen. One ended up back in rehab for the 6th or 7th time over a six-month period with burned hands from an accident involving gasoline. Some get served divorce papers. Others wake up in jail or the hospital. The stories are absolutely heart-wrenching. Many pay the ultimate sacrifice. Their death certificates never read "alcoholism" or "drug addiction," but that's what kills them. All of these kinds of behaviors involve out-of-order thinking that puts "self" above all else.

Sadly, so many of us require one or more painful "rock bottom" experiences to find the willingness to surrender. After learning things the hard way, I have had the privilege and blessing of understanding and experiencing life under grace and humility instead of pride. I can ALSO tell you from experience that, in as much as God OPPOSES the proud, he gives the same amount or more of grace to the humble. Properly ordered thinking like this is foundational for living as TRUE men, in congruence with our TRUE selves.

So how do we bring things BACK into order when our thinking has been OUT OF ORDER? Well, there MIGHT be another way, but I don't know what it is. MY personal experience is that I needed help from GOD and from other people that I could trust to assist me in getting my thinking back in order. This was done only through my own WILLINGNESS to be TRANSPARENT and to be involved in true COMMUNITY.

I learned transparency through diligently and fearlessly working through the 12 steps of recovery with a trusted friend, my sponsor. I learned to live in true community by intentionally seeking out and building relationships with other men that I could trust, actively participating in my church and regularly attending recovery meetings with the intention of helping those that are still suffering. The secret to putting disordered thinking BACK into proper order is:

Transparency - a willingness to be honest with myself, God and others

Community - a willingness to interact with and help others

I discuss some ways to develop both of these things in another of my books entitled, *"Break It Now! The Secret to Living in Freedom from Bad Habits, Negative Patterns and Addiction" (available on Amazon.com).* These are both key, CRITICAL elements in the PROCESS of recovery and spiritual formation.

The fruit of transparency and community do not grow overnight - we claim spiritual progress, not perfection. We willingly submit ourselves to the PROCESS of recovery...the RE-ORDERING of our thinking. Our state of sin on this earth has put everyone's thinking OUT-OF-ORDER to one degree or another. Transparency and community are the secrets to getting our thinking back into congruency with the way God originally intended when He created us.

BULLETPROOF GLASS CHALLENGE:

Honest IN (Being authentic with myself, self-assess) –
- Can you think of a time when your own thinking was "out-of-order" making way for selfish, sinful behavior?
- Explain how you put your own will above God's in those situations.

Honest UP (Being authentic with God, pray, confess) –
- PRAY THIS: (I call this the "Arrangement Prayer") "God, please arrange my thoughts, hopes, dreams and desires so that the actions I take and the decisions I make

will drive me towards helping others, your best for me and my family and away from the fulfillment of my own selfish will."
- Is there something specific you need to confess in regards to your own "out-of-order" thinking and the resulting behavior?

Honest OUT (Being authentic with others, share, discuss) –
- Discuss with your "Bulletproof Brothers" about the times when your thinking has been "out-of-order".
- Ask them for input on what you should do to bring your thinking back into proper order, rightly understanding your position and relation to God.
- Can you think of a time when you knowingly acted out in sinful pride? Discuss this with your group.

CHAPTER EIGHTEEN

THWARTED EFFORTS

The path that God allowed me to travel which eventually brought me to the place where I am today is an absolute miracle. While I can remember having a desire to know God since I was young, I had no idea how to know Him or live to please Him. I didn't grow up in a Christian home – my parents weren't opposed to church, but they never pursued a relationship with God themselves as far as I was aware. Looking back, now I can see so many turns that my life took, which at the time seemed painful and confusing, but whose purpose was to put me on the path to where I am today. I definitely had my own brilliantly thought-out plan for my life and I set myself out like a rocket to pursue it by getting what I wanted, the way I wanted, when I wanted. The problem is, MY path seemed to be headed in the opposite direction of the way God wanted me to head and he was opposed to it almost every step of the way.

"A man's heart plans his way, but the LORD directs his steps."

– Proverbs 16:9

What else would a loving Father do for a child that was running with complete abandon in the wrong direction, into imminent destruction, other than try to redirect his path? That's how I can look at so many painful events in my past now when, at the time, I thought God was punishing me at best, simply absent at worst. In reality, He was masterfully allowing the pain and natural consequences of my actions to redirect my steps in the direction He wanted me to go in life. I want to share some of the key emotional and physical injuries (most of which I caused myself) that I experienced throughout my life so I can put them in perspective with the big picture of God making me who I am today.

Apart from God's perfect, unfailing love for me, I know I could look back on all of these painful events and be bitter, angry and resentful at Him or at life in general. Instead, I've learned to see these events as examples of His love and grace in my life. These kinds of consequences, though painful and confusing at the time, eventually set me on a path into the BEST things God had for me and for becoming the true man He had created me to be all along...

"When you follow the desires of your sinful nature, the results are very clear; sexual immorality, impurity, lustful pleasures, idolatry, sorcery, hostility, quarreling, jealousy, outbursts of anger, selfish ambition, dissention, division, envy, drunkenness, wild parties and other sins like these. Let me tell you again, as I have before, that anyone living that sort of life will not inherit the kingdom of God."

- Galatians 5:19-21

We tend to read a verse like this and focus in on the "results" which look like a list of "things you shouldn't do." I think this is a huge mistake to read this verse in that way. The church has (unwittingly) used lists like this in the Bible to create a doctrine of "right and wrong." It is the unspoken message of the spirit of "religiousness" that has permeated our churches: "If you don't DO this list of things you are OK, acceptable to God." It's a deadly doctrine that communicates a message that we can make ourselves acceptable to God in our own power by checking off the prescribed list of do's and successfully avoiding the don'ts. I think the proper emphasis on this verse is to simply understand that this is part of the way things now work in this world, that there are the natural consequences to what happens "when you follow the desires of your sinful nature."   If you DO "A," the result is "B, C, D, E and F."

Our collective shame and fallen, sinful nature tend to cause us to look at the last verse as the punishment we'll receive if we do these things. We read it with a tone of shame as if from an angry father shaking his finger at us... *"If you do these terrible things I'm not letting you into my house!"* SO many valuable, precious hearts have been crushed with this lie. That's just not the message here in the way I understand this verse now.

I see it now as simply a factual statement that says, "This is how things work. When you do 'A,' you get 'B' and that's not going to get you the results you want." These are the words of a loving, wise Father. And that's EXACTLY what I experienced in life. God isn't an angry father shaking his bony finger at me as he threatens to take away the fun stuff if I'm not good. He loves me with an everlasting love. If he failed to explain clearly, truthfully, exactly how things work in the world where I'm living, He would NOT be loving me - He would be ABANDONING me. It's SO easy to misunderstand God's sovereignty in this way.

God wants us to know a couple of things about our desires. He wants us to know that He understands that we have them (He created them in the first place!), that we can be easily deceived by them and that we must take special care in handling them in our lives so that we can receive HIS best for us. That's what this verse is about. The collective shame of this world causes us to read it through a shame-tinted filter. For me, I learned the truth of this verse the hard way – by actually FOLLOWING my own sinful desires. True to God's word, that action produced the results of the laundry list of Galatians 5:19. God knew that these things would come up empty for me, only causing me to cry out in surrender for something that would last.

So before I explain how God thwarted my plans, let me give you some of the back-story. My father is a retired PGA Golf Professional, so I grew up around the world of golf and started playing the game myself around the age of 5 or 6. By the time I was 9 or 10, I was playing competitively in local junior golf events in North Carolina...and won often in my age group.

By the time I was 13 or 14, my skills were improving and somewhere along the line I decided in my heart that I was going to be a golf professional just like my Dad. This was before I had a relationship with God, so this decision was made completely absent of any consideration of it being a path God wanted me to take – turns out, it WASN'T - at least not as a destination for my life. As wonderful as it may have seemed at the time, God did not want that for me. My father and the other successful golfers I was around were my golf heroes – they were all self-made men. So I patterned my life after how I saw them live theirs. This is a HUGE mistake – to pattern our lives after the lives of others WITHOUT consulting the God of heaven and earth FIRST. This is how men like me often miss God's great calling on our lives and end up in a place we never intended...by following our own desires before consulting the God of the universe.

I threw all of my strength, effort and time towards becoming the best golfer I could possibly become. I read every article in Golf Digest, GOLF Magazine and Golf World. I read books about my golf heroes; the legendary Ben Hogan, Arnold Palmer and my biggest hero – the Golden Bear, Jack Nicklaus. In my heart, I made a SOLEMN VOW to be better than them all.

Being skilled at golf at a young age attracts a lot of attention. Golf is a hard sport to become really good at. There are hundreds of thousands of "golfers" around the world but there are only about

430 currently on the PGA and Senior PGA Tours combined. When you're a kid that knows how to strike a ball well and you win a couple of tournaments, people notice you. The golfers around the club that weren't so good and wished to be better (and that was MOST of the country club members) started watching me. Many would come and stand around to watch me hit balls on the practice tee as my Dad gave me a lesson or they might stop by to watch me hit a shot or two out on the course. Many of the junior events I played in had considerable galleries and even some press attention. Hit a big drive or make a crucial putt and the crowd would ROAR with applause. I loved the attention I received from those that watched me and the feeling of bringing home a trophy or a great scorecard to my Dad. I became enamored with the kind of praise I received from others and from my father because of my ability at golf. Playing good golf earned me lots of attention...and made my Dad proud. Golf was becoming my life, my identity. It was a way in which I was seeking to validate myself as a true man. Later on, I would come to understand that I had actually made the game of golf into an idol which took the place of God in my life.

    Being skilled at golf and being the son of a PGA Tour player also afforded me many other benefits. I was able to play at some of the country's most beautiful and exclusive golf courses, many that golfers around the world only DREAMED of playing...and we played at almost ALL of these places for FREE! I didn't ever have to pay for a round of golf until many, many years later as an adult.

    Because my father was a PGA Tour pro, we also regularly received free golf equipment from his sponsors. I usually had a new set of clubs each year. New shoes, new gloves, new golf balls, new golf bag – expensive stuff...much of it for free (or heavily discounted), given to my father by the manufacturers and sponsors because of his professional status. My father also received two new cars - one for himself and one for my mom to drive each year, provided by one of his sponsors. We lived on a golf course since my early childhood. I could almost always walk out my back door and hit putts and chips to the green any time I wanted.

Golf also allowed us to travel with my father to many of the professional tournaments he played in at beautiful, exciting destinations like Orlando, FL, Washington, DC, Pinehurst, NC and Hilton Head, SC, Monterey and Palm Springs, CA, Canada and many others. Because my Dad was a pro, I got to spend a lot of time "inside the ropes" at these tournaments and was able to actually meet many of my golf heroes including Jack Nicklaus, Lee Trevino, Arnold Palmer, Johnny Miller and so many others. My Dad took my brother and me for lessons with some of the top teaching pros in the country at the time. When we moved to Southern California, I was often able to play with PGA tour pros that frequented the club where my father worked. This lifestyle developed a tremendous and dangerous sense of pride and entitlement in me, causing me to become driven, selfish and arrogant...ENTITLED. Basically, and sad to say, I was a bit of a spoiled brat.

This lifestyle caused me to become driven, selfish and arrogant...ENTITLED.

Being around golf, country clubs and professional and amateur golfers also created in me and my family a desire to keep up what I've now come to call the "country club look." It was, in essence, a kind of "mask" that we wore which projected a persona of success, intelligence, talent and status. My family was fairly well off and my mom and dad made sure my brother and me were always dressed in the most appealing styles and brand name clothing of the day and we always had the best golf equipment supplied from my dad's sponsors (am I starting to sound like a typical spoiled little rich kid? I knew people perceived me that way and I really tried to work against it as best I could!). I think keeping up the "country club look" really became a source of striving for my mom and dad and that attitude was later passed on to my brother and me. To me, I developed a belief that my parents were always more concerned with the way things appeared on the outside rather than how things really were on the inside, in my heart. Because they never developed any kind of spiritual relationship with God, they weren't equipped spiritually to do anything different.

By the time I was 15, I had won the North Carolina State Jr. Championship. The prize: an all-expenses paid trip to Orlando, Fla. to play in the PGA National Jr. Championship as the ONLY male representative from our state. It was my greatest accomplishment as a junior golfer. I was headed to the "BIG TIME" of junior golf. My plan was coming together perfectly.

THAT'S when the thwarting began.

Two weeks later, while on vacation in Myrtle Beach, SC, with my family, while having some irresponsible teenage fun, I jumped off of a six-foot high wall onto the sand at the beach (sheepish grin: yes, I was showing off for a girl!) and severely broke my right ankle – turning it a full 90 degrees inward - which put me in a cast for ten weeks. This was a major injury, ultimately causing me to have to withdraw from the tournament and give my spot in the PGA National Jr. Championship to the runner-up of the qualifying event. Missing this event was one of life's MAJOR disappointments for me and I'm sure for my parents as well. Looking back now, I see it as the first of many "thwarted efforts" – times when God interrupted my plans to get me to move in a different direction...His direction instead of MY OWN. Today I see this, not as punishment, but as an act of love, natural consequences and discipline to a son He values.

Today I see this as an act of love, natural consequences and discipline to a son He values.

At the beginning of my junior year of high school, just after we had moved to Southern California from North Carolina, I experienced a significant spiritual event in my life. I had never attended church as a boy. Of course I had been to the token wedding and attended an Easter or Christmas Eve service here or there, but we never attended church regularly. While my mom and dad would say they were "Christians," they had never formally made a commitment to Jesus that brought about any significant life or heart change. I don't want it to sound as if my parents were "godless," because they were not. They were and are good, moral upstanding people that believe in God like many Americans probably say they do. While I'm not sure I had any idea what a "Christian" really was, there came a time when I desired something deeper out of my relationship with God.

We had just moved from North Carolina all the way across the country into a condo in Southern California and I had my own room. One night, I was sleeping and had a vision...a dream, if you will...from God. I remember seeing a pinhole of light far off in the distant blackness of night as I lay staring upward in my bed. The light approached me slowly and grew in brightness. As it got closer, I finally realized it was Jesus, hovering over me in my bed with his arms open wide, lovingly staring into my eyes. Suddenly, a bright beam of light came out of his chest and went into mine like a cannon shot. I felt an "emptying" sensation, as if he was vacuuming out my soul, my sin. This went on for only a few seconds and then the light retracted back into Jesus. He closed his arms, smiled at me and then receded back into the darkness and was gone. I woke immediately, soaking wet in a cold sweat...terrified. I didn't tell anyone about my dream for fear that my family or friends would think I was crazy. I don't think I told anyone at all until I shared the experience with my wife many, many years later after we were married.

Why did I have a dream like that? Where did that dream come from? Does God really talk to people in dreams? Jesus was the farthest thing from my mind at the time as a 16 year old kid in high school. At that time, I was really only interested in two things: GOLF and GIRLS. Jesus simply wasn't on the radar.

Several months later, after I had started my junior year at a new high school, I joined the golf team and became fully enmeshed in my new Southern California lifestyle. It was about that time that I was invited to church by a friend that played with me on the golf team. I went to church several times with him and his family. The pastor usually held an alter call, and finally after many Sundays of testing the waters at church and learning about God, I responded to the altar call and prayed to receive Jesus Christ as my Lord and Savior. The dream I had had months earlier resonated with me. I wanted to know God and I wanted his help in my life. I remember an amazing feeling of weight being lifted off my shoulders when I walked out of church that day. I had been forgiven of all my sins. It was the beginning of a life-long relationship with Jesus and the first step in a long, continual process of sanctification of which I secretly resisted for most of my life.

During the summer between my Junior and Senior years of high school, I was Runner-up in the Riverside County Amateur Championship playing against more experienced adults (I ended up losing in a sudden death playoff to a man much older than me). As a senior, I was among the top players on the junior golf circuit in Southern California. I co-led the CIF Championship winning Palm Springs High School golf team, and later earned golf scholarships at UC Irvine, UCLA and Fresno State - all major accomplishments in my golf career. The day my high school team won the CIF Championship, I dove head-first into a lake on the last hole with my teammates and nearly broke my neck when I hit the sandy, shallow bottom. While I dodged a major injury at the time, I definitely hurt myself again and caused some real damage to my neck, eventually requiring a major surgery many years later. It still hurts today (and is hurting even now as I write this!).

I began attending Fresno State University on a golf scholarship in the winter of 1983 and was a member of the golf team, all the while still working to keep MY plan on track. I was learning how to include God in some areas of my life, but I resisted Him or outright EXCLUDED him from others. I was happy to include God and give Him the credit when things were going along according to MY plan, but there were other times I sensed Him wanting me to do things differently in my life, and I ignored Him or just rebelliously refused.

By the middle of my first year of college, I began suffering severe back problems including sharp pain down the back of both of my legs. The pain and tightness began keeping me from walking, carrying my bag and being able to swing smoothly during practice. The diagnosis – a ruptured disc in my lower back requiring surgery. I red-shirted the first year, had the surgery and went through intensive physical therapy and rehab, but my back...and thus my golf game was never the same. I withdrew from the team at the end of my first year and gave back my scholarship - another MAJOR disappointment for me. This was also another example of God thwarting my plan to live life according to my own design. It resulted in me making major, life-altering decisions about my major in college, how I spent my time and the people I hung around with.

Don't get me wrong. I don't believe God CAUSED these kinds of things in my life. We live in a fallen world and decisions made apart from God will typically take us to God-forsaken places in life. I believe God providentially allowed me to make these choices, knowing all along the way He was moving me into a place where I would be <u>willing to HELP OTHERS</u>. God has given me tremendous gifts and my experiences in life have equipped me perfectly to help others. He has given me the gifts of encouragement and discernment and He has made me a leader, someone that others respect and will follow. My problem is that, for most of my life, I almost exclusively used those gifts to advance MY OWN AGENDA – getting WHAT I WANTED, WHEN I WANTED, THE WAY I WANTED. I irresponsibly misused my gifts to meet my own desires. I was willfully resisting God's BEST for me by insisting on living a selfish, self-centered life of my own making. NO WONDER God thwarted my efforts so often! Now I can honestly say that I am so grateful that He did.

I used those gifts primarily to advance MY OWN AGENDA – getting WHAT I WANTED, WHEN I WANTED, THE WAY I WANTED.

These are just a few examples of God's gracious thwarting of my own plans. I made MANY other poor, godless decisions that took me in a direction AWAY from Him and His best for me. These decisions, my best thinking and strategizing, only produced pain, misery and a ton of negative consequences for me. I love to quote my Bulletproof brother, Mark, who often says, "I was a terrible CEO of my own life." I tried to fulfill my own desires with things from MY OWN hand instead of gratefully receiving God's provision.

Today, on the recovery side of addiction, I can look back at all of these events and experiences and see them as the pieces of a puzzle that God was slowly putting together, one that would display a picture of who HE truly created me to be – a much more beautiful picture than the one I was trying to create in my own selfish, self-centered life. God loves us enough to never give up on the task of making us into the person He originally intended for us to be.

If he had not allowed me to get a golf scholarship and attend Fresno State, I never would have met my amazing wife and we never would have had our four phenomenal daughters. ANY thwarting of my own plan was worth those two things alone! God doesn't waste ANYTHING. He causes ALL things to work together for the good of those who love Him (Romans 8:28). If we truly love Him, He won't allow us to squander our lives on our own selfishness without thwarting our efforts out of love.

> ***If we truly love Him, God won't allow us to squander our lives on our own selfishness without thwarting our efforts out of love.***

Now, instead of pursuing my own selfish agenda, I can live with anticipation and excitement of HOW God is going to use me next in the life of someone else that is hurting, depressed or struggling with addiction. Because of His providential "thwarting" of my efforts, he has allowed me to travel a path and experience life in such a way that now I have something of VALUE to offer others in need. What I previously perceived as painful tribulation – a liability in my life, I can now view as necessary experience – an asset of untold value that God will pour out through me to bless others…if I will only allow Him.

As I've grown in my relationship with God, I've come to realize that I really don't have much control over the "birth" of my desires – they will sprout up in my heart seemingly without provocation. I DO have control over what I do with them though. So here is a prayer I have prayed often along the way in an effort to stay on God's path for me as I turn those desires over into His loving hands. Maybe you'll find it useful and inspiring as well. I call it the "Arrangement Prayer."

"God, arrange my thoughts and desires in a way so that the actions I take and the decisions I make move me constantly in the direction of YOUR best for me, my family and those I would help along the way. Amen."

BULLETPROOF GLASS CHALLENGE:

Honest IN (Being authentic with myself, self-assess) –
- If you're brutally honest with yourself, how have you followed the "desires of your sinful nature?"
- What have been the results of those choices? Have you experienced the results listed in the *Galatians 5:19-21 passage?*

Honest UP (Being authentic with God, pray, confess) –
- Ask God to reveal the ways in which He has allowed your plans to be "thwarted" in an effort to move you in HIS direction.
- Has God's "thwarting" resulted in an improved life situation, a blessing or a special experience of God's glory? Explain.

Honest OUT (Being authentic with others, share, discuss) –
- Share one or two of your experiences of having your plans "thwarted" with your "Bulletproof" brothers.
- Ask your "Bulletproof" brothers if they see you heading off in a direction that seems counter to what they perceive would be God's way.
- WILLINGNESS CHECK: Are you truly willing to listen, consider and pray about how they respond? If not, why?

CHAPTER NINETEEN

SEX AND GOLF
Duck Hooks and Swiss Cheese

I am 15 years old, standing on the tee of the last hole of the qualifying round for the National PGA Junior championship in Wilmington, NC. It was a two day event of the best boys and girls in golf in the state. One boy and one girl would qualify for an all-expenses paid trip to play in the championship in Orlando, Florida later that year. This was junior golf's version of the PGA Championship. I was leading the boys division by one stroke and was even par for the two days. During both rounds, I had a string of three birdies in a row, something I had never done before. I was on fire, in the zone. I was playing with the boy that was one stroke behind me, the only one that really had any chance at all to beat me at that point.

Then I stepped up to the 18th tee and duck hooked my drive deep into the left rough. Awesome.

My opponent DRILLED his drive right down the middle. It looked like he would easily make par (4) and I was in big trouble. When I finally found my ball and assessed the next shot, there was little hope. A massive grove of super-tall eucalyptus trees stood between my ball and the green, which I couldn't even really see from where I stood. On top of that, I had a weird lie on a patchy area of deep, thick grass. I had a choice of either pitching out into the fairway and playing it safe or trying to hit a HUGE hook around the grove of trees. The trees were too tall and I was too close to try and hit it over the top of them. Because my lie was bad, I felt I couldn't get enough spin on the ball to hit the hook and if I pitched into the fairway, I'd have to hit my approach close and then make the putt to ward off my competitor and win.

That's when I saw it. A Swiss-cheese styled hole in the grove of trees about ten feet in diameter. If I stepped to the left a few feet and stood on my tip toes, I could see the flag waving in the soft breeze on the green. Could I really pull that off? I would have to hit a high fade with a three iron and thread the needle through the trees, clear the front sand trap and hope the ball stopped before it rolled off the back of the green. It looked like an impossible shot. Exactly the kind I liked.

As a boy and a young man, I remember wanting to be a golf pro just like my dad. We spent long hours together, my father teaching me the intricacies of the game of golf; how to put spin on the ball, how to control the ball's flight path, how to use different clubs in different situations and in different conditions, how to control my emotions and thoughts under pressure. I worked hard at it, sometimes leaving the driving range long after dark with blistered, bleeding hands. I wanted so badly to be a golf pro and I wanted to win. I spent hours every day playing, practicing and studying the game of golf. As a kid, I loved it. Golf was my life.

So what does all of this have to do with sex? I never would have connected the two until I found myself late in life struggling with sex and pornography addictions and my entire world collapsing around me. It was during a conversation with an addiction specialist that my sexual desires and my well-learned golf skills came together perfectly to complete a puzzle that had long been a confused, jumbled mess in my heart, mind and life. This wise doctor basically gave me the sex talk I wished I had heard as a young man. Here's how the conversation unfolded...

Doc: "So, this sex stuff you're struggling with...you know it's a lot like golf?"

Me: "Huh?"

Doc: "You used to be a great golfer, right? You were a competitor. You worked hard to become great. You were a student of the game right?"

Me: (feeling like he was trying to appeal to my ego) "OK, sure."

Doc: "I bet you had to work pretty hard to learn the nuances of golf, didn't you? You had to learn how to hit different kinds of shots, put spin on the ball, how to hook it, slice it. You had 12 different clubs you had to learn how to use."

Me: "14. Regulation is 14 clubs." The doc wasn't a big golfer, but he was doing his best with this analogy.

Doc: "Ok. You had 14 different clubs you had to learn how to use. The driver you use to hit it long off the tee. The sand wedge you use out of the sand. The putter you use on the green. Every shot is different depending on the course, the distance, the wind, the lie. Am I right?"

Me: He had my attention now. "Yep."

Doc: Look, it's the exact same way with your wife. You have to become a student of HER the same way you were a student of the game of golf. If you truly love your wife as much or more than you loved golf, you'll learn everything you can about her needs. You need to learn exactly what to say and how to say it during different situations. You need to learn how to touch her and talk to her in different ways that communicate how much she is loved and valued – and I'm not talking about just in the bedroom. I'm talking about throughout the day. You need to figure out how to meet HER emotional needs and how to SERVE HER in every different situation, when she is in different moods. What are the things she likes you to do for her that make her feel loved and valued? Make it about HER *and making her feel good emotionally and physically. Just like you would study golf so you could become a master of hitting the right shot at the right time, you have to study her and become a master at meeting her needs. Be a servant, be a giver and learn what to say and do to meet her needs in every different situation.*

If you spend HALF as much time and energy getting good at knowing your wife as you did getting good at knowing golf, you won't have any more problems with sex. If you do THAT, sex will just happen naturally and it will be a by-product of your true love for her. It won't be something you guys are struggling with. It will be a place of mutual trust and a natural response to how you're treating her throughout the day. Study your wife the way you studied golf and all of this sex stuff will all come back to normal."

That talk changed me. It helped me get out of myself and to stop looking at sex as a way to GET PLEASURE. I had only been in it for what I could get out of it. If she happened to get pleasure through it as well, great. If not, I was still having my needs met. I was SO INCREDIBLY SELFISH in my sexuality! It had NOT become a natural outpouring of emotional intimacy with my wife. I was a TAKER, not a giver, which is COMPLETELY opposite of what God created sex to be. I had a completely UNHEALTHY view of sexuality. Untangling my misplaced sexual desires and intimacy with my wife took some time and much grace from her for sure. But this talk was the beginning of me being able to view sex in a completely different way. It started me on a path of loving and serving my wife, becoming a student of how to meet her needs instead of expecting her to provide sexual satisfaction for me.

So what does HEALTHY sexuality look like? Here's a side-by-side comparison of UNHEALTY verses HEALTHY sexuality:

Addictive/Unhealthy Sexuality	vs.	Healthy Sexuality
Feels shameful		Adds to self-esteem
Is illicit, stolen, or exploitive		Has no victims
Compromises values		Deepens meaning
Draws on fear for excitement		Uses vulnerability for excitement
Reenacts childhood abuses as an adult		Cultivates sense of being an adult
Disconnects one from self		Furthers a sense of self
Creates a world of unreality		Expands one's reality
Is self-destructive, dangerous		Relies on safety
Uses conquest or power		Relies on intimacy
Serves to medicate and kill pain		Takes responsibility for needs
Is dishonest		Originates in integrity
Becomes routine		Presents challenges
Requires a double life		Integrates most authentic parts of self
Is grim and joyless		Is fun and playful
Demands perfection		Is imperfect

Unhealthy sexuality is "me focused." It does not take my wife's needs and desires into account or at least makes them secondary to my needs (remember having our thinking "out of order?"). Healthy sexuality within the context of marriage is "wife" focused. When I was able to change my perspective and start studying her needs, becoming a student dedicated to learning everything I could about her, I was able to move into healthy sexuality.

Sexuality in our culture today has become incredibly selfish. Pornography, masturbation, strip clubs, prostitution, voyeurism, nudism, homosexuality, trans-genderism, etc. – I challenge you to find the selflessness in any of that. It is all a warped, twisted abomination of what God originally created sex to be. Woman, created to be a man's helpmate and companion, has been reduced to body parts, objects to be selfishly used by men to TAKE pleasure from. There is no love. There is no sacrifice. There is no intimacy. Pornography teaches men to view women as a pair of breasts and a vagina. Becoming the true man that God created us to be means we learn how to see women, not as objects, but as God's precious daughters, real people made in His image, worthy of being valued, loved, cherished, respected and protected.

Pornography teaches men to view women as a pair of breasts and a vagina.

God created sex to be the most exhilarating, passionate and pleasurable experience on earth because it is a celebration of life. It is a mysterious mixture of the physical, emotional and spiritual aspects of man and woman working together in an act of mutual worship of God, just as it was designed. It involves the spiritual components of love, tenderness, vulnerability, selflessness and faithfulness (loyalty). Engaging in the self-sex of pornography and masturbation LEAVES OUT the emotional component and manifests as a warped physical act that includes the spiritual components of selfishness and disloyalty. This is why Jesus told us that "anyone who looks at a woman lustfully has already committed adultery with her in his heart." - Matthew 5:28 The adultery happens in our hearts when we emotionally defect from our wives and enter into sex with another woman in our minds and hearts through pornography. God did NOT design men to live like that and He has made that clear in His word. Pornography is not even CLOSE to being God's best for us. As a matter of fact, it has NO PLACE in the life of a man seeking God...

> *"But among you there must not be even a hint of sexual immorality, or of any kind of impurity, or of greed, because these are improper for God's holy people."*
> *- Ephesians 5:3*

Unhealthy sexuality in any form is simply a symptom of the REAL problem in our lives - a heart that is secretly bound up in resentment, shame, selfishness and self-centeredness. Seriously working the 12 Steps of recovery solves these problems and helps us develop a new set of spiritual tools to live an emotionally and spiritually healthy life - the way we were created to live.

I don't want to leave you hanging with my golf story though. I DID in fact end up hitting a near perfect shot through that hole in the trees. The ball landed just over the sand trap and rolled to the back fringe of the green. I two putted for a par, tied the hole with my competitor and won that tournament. Like I said in the previous chapter, I DID NOT, however, ever make it to the PGA National Junior Championship in Florida due to a serious injury not long afterwards when I broke my ankle. To me, becoming the true man that God created meant becoming a successful golf professional. Here's yet another amazing example of how God works - He used my relentless pursuit of success in golf to teach me the much more valuable and pleasurable lessons about healthy, God-honoring sex with my beautiful bride.

BULLETPROOF GLASS CHALLENGE:

Honest IN (Being authentic with myself, self-assess) –
- Are you able to admit to yourself if you've used your own sexuality in selfish, harmful ways? If so, how?
- How could you have used your own sexuality differently in ways that would honor God's design and will?
- How have you hurt others or taken from them in your sexuality?
- Have you or do you struggle with seeing women as objects to be used for the taking of pleasure?

Honest UP (Being authentic with God, pray, confess) –
- Ask God to reveal any other ways in which you've used your own sexuality selfishly.
- Confess them to God in prayer and claim His forgiveness through Jesus' sacrifice. (See I John 1:9)

Honest OUT (Being authentic with others, share, discuss) –
- Discuss these revelations with your "Bulletproof" brothers and confess your sins to them so that you can experience healing. (See James 5:16)
- Ask your friends to pray for you that God would give you the courage and strength needed to honor him with your sexuality.

CHAPTER TWENTY

THE PAIN
Will I STAY...or will I GO?

> "If you are distressed by anything external, the pain is not due to the thing itself, but to your estimate of it; and this you have the power to revoke at any moment."
> - Marcus Aurelius Antoninus

  I don't believe Marcus Aurelius to be a Christ follower, but what he said is true because this is the choice that God has given to all men. We have the power within ourselves to change our minds about a matter, to decide, to commit, even to vow to think about things differently – BECAUSE GOD HAS GIVEN US THIS GIFT.

  Remember the scene at the end of the movie Braveheart when the torturer is tearing away at William Wallace as he's tied down on the cross? The torturer tells him that if he will just say "mercy," this can all end quickly. But Wallace is relentless and guts it out (no pun intended) as they carve away at his manhood. Remember, now, that he is TIED down to this cross (if he hadn't been tied down, we all know he would have hopped up off that cross and kicked the torturer's ass – just sayin'). Still, the one thing he is still in control of is his own will. He took a pass earlier on the anesthetic brought to him while he was in chains in the previous scene and then he bravely takes a pass on "mercy" just as the movie ends with him screaming "FREEDOM!"

  This scene resonates SO deeply with me, especially when I am experiencing the spiritual pain and the force of shame in my own life. Wallace is committed <u>to living TRUE to himself, his values,</u>

his God in every situation, no matter the consequences. He will not abandon this commitment even unto death – definitely making him a "Christ-type" in a literary sense. I WANT this admirable quality, this commitment in my own life, in every area of it...in every circumstance. This kind of commitment is at the heart of becoming the TRUE man that God created us to be.

This commitment is at the heart of becoming the TRUE man that God created in each of us

During more than 24 years of marriage, my secret life embattled by addictions wrought immense emotional and spiritual injury upon my wife. I created a tremendous sense of mistrust, disappointment, embarrassment, and righteous anger. When she so graciously and bravely offered to stay and fight for our marriage and our family instead of just walking out and starting over, I knew we had a long, difficult path of healing to walk together. I had been given a gift – from God and from her – a chance to do the right thing now and to start building back everything I had selfishly torn down.

My wife writes bravely and honestly about her experience of our journey together and how God healed us in her own blog (www.celestewilcox.com). This is just one of the places the Lord gives her a voice to help other women struggling in difficult marriages like we had. During our journey of recovery together, there were many long, painful and difficult conversations we had together trying to untangle all of the hurt and disappointment of my secret life and addictive behavior. Some of this was done with counselors, some with loving and brave friends willing to get down in the muck with us and some done just between the two of us.

These tough talks were critically necessary for both of us to heal. I think we both had the understanding that this was just going to be part of the journey we would have to endure with God's strength.

My wife has shown (and still does today) amazing patience with me as I have done my own work to heal and learn how to take responsibility for my actions. In the beginning of my recovery, I FOUGHT taking responsibility and this created a lot of conflict in our healing together. Many of these conversations left us both in tears, confused, angry or even in despair, wondering if there was any way we were going to make it. I had caused A LOT of damage. God had a HUGE disaster area to clean up when it came to our relationship. The question was, would I ALLOW Him to clean it up or would I stubbornly refuse the power of His grace?

When I was in conflict with my wife and having some of these difficult conversations with her, I would typically experience a tremendous sense of shame, regret and despair feeling like the things I had done were just too awful for us to ever heal from. I struggled with being able to listen to her pain while she was healing from the emotional wounds I had inflicted upon her. She needed to verbalize her pain in order to be free of it, to heal from it. When she would recount the things I had done and expressed her true feelings, it could get pretty nasty and painful for us both. She could sometimes get very detailed and even graphic in her explanation of how the things I did made her feel. She'll confess that, when she was at some of her worst moments, she gave way to anger and lashed out at me with hurtful words – understandably so. While I was still figuring out how to listen and take responsibility, many times I'd deflect or defend myself, only making the arguments worse. Sometimes I'd just sit and commit to not saying a thing in response, feeling like anything I'd say would only make matters worse. But when I didn't react, in her mind, I must not be truly hearing her.

Don't get me wrong - I am NOT blaming my wife for this. I caused this pain for her. I accept the responsibility for it. NONE of this is her fault. What I struggled so deeply with was, as she processed her pain in this way, it would directly cut into my old wounds of self-loathing and rejection and lack of self-worth (recall the way I viewed myself in chapters 8 & 9, incompetence, insignificance, impotence). When I was trying so hard with all of my being to leave my past behind me, to recover and to repent, it would all suddenly be brought back, front and center in vivid reality through the mouth of the one person in the world that I love and trust the most. My awful behaviors were being recounted over and over again every time we'd have one of these talks, reminding me of just how very much I had hurt her. The message I would hear from the enemy was, "See, you ARE worthless! Look what you did to her! You ARE a piece of crap! You ARE a liar! An adulterer! HA HA HA! WHAT a loser." And the problem was that it would ring SO true because it was coming from my wife. She was confirming all of these lies in my heart when I was trying to break their power and get well. It is a form of torture I would not wish on anyone. In an emotional and spiritual sense to me it was just the same as that torturer taking out the different tools and carving away at William Wallace. The spiritual and emotional pain is immense and unbearable.

My love languages are "words of affirmation" and "physical touch" (see Gary Chapman's excellent book, The Five Love Languages, Zondervan, 2010). I receive and perceive love best when it comes at me in those forms. So when my wife was processing pain in words of anger, blame, accusation and shame, physically and emotionally pushing me away, it would re-open all of the old wounds of shame I had amassed over the years since childhood.

The problem for me with this process is that I'm NOT tied down on that cross like William Wallace was. I am free to get up off of the cross at any time and exercise my own free will. This could include any number of my own strategies to eliminate the spiritual and emotional pain - I could react in anger, yell louder, get physical even (thank God I never did this). I could leave, physically or emotionally. I could medicate (another form of leaving really) through alcohol, drugs, pornography, food. The fact is that any of these methods actually work to one degree or another at stopping the pain...at least for a while. Because this is hitting very tender, old wounds and because I am NOT tied down, the reaction to get away from the pain was reflexive for me – stimulus/response – a very real example of "fight or flight" syndrome.

If someone came into the room and fired up a propane torch and started burning your face with it, would you not jump back and shield yourself? If they did it again immediately, would you not take action against the person or leave the room? If they followed you into the next room and did it yet AGAIN, would you not leave the house or react physically in some way? That's the only way that I can explain what these kinds of exchanges with my wife felt like to me. Again, NOT my wife's fault – this has to do with what I WAS HEARING from her, NOT what she was saying. This is the enemy's tactic of "confusion" – a mistranslation of meaning between two parties that are communicating. My wife was simply saying, "this is how you've hurt me," something she has every right to say. I was hearing "because you've hurt me, you are BAD" – the devastating message of SHAME.

I remember a counseling session we had together about a year or so before I made total disclosure to her. I was explaining to the counselor how it felt when my wife would unload on me with what I felt were painful, cutting, accusatory and disrespectful words. I told him how sometimes she would just melt down and scream obscenities at me (this really was me just trying to shift blame, deflect, put the responsibility for our problems on her). I told him, the way I saw it, when she talked to me like this, I have three options:

- *I could raise my voice OVER her and win the screaming match.*
- *I could physically respond and strike her – which I never had and NEVER would – but nonetheless, it remained one of my choices.*
- *I could "leave" – I could just physically run away from the situation or leave emotionally by checking out through the use of alcohol or drugs.*

 To me, these were the only options that I could see. The problem is, this is NOT what God was calling me to do. Therefore, if I were to take any of these options, I would be in sin, deciding to exercise my own will over His. I am ceasing to trust in the Lord and in his strength and mercy to deliver me from the pain. I have tried both options #1 and #3 in the past – never choosing to harm my wife physically in these situations. I usually opted for #3, the "leaving" option. I chose to run away. I would just go get in my car and drive to the mountains and escape. I was a runner. SO cowardly.
 The counselor pointed out that I actually had a FOURTH option. I was dumbfounded. That's how screwed up I was.

> *Me: "Look, there IS no other choice."*
> *Counselor: "You could just stay and listen to her."*

The reason there was no other choice as far as I was concerned was that, in my own spirit, I REFUSED to listen to my wife. I had stubbornly and selfishly made up my own mind: I WOULD NOT ALLOW HER TO TALK TO ME LIKE THAT. I had made a vow, a solemn oath that I would never let a woman hurt me or control me and it was a vow I LIVED by.

I had made a vow, a solemn oath that I would never let a woman hurt me or control me.

By choosing to sit and listen to her, I would be being UNTRUE to my system of values – a system I had created ON MY OWN! Do you see how believing the lies of the enemy puts us in a position of slavery to sin? I WANT to be true to myself, but I've made a vow that is totally against God's word and will for me. In this case, being true to myself resulted in hurting my wife...over and over and over. It is in these kinds of defiant acts of refusal that we DISALLOW God from working in our lives with the power of His grace and love. These kinds of vows MUST be broken, SMASHED against the rock of Jesus' sacrificial grace by being brutally honest in, up and out.

I remember one time after I was beginning to understand this vow and how it was affecting me. Celeste and I were having an argument and I was contemplating just getting in my truck and driving away to go get drunk. I remember thinking the same old thing...that I wasn't going to let her talk to me like that. That's when I heard the Lord say something to the effect of, "What if I have something to say to you and I choose to say it through the mouth of your wife? Are you going to refuse to listen to ME also?"

Ouch.

"What if I have something to say to you and I choose to say it through the mouth of your wife? Are you going to refuse to listen to ME also?"

Here is what God was saying to me in all of this, "Tony, I know you love your wife and the way I am going to heal her heart from the things you've done to her and the way I'm going to heal your heart from the things that have been done to you and the things you've done to yourself is for you to stay and listen to her pain. This is open heart surgery and you must willingly lay down on the table, multiple times, no anesthesia and endure it until I am finished. Here's my promise to you: I will give you the strength to do this if you will trust me."

So the question then becomes, "Do I trust you, Lord?" "Do I love Celeste?" Jesus went willingly to the cross OUT OF HIS LOVE FOR US. He calls me to do the same in these situations. This is what the mystery of carrying the cross of Jesus looked like in my life: choosing to walk into pain and STAY IN IT, in spite of my own fear, fully relying on God to get me through it.

Therefore, I will take the advice of Marcus Aurelius, whom I quoted at the top of this chapter. I choose to change my mind about the matter, to decide, to commit, to vow even…to say YES, I trust you, Lord. YES, I love you Celeste. I will choose to rely on God's strength because I DO trust him and I will stay in those painful situations because I love my wife. The fact is, she NEEDS me to stay and listen in order for God to heal her from the wounds I have caused. Not to mention the fact that I need to do it for God to heal me of what I have done to myself.

> *"Therefore, I urge you brothers, in view of God's mercy, to present yourselves as living sacrifices, holy and acceptable to God, for this is your spiritual act of worship."*   - Romans 12:1

You know what they say about living sacrifices - they have a habit of jumping off the altar! Becoming the true man God created me to be means learning to trust Him through these kinds of "deaths." But herein lies the mystery of the crucifixion and how it applies to our own lives - it is not until we DIE that God can raise us. It is in these painful, yet amazing spiritual exchanges that Jesus invites us into DEATH so that we can experience the miracle of RESURRECTION.

BULLETPROOF GLASS CHALLENGE:

Honest IN (Being authentic with myself, self-assess) –

- Can you relate to the kinds of spiritual situations described in this chapter?
- Do you have any similar vows that you may unwittingly live by, such as *"I will not let a woman hurt me or control me"*? If so, what are they? Write them down and bring them into the physical world.
- What are one or two situations you can remember when you felt the powerful spiritual force of shame that put you in a position like was described above where you were tempted to FIGHT, RUN or simply stay and endure?

Honest UP (Being authentic with God, pray, confess) –
- Do you trust God to give you the power to stay and endure when you find yourself in these kinds of spiritually taxing situations? Do you truly believe he will actually show up and do His part?
- Pray that God will break the unrighteous vows you have made and live by.
- Pray this: "God, I trust you to pour out YOUR spirit of peace, patience and self-control on me when I come face-to-face with shame, guilt, despair or fear. You are my rock and my redeemer. I trust you, God. Deliver me."

Honest OUT (Being authentic with others, share, discuss) –
- Discuss the situations you can remember where you were faced with a choice to FIGHT, RUN or simply stay and endure with your "Bulletproof" brothers.
- What kind of situations (where you are faced with shame, fear or guilt) seem to be the most challenging or troubling for you personally?
- Can you or any of the men in your group share specific examples of times when you trusted God to show up in situations like this? Explain and discuss how it happened.

CHAPTER TWENTY ONE

APPEASEMENT
Jacob's Fear of His Brother Esau

I introduced the strategy of "appeasement" in Chapter One and I want to dive deeper into it in this chapter because this strategy is used by so many of us, so often - especially those who struggle with addiction to a behavior or a substance. Understanding appeasement, recognizing when we're doing it and learning to allow God to replace these strategies with the power of His Spirit brings new life, recovery and redemption.

Genesis Chapter 32 tells the story of Jacob's brother, Esau coming towards him. They have been estranged brothers for many years and Jacob is fearful of Esau's vengeance because Jacob had stolen his brother's birthright long ago before their father Isaac had died.

As Esau is approaching, Jacob's fear is getting the best of him. His servants tell him, *"We came to your brother Esau, and furthermore he is coming to meet you, and four hundred men are with him." (verse 6)*

This puts Jacob in a state of fear. He immediately goes into a panic and starts devising a strategy. *"Then Jacob was greatly afraid and distressed; and he divided the people who were with him, and the flocks and the herds and the camels, into two companies; for he said, If Esau comes to the one company and attacks it, then the company which is left will escape." (verses 7-8)*

Then it seems as if Jacob has a moment of clarity and he cries out to God, *"Deliver me, I pray, from the hand of my brother, from the hand of Esau; **for I fear him**, that he will come and attack me and the mothers with the children. For You said, 'I will surely* *prosper you and make your descendants as the sand of the sea, which is too great to be numbered." (verses 11-12)*

Jacob is in a situation where he perceives that things might not work out according to God's promise to "prosper him." Did God *lie* to him? Jacob is familiar with lies. His very name means "deceiver." He is a liar and deceiver to the core. It is terrifying to him to think that his God might have turned the tables on him! However, turning to God and asking for deliverance is the first smart thing Jacob has done in this story. It is ALWAYS wise to turn to God immediately when we are in fear.

It is ALWAYS wise to turn to God immediately when we are in fear.

He turns to God and acknowledges His promise to him. He claims God's promise as his own. Then he immediately fails miserably again! He just can't stand it and his fear overtakes him yet ONE MORE TIME. *"So he spent the night there. Then he selected from what he had with him a present for his brother Esau: two hundred female goats and twenty male goats, two hundred ewes and twenty rams, thirty milking camels and their colts, forty cows and ten bulls, twenty female donkeys and ten male donkeys."* (verses 14-15)

Jacob refuses to wait for God to show up, takes matters into his own hands and uses the strategy of "appeasement" in an attempt to pacify his brother..."*For he said, I will appease him...*" (verse 20).

I opened this book in Chapter 1 by introducing the impactful sermon by Dr. David Wilkerson written before his death in 2011 entitled "Jabbok" in which he comments brilliantly about Jacob's appeasement strategy. Here are Wilkerson's words...

> "But this humble, obedient, praying, God-fearing, truth-loving servant of God was still into appeasement! That means, "giving in to a dangerous power to avoid trouble." Peace at any cost includes compromise!
>
> Instead of trusting God in his crisis, he worked angles. He tried to think his way through his problem. He divided his cattle into separate droves, sending them on ahead to soften his brother's heart. He would bombard Esau with wave after wave of gifts of goats, camels, bulls, sheep, donkeys, and rams.
>
> Appeasement! That is what multitudes of Christians are into! They give in to a dangerous power, because they are afraid they are helpless! You hear it everywhere nowadays "I just can't help it! I don't want to do it. I hate my sin. But in spite of all my super efforts, I give in and fail!
>
> So over and over again, we appease! We sin and confess, weep and confess, try to think our way out. Oh, the angles, schemes, justifications, excuses, plans - all in vain. We seem powerless against overwhelming needs and desires.
>
> Obedient! Praying! Seeking the truth! Humble! Loving! Kind! God-fearing! But there is still that fly in the ointment! There is still a secret holdout deep in the heart. There is still appeasement, scheming - one idol still standing - not yet totally yielded. Not yet under the total Lordship of Christ." [12]

Appeasement is about submission. Wilkerson defines appeasement as "giving in to a dangerous power to avoid trouble." One of the world's great leaders and war strategists, Winston

Churchill said, *"Appeasement is like feeding a hungry crocodile, hoping it will eat you LAST."*

"Appeasement is like feeding a hungry crocodile, hoping it will eat you LAST."
- Winston Churchill

In Jacob's case, the dangerous power is the power of FEAR. He gives in, submits to fear and submits himself to HIS OWN WILL over trusting God. At one point in the story, he takes a shot at turning to the Lord in his struggle when he prays, but he doesn't have the strength to wait patiently for the Lord to work his purposes, to deliver him from his situation. He is impatient. He won't "sit in" the uncomfortable spiritual struggle with fear and allow God to fight it for him but instead, relents and turns to his own scheming and devices *to relieve the discomfort of fear.*

This strategy of "appeasement" IS the hallmark of habitual sin, the addictive cycle. In my own life, when I was faced with *the emotions* generated from a difficult situation, angry words from my wife, financial pressure, a hard discussion with my boss, a challenging legal issue, physical pain (in the world of addiction and recovery, these things are called "triggers"), etc., I would *almost always* turn to, reach for a substance or selfish behavior to *avoid trouble*; the uncomfortable spiritual struggle of waiting for God to heal these emotions.

Be honest with yourself. Haven't you had experience doing this with almost any difficult emotion – positive and negative? We experience strong feelings of anger, resentment, frustration, disappointment, embarrassment, shame or physical pain and we are suddenly faced with the question WHO (or what) WILL I TURN TO AS I EXPERIENCE THE POWER OF THESE FORCES that may be greater than I know or understand how to sustain? Will I turn to God in prayer or praise and "sit in" the uncomfortable spiritual struggle of the emotions or will I submit to the "deep desires" *(epithumia)* that cry out for the discomfort to stop and *turn to my own ability to solve the problem?* When I'm honest with myself, I have to admit that I've resigned to the strategy of appeasement to deal with these things for most of my life. This is why I need a power greater than myself to live life in congruence with my TRUE self.

Who will I turn to as I experience the power of these forces that may be greater than I know or understand how to sustain?

More than anything, God desires DEEP INTIMACY with us. This is how he designed us to live, how he created us. His desire is for us to turn to Him FIRST and be willing to wait for Him to work in our hearts, our spirits to relieve the spiritual discomfort of these powerful forces against us. If we submit to them, to our own devices and schemes instead of our God, we are actually committing TWO sins – the sin of unbelief and the sin of idolatry. We are unbelieving in that we refuse to believe that God is GOOD and that He WILL show up for us in times like this and deliver us. We are idolatrous in the fact that we are, instead, turning to something other than our loving Creator to appease the pain. This is why God warned us, "Do not worship any other god, for the LORD, whose name is Jealous, is a jealous God." – Exodus 34:14

Here is the question God asks of us: When you experience the emotions that come from strong spiritual forces, will you turn to Me in prayer and meditation and trust Me to work with my Spirit in the difficult, uncomfortable struggle within OR will you reach for the closest thing in your general vicinity that will soothe the spiritual discomfort – a pill, a drink, a snort, a joint, pornography, sex, masturbation, a gallon of ice cream or a bag of chips, gambling, vigorous exercise, a TV show, ESPN, social media, a game on your phone – ANYTHING to distract you from the spiritual struggle? THIS IS THE ESSENCE of idolatry in the 21st century.

This is the essence of idolatry in the 21st century.

If God is truly our God, we will turn to Him in prayer and through the wise counsel of our trusted, godly friends...our "Bulletproof" brothers. This is where TRANSPARENCY and COMMUNITY are critical - being honest with ourselves, God and others - **Bulletproof Strong.** It is the place where we move one step closer to becoming the TRUE man that God created us to be from the very start. Most importantly, it is where God and His Spirit do their most powerful, transforming and amazing work in our hearts – when we choose HIM over anything and EVERYTHING else.

BULLETPROOF GLASS CHALLENGE:

Honest IN (Being authentic with myself, self-assess) –
- Identify and list the powerful emotions or situations (triggers) that put you in a position where you are tempted

towards appeasement and have to choose between God and your own devices and schemes.
- Are you able to recognize when you experience powerful emotions like anger, fear, regret, resentment, confusion, disappointment? Are you able to call them for what they are and turn properly to God with them or do you typically medicate their impact through a substance or negative selfish behavior?
- Do you really believe God has the power to overcome the power of these negative spiritual forces when you come under their influence?

Honest UP (Being authentic with God, pray, confess) –
- Ask God to convict you of any idol in your life that you have a tendency to turn to when you experience these kinds of spiritual forces. Sit quietly with Him for a while and wait to hear His response.
- Are you willing to really listen to what He has to say about these things?

Honest OUT (Being authentic with others, share, discuss) –
- Tell a trusted friend (or friends) about your list of triggers and what God revealed to you about the idols in your life. Ask him to pray for you for wisdom and courage to lay it down and begin turning to God faithfully each time instead.
- WILLINGNESS CHECK: Are you truly willing to commit to call or text your "Bulletproof" brothers the very next time you experience one of these negative forces or triggers? Do it! Discuss how these things are making you FEEL and ask them for prayer so you can experience God's voice and transforming touch THROUGH your friend.

CHAPTER TWENTY-TWO

EVERYTHING BROKEN

Sometime after my full confession to my wife, Celeste, we experienced one of the most painful times in our healing and recovery. I had broken my wife's heart with the crushing news of years of secret addictions and betrayals several months earlier. Celeste had been struggling with processing the pain that comes with getting this kind of news, trying to figure out what moving forward looked like with a man she loved but didn't trust. To her, all of her dreams had been shattered, crushed, trampled – what she had hoped to find in a man, her dream of having a husband that was faithful to her, her image of who I was and the kind of man she thought I was, and even her own, already shaky self-image...all smashed to smithereens. What's worse, she felt like a fool, struggling with thoughts of...

"How could I have not seen this happening?"

"What are all of my friends going to think when they find out? I'm totally embarrassed of myself and him."

"What will everyone think of me when they find out I am staying with him? They'll all think I'm weak."

"What did I do to deserve this?"

The enemy was attacking her in every direction. Not only was she experiencing these kinds of hellish thoughts, but she was also being attacked physically. She had a nagging rash on one arm that would flare up and itch and swell when she was under stress or not getting enough sleep – which was pretty much constantly. She had an eye condition that would cause one or the other eye to flare up and become terribly red and painfully irritated. On top of that, she had brutal bicycle accident one Saturday, flipping head over handlebars and crashing onto the pavement in front of our eleven-year old (youngest) daughter. This resulted in multiple, nasty scrapes, bruises and contusions on both her arms and legs. She literally looked like she had been beaten.

She was also scheduled to have a surgery due to heavy bleeding she had been experiencing with her periods. This was a painful procedure that would take several weeks to heal from. On top of everything else, she ended up getting a staph infection during her time at the hospital. The enemy was attacking my wife in every way possible and I felt responsible for it all.

These kinds of thoughts and physical stresses culminated in a downward spiral of her emotions. Personally, I was also struggling to get my own behaviors under control. While I had been getting some help from friends and working through what it looked like to submit all of the things I was struggling with to the Lord, the truth was, I still wasn't creating a safe or completely truthful environment for her. While I may have thought I was being pretty heroic in my recovery efforts, Celeste was struggling greatly with the pain of my betrayal. During one, very painful 48 hour period, her despair turned to such anger and rage against me for what I had done, that she smashed all of our wedding china, broke my fly rod, flushed her wedding ring down the toilet and packed all of my clothes into seven large garden-size trash bags while I was away at work. When I got home, she had made up her mind that she wanted me out and we were finished.

"I flushed that ring down the toilet! It means NOTHING to me! I will learn to get along without you. I feel sorry for the kids, but I can't do this anymore. I don't love you. Get out. Just leave! Get out!"

I was desperate to fix the things I had broken, but I was helpless, powerless to do it. I got down on my knees in our bedroom and I told her, "You are getting ready to make the biggest mistake of your life. You are going to look back on this one day and wish you had never done this babe. Please don't do this. We can get through it. Let's go talk with some of our friends and get some help. We need someone to help us. We can't do this alone. We are getting attacked spiritually here. Why aren't we down on our knees begging for the Lord's mercy to save our marriage? Will you pray with me, please??!!" I wasn't being heroic – there were just no other options.

I got down on my knees at the foot of our bed, hoping she'd join me. She didn't. She just wasn't capable. While I was praying, begging the Lord to intervene, to save our marriage, she walked out of the room and dragged all of the garbage bags with my clothes down the stairway and threw them into the driveway. She stood at the base of the stairs screaming at me to get out...at which point I did. I threw all of the garbage bags in my truck and drove away. Where I was headed, I had NO idea.

An hour or so later, she sent me a text and agreed to go meet with some friends to talk. They graciously agreed to sit with us and try to help however they could. We met and discussed the entire scene with them in their living room and really got nowhere. I thought it was all over and I had no idea where I was going to sleep that night or what I was going to do. I drove away from our friend's house in complete despair. My marriage was over. I had crushed my wife's heart beyond repair. I would wake up the next day effectively divorced – the paperwork would just be a formality that would sustain the agony for several weeks while some attorney put it all together. I had no idea how I was going to live my life from there on out. How were the kids going to deal with this? How do we do custody? Visitation? Alimony? Child support? All words I thought I would never have to deal with so personally. The only thing I knew for sure was that my marriage to Celeste was OVER and I had caused it.

I wanted to die.

While I knew about the broken china and that she had flushed her wedding ring down the toilet, she forgot to tell me that she had broken my fly rod.

So how does God redeem all of THAT?

Somehow we got through those next few days and weeks. Things eventually settled down and we were doing our best to make things work, one day at a time. Several weeks later, we had healed to the point that we planned to take our whole family on vacation to Colorado – our favorite place to go almost every summer.

About three days before we are scheduled to leave, we were in her car and heading out to get something to eat one evening. I asked her where she wanted to go for dinner and she said, "I don't care where we go for dinner, but after we eat, I'm taking you to Bass Pro Shop and we're buying you a new fly rod."

"I don't need a new fly rod – I bought a new one last year," I replied.

"Well...remember the day I broke the china and flushed my wedding ring? I forgot to tell you I broke your fly rod that day too," she said sheepishly.

Nice.

Sad about the old fly rod, but in reality, I'm really the one that broke it when I broke her heart. So we go to Bass Pro Shop and I'm checking out the different rods (I ended up buying an Orvis 9', 5/6 weight, four-piece rod if anyone cares to know – great rod!) and she says, "Hey honey, look at this." I turn around and she's holding a bright, fluorescent-pink fly rod – her favorite color. She gives me a grin and says, "Wanna buy this for me and we can fish together in Colorado?"

Now, for a guy getting ready to go on vacation where he is looking forward to spending some relaxing, quiet time communing with the fish on a mountain stream, this might seem like a dangerous question coming from his wife. But this vacation was not going to be about me and fulfilling my personal passions like it had been every other summer before. It was about rebuilding our marriage, our friendship, our family...from all that I had put us through. It was about making NEW memories together and moving forward together. I bought the pink rod without hesitation.

Several days later in Telluride, Colorado, Celeste and I headed out alone to fish together. On the way in the car to the stream we ended up having a deep, somewhat painful conversation about my tendency to talk, check my email or the news on my cell phone while I'm with her and how that made her feel ignored, unwanted, rejected. Instead of getting offended, blaming her for doing the exact same thing or reacting with hostility, the Lord gave me ears to hear her heart and to have compassion on this beautiful woman whose heart I had trampled on for so many years. I heard the Lord's voice spoken clearly through my wife during this conversation...I truly listened. His Spirit convicted me and something in me shifted – one more little piece of me that was out of place was moved back to where he wanted it to be in my own heart. The vow I had lived by for so long, to "never let a woman control me" was smashed and I allowed the Lord to speak his deep, although painful truth to me through my wife. I told her how sorry I was that I was making her feel that way and I took responsibility for my actions. If I was doing something that was causing her emotional pain, I wanted to stop – regardless of what I may have been gaining from it. This was a beautiful example of how I began to make a "living amends" with my wife, doing my part to repair our broken relationship. We held each other and cried as we sat in the gravel parking lot next to the San Miguel River that runs out of the valley in Telluride. This is what it looks like when God starts healing a broken marriage.

After the tears had dried and we collected ourselves, I set up both of our rods and reels and we headed down to the stream. Celeste had learned to fly fish many years ago, so she still had a good grasp of the basics. We got down into the water and she says, "Umm…I'm not sure I really remember how to do this. Where should I throw the fly?" I pointed ahead of her and told her, "Throw it right up into that riffle where the two segments of water come together right below that little island in the middle of the stream. That's where the fish like to hang out."

She casted it perfectly to where I told her and on the second cast, BAM! She got a strike and landed the first fish of the day – a beautiful 10" rainbow trout. Now as I look back, I see that the Lord was saying, if you two will work together, love and respect each other for who I have made you, I will provide amazing, beautiful things for you. No, it wasn't a monster fish to be proud of. Nothing to mount on the wall, but SO much more than that – an amazing gift from the Lord, caught on a fluorescent-pink rod. It was a whisper of His deep love for both of us and a symbol of his beautiful, perfect provision.

> *"Follow me and I will make you fishers of men."*
> *— Matthew 4:19*

Fast forward again several years later. Now we are truly best friends. We share our deepest hurts, worries, fears and joys with each other. We are transparent, real, authentic, honest with each other about what is going on at a heart level and in our lives. We are committed to each other to stay in the difficult process of recovery TOGETHER and to give each other grace in that process. We are committed to listening well to each other and staying in the difficult, painful conversations with each other that God uses as His refining fire to mold us into the TRUE man and woman He wants us to be. God has restored and continues to polish our marriage and friendship. I am learning to love her like Jesus loves me and she is doing the same for me. God has truly made beauty from ashes.

Today, things are so very different in our lives. Our home is a place of peace, rest and love. As I'm writing this, our youngest daughter is napping on the couch with Gunny the Wonder dog snuggling under her legs – they are both snoring! Our kids are thriving and pursuing Jesus and have good relationships with good friends. Celeste and I spend a lot of our time now reaching out and helping other people that are struggling in some of the same ways we both did. We work with people at our church, mentor them, guide them, encourage them and pray with them through difficult times. I personally mentor/sponsor several other men dealing with difficult addictions like I suffered from and walk them through the 12 steps of recovery and I lead a couple of groups that do the same. Celeste does similar work with women in the crisis of a difficult marriage or relationship. Our lives changing like this is not the result of something we did – we can't take any of the credit. It is purely the result of us both ceasing to resist and allowing God to do in us what He does best, what He wanted to do all along – take *everything broken* and make it **beautiful.**

BULLETPROOF GLASS CHALLENGE:

Honest IN (Being authentic with myself, self-assess) –
- What parts of this story can you relate to on a heart level?
- Are you able to take responsibility for the ways in which you hurt a close friend, a family member or your spouse?
- What things are "broken" in your own life and relationships that need God's healing touch?

Honest UP (Being authentic with God, pray, confess) –
- Spend some time meditating about what it would look like for God to redeem the broken things in your own life.
- Now ask God to heal, recover and redeem those broken things and make something beautiful out of them according to His purpose for your life.

Honest OUT (Being authentic with others, share, discuss) –
- Is there someone you need to make "amends" with in doing your part to help heal a broken relationship?
- If so, do you have a game plan and the courage to carry it out?
- Ask your "Bulletproof" brothers to pray with you about it before you go to make amends.

CHAPTER TWENTY THREE

BULLETPROOF GLASS
Esse quam videri

      As my wife and I navigated the rough waters of recovery, we had MANY pointed, painful conversations about my past. There was so much I had hidden and she wanted to know. She would be triggered by a place, a song, a news article, a movie (the enemy likes to use these things to open old wounds, press on a bruise)...and it would bring back painful memories of the past; times I had lied to her, got drunk or acted out in some way. In order to process the pain of these real experiences, she needed to "re-live" them in a sense, by asking me questions that shed light on them for her. This allowed her to put them in proper context with the newfound truth God had revealed. This was the only way my wife could regain her own sanity. Like I've discussed in earlier chapters, these conversations were EXCEPTIONALLY difficult for me, bringing up tremendous amounts of shame and guilt.

      I was a recovering addict, a runner. The habitual pattern I had developed in my life was to opt-out of ANY painful circumstance in the fastest, easiest way possible. Instead of staying in a difficult circumstance or conversation, it was ALWAYS much easier and less painful to simply say to myself "F-THIS," pack a bag, jump in my car and go get hammered. In my men's group, we have affectionately dubbed this curious mental state-of-being that precedes an act of selfishness and stupidity as the "EFF-its" (as in "he's got a bad case of the eff-its"). Alcohol ALWAYS works in these situations...albeit temporarily and with the added bonus of LOTS of negative consequences. The shame of the things I had done, the secrets I kept, was SO TREMENDOUS that I had lost the ability to face them, acknowledge them, discuss them or even consider them. My soul could not take the pain of these conversations before I had confessed and began to recover, before I developed a sense of "shame resilience" as Brene' Brown describes. Shame and fear were the primary motivators of my secret life.

After my confession and my wife's grace-filled, courageous response and decision to stay with me, RUNNING was no longer an option. If she was willing to stay with someone as screwed up and spiritually ill as I was, then I needed to make the same commitment – the one I SHOULD HAVE KEPT from the day we were married. So instead of running, now it was my responsibility to stay and listen, consider the ramifications of my actions and MOSTLY, validate how important and valuable my wife is to me by LISTENING to her pain.

Celeste was angry and she had every right to be. She will confess that, in her anger, she said many hurtful, painful things to me as she processed her pain – things she wishes she could take back. The truth is, even if she HADN'T unleashed her anger towards me as she processed, just bringing up my past indiscretions and sinful behaviors brought enough shame to sear any soul. Without supernatural help, it would have crushed me for sure. I hung on to Romans 13:12 and Jesus' imagery to me of "bulletproof glass" like my life depended on it. Looking back, it probably did.

I remember a turning point for me. It was several months into my sobriety and she was having a hard morning (she would have good days, bad days and awful days that came like emotional tidal waves at her). She had been triggered and was experiencing deep pain and grief over the loss of what she had hoped our marriage would have been. I was getting ready for work trying to get out of the house to avoid the conflict. She railed against me hard, raising her voice, pointing her finger at me in accusation, reminding me of the awful things I had done and how it made her feel. This was definitely a trigger for me and one of the times I wanted to run. In the past, I would have said to myself, "I'm not going to let her talk to me like that! I know I hurt her, but I deserve more respect. She's not going to talk to me like I'm a little kid." It would have been the perfect scenario for a good case of the "eff-its" where I would just give her the middle finger, pack my bag and go on a bender. Just writing that now makes me shudder – SO cowardly and immature. This is my FALSE self. This is what it looked like when I lived FULLY COMMITTED to the man I WANTED to be, NOT the man God wanted to make out of me.

It is also where and how I learned to FULLY lean into Jesus for the strength and courage needed to ENDURE these kinds of painful discussions without running away or lashing out. I needed to NOT just hit the eject button and go back to my life of addiction, medicating my pain which had been my pattern for so many years. She followed me out to my car as I needed to leave for work. I remember standing next to my truck with the driver's side door open, feeling torn and wanting to get in and drive away but knowing she needed me to stay and listen. She DESERVED for me to stay and listen. The spiritual pain of shame and fear was palpable, overwhelming for me. I wanted to rescue her and somehow redeem all of the terrible things I had done but I felt completely helpless. Suddenly, as she was speaking harshly to me and everything in my heart and spirit was just wanting to RUN...I had a crystal clear vision and experienced the Lord's presence, His gentle, yet strong whisper to me again. It was like a vision-flash: Jesus standing in front of me, between us, facing my wife. He moved his right arm around behind himself and embraced me gently with it, still with his back to me. He held is left hand out to her, palm up as if to say, "It's OK. Say what you need to say." He turned his head slightly to the right so I could hear him and he whispered quietly to me, "You're OK. I've got this. Don't run. Stay right there and listen to her." In this lightning flash of a vision, Jesus became the shield of bulletproof glass between us. I felt a humble courage rise in my heart as my Lord stepped between us and validated how important we both are to Him. That gave me the courage to patiently stand there...and listen.

I let her finish, told her she had every right to feel that way and that I understood. I said the serenity prayer in my mind, got in my truck and broke into tears. They were tears of joy-filled grief, if that makes any sense. Grief for all of the pain I had caused my beautiful wife, God's precious daughter. Joy that Jesus' grace had eclipsed all that I had done and shone a light on how valuable I am to Him. It was one of the most amazing spiritual experiences I've ever known. This was a turning point in learning how to listen well to my wife's heart, having empathy for her, taking responsibility for all that I had done and having the courage to sit in that pain WITH her.

I want to pause here and say a little about these kinds of experiences when Jesus revealed himself to me like this. I absolutely don't want to sound as if I have some kind of direct line to God. And I'm sure it sounds strange or even crazy when I say things like, "I heard the Lord say to me" or "That's when God spoke." I understand how that must sound. But here's the thing - when I talk like that, I'm simply just doing my best to communicate an unseen, "spiritual" experience or exchange with God. Because you can't see it and it can't be validated by an eyewitness, it probably sounds preposterous. If there's ANYTHING I've learned through this process, it's this: God is...well, He's GOD. And because He's God, He reserves the right to reveal Himself to us in any manner He so chooses. He does not need our permission...but at the same time, God is a gentleman. He will not FORCE Himself upon us. Instead, He wants us to want Him. And so He woos us. He romances us. He whispers to us. He invites us. The only thing He requires of us is our complete willingness to experience Him in whatever way He so chooses. When I finally understood that and truly became willing to let God come to me on HIS terms and not demand that He only come to me on MINE, that's when I started experiencing Him in these ways I've been talking about.

So many of us want to "box" God in. We demand that He come to us in the way WE want or the way that is comfortable to us or in a way that best suits OUR needs. Many of us view God as some sort of great "vending machine" in the sky whose job is to produce the things we want and need and when He doesn't...we shut Him out, discard Him, ignore Him, turn our backs on Him. For many of us, when we experience something difficult or painful (the death of someone close to us, a tragic accident, a serious illness, etc.), we can be tempted to shut Him out because we simply don't understand His sovereign purposes in things like that.

Here's the other thing I've learned: God is dangerous. The Bible says "It is a terrifying thing to fall into the hands of the living God." (Hebrews 10:31). It's true. A personal encounter with God can be frightening...and He knows that.

It is a terrifying thing to fall into the hands of the living God.

But as terrifying as God is, He is equally GOOD. That is why He can be trusted in EVERY way. Once I was able to come to grips with these things, God started showing up in my life and communicating to me in any number of ways - in a song, the words of a friend, the words of my wife or my kids, a picture in a magazine, a sunset, a child's smile, a news article, an email or text message, a passage of scripture, a movie, a sermon...and yes, even a dream or a vision (and at the risk of sounding totally dumb, God has even revealed Himself to me through my dog!). He is God and if I'm willing, He'll come to me in the most awesome, interesting and amazing ways. I LOVE this about Jesus!

Fast forward about two and a half years into our journey together, my wife asked me a pointed question one evening. She had read several news articles about the data hack of a large, worldwide adult cheating website and how it was ruining so many lives and marriages (this was a website that connects people that want to secretly have an affair). The website's database had been made available to the general public on the internet, revealing the names of everyone that had an account. She asked me, "If I were to search that database for your name, what am I going to find?" The articles had triggered her. Fear and mistrust were rising up in her, rearing their ugly heads. I instantly recognized these enemies as spiritual forces and felt the strikes of their projectiles of accusation and shame at my soul.

My addictions had taken me into many dark places as I struggled to satisfy the deceitful desires of my heart, driving me to do things I would never allow my true self to do, engaging in behaviors that were shameful, disloyal and hurtful to my wife and family...not to mention to my Lord. I had effectively hidden these behaviors from everyone through the presentation of a "false self" for most of my life. I wore a mask that communicated that "I have it all together," portraying myself as a loyal, devoted, church-going, family man, husband and father. I kept this mask in place through an elaborate system of lies, manipulation and deceit. I truly wanted to stop doing the things I was doing, living in duplicity...but the reality was that I was powerless to become the true man that God wanted me to be.

This time, shame and fear would not win. Even though I had never created an account on this website, I very well COULD have and so the shame and fear still presented themselves in her question. Their impact upon me was noticeable, but without the expected spiritual or emotional pain. I realized they had struck me, but it didn't hurt – maybe like it feels when someone throws something small and soft at you...like a grape or a marshmallow. Spiritually, I felt it, but it didn't bring any pain if that makes sense? I was able to see my wife as a friend who was in pain herself, still suffering from the wounds I had caused in the past. Instead of being offended and trying to deflect the question, I asked myself, "How can I help her in this state?" I could answer honestly now.

"You can search it. There's nothing there. I never created an account. I definitely could have, but I didn't. You know everything I've done, Love. I've told you everything. I didn't leave anything out. I totally understand why you'd ask me though. I don't blame you at all."

I have lied to my wife in so many ways in the past that she still has a hard time believing me in a situation like this. She has every right to question my truthfulness and you know what? That is totally OK. How SHE responds to my answer is not up to me. All I can do is to respond truthfully, respectfully to a person that I've caused great harm to, someone I love more than anyone on the planet. She deserves the truth. She is worthy of my love, my loyalty. Now instead of these kinds of conversations being opportunities for shame and fear to overtake me, they are opportunities for God to show HIS omnipotence...and He does.

Shame and fear are two of the most powerful negative spiritual and emotional forces in God's universe. Thankfully, grace and love are so much more powerful. Shame and fear work together in the process of addiction to keep people like me in bondage and this was exactly what I had experienced. It is why I worked so hard to keep up my elaborate system of lies, manipulation and deceit; I was a slave to my own silent fear and shame. Fear of being exposed, known and condemned for my deplorable secret life. Being exposed would bring on shame – the "fear of disconnection." To avoid shame, people (and especially addicts) lie. It's that simple.

The antidote to shame is transparency. It is living a life in fulfillment of the Latin expression, "Esse quam videri" – to BE, rather than to appear. The secret of Bulletproof glass is this: live life transparently. Remove the mask. Stop pretending to be something you're not. Stop manipulating others. Let others see you for who you TRULY are...shortcomings and all. Take responsibility when you do wrong or fail, when you act in a way that is contrary to your true values or when you hurt someone else. It is here that God begins to work his miracle in our hearts, in the midst of our exposed weakness, our acknowledged shortcomings – this is where he does his greatest work, moving us towards our TRUE selves, the authentic men that He created us to be. It is where he makes us strong, more than conquerors, with hearts of flesh protected behind the armor of light...like a clear sheet of bulletproof glass.

"The night is nearly over, the day is almost here, so let us put aside the deeds of darkness and put on the armor of light."
- Romans 13:12

BULLETPROOF GLASS CHALLENGE:

Honest IN (Being authentic with myself, self-assess) –

- Recall a time when you experienced shame and fear. Write them down in a journal. How did you respond to them? By hiding, lying? By minimizing or deflecting? Or could you call

it what it was and speak honestly to others about how you felt?
- What is the ONE THING about yourself that you don't want anyone else to know...the thing you'll probably take to your grave with you?
- Think back to a time when you know you were "wearing a mask". What is it that you were hiding? What spiritual force were you avoiding – fear, shame, grief, anxiety?
- What would it look like for you to tell someone else about it?

Honest UP (Being authentic with God, pray, confess) –
- Ask God to show you the ways that you hide behind a mask and what steps He'd like you to take to dismantle the strategies you've formed to hold it in place.
- Pray that God would give you the courage and the spiritual resources you need to tell someone else about this dark secret or secrets that you have hidden.

Honest OUT (Being authentic with others, share, discuss) –
- Are you withholding something from your "Bulletproof" brothers that you should be disclosing to them?
- Ask your closest friends, your wife or someone you trust this dangerous question and be willing to hear their honest response: "Do you think I'm generally headed in the right direction in my life?"
- WILLINGNESS CHECK: Are you truly willing to listen, consider and pray about how they respond? If not, why?

CHAPTER TWENTY FOUR

BULLETPROOF BROTHERS
Full disclosure is the path to healing

After I came clean with my wife about my alcohol and drug abuse, pornography and sex addiction and betrayal, there was one other group of people to whom I needed to disclose. I had been in a men's group for the past several years. We meet weekly to hold each other accountable, share our struggles, pray for each other, etc. Sometimes we might study a book from the Bible or another source, but most of the time we are just talking with each other, praying for each other and keeping up with one another's lives. I had kept my secret life hidden from these guys the whole time. None of them had any idea of the depth of my secret sin. I had been lying to ALL of them as well.

They knew my wife and I were struggling. They knew I would sometimes abuse alcohol. They knew I'd stumble and look at porn once in a while. But the truth was, I was only giving them about 20% of what was really going on in my life. I kept my mask firmly in place for the most part with these guys because I wanted their approval. The sad part is, these guys are my very best friends in the world. They love me, they respect me, they support me. If there is anyone on the planet I could trust with shameful admissions it would be them. Still, my shame was so intense and I was so committed to keeping up the façade I had created that I didn't let them see me for who I truly was.

I had floundered through life up until this time. I called myself a Christian, yet I lived a duplicitous life, bound up in addiction, trying everything I knew possible to break the chains...but NOTHING worked. I went to counselors. I went to my pastors at church. I went to the elders of the church. The problem was, I wasn't being FULLY honest with any of them - I had too much shame and I didn't perceive any of them to be "safe" enough for me to share the full extent of my brokenness with them. When I finally reached "rock bottom," I really had nothing left to lose. So, after I had fully disclosed to my wife, I went and told the men in my group EVERYTHING as well.

I remember the day I spilled the beans with these guys. I came clean about all of it; the porn, the alcohol, the pills, the strip clubs, the massage parlors, the unfaithfulness and lying to my wife...the lying to them. I cried and blubbered a tearful confession and asked their forgiveness with tears and snot running from my face. I was making myself more vulnerable than I ever had and certainly more than common sense or instinct would dictate. This was seriously dangerous ground for me. I fully expected to be lectured, shamed, scowled at and rejected.

Instead, what I received was grace.

All of them stood up, walked over to the chair I was sitting in, laid their hands on me and wept with me and told me how much they loved me...and that they forgave me. It brings back a flood of tears even as I write this and remember that day. Something shifted in my heart again, tectonic plates sliding across each other setting off an earthquake in my soul, relieving decades of built up spiritual pressure and pain. A bond was formed right then and there between all of us that can never be broken. These men went from being simply good friends at a men's group to what I now call my "Bulletproof brothers" in a matter of a few minutes. This was where I was joined in my journey of recovery by some courageous, godly men that have become my very best friends in the world.

What was even more miraculous was that, after the crying had subsided and the tears and snot had been wiped away, several of them spoke up and told the group that they, too, had some secret behaviors they had been hiding because of shame that they needed to confess to the group and to their wives as well. My personal transparency had spawned the same from other members of our group. That put ALL of us on a life-changing journey of recovery, healing and redemption that would likely have been impossible without my brutally honest disclosure to them first. My disclosure started a small revolution...at least within the bounds of this group of men.

    I want to briefly share some of their stories with you as an example of how God uses a community of broken, banged up knuckleheads to heal each other and create new men with vibrant, abundant, fruitful lives. In consideration for their own anonymity, I'll use only their first names, but I assure you that they ARE real men with real stories of recovery and redemption that I've had the privilege of watching.

MIKE

    Mike confessed a long-hidden secret of molestation that he had suffered as a young boy at the hands of a family member. It was an area of shame that he had carried all of his life. It had been the driving force in many negative and hurtful behaviors over the years including the use of pornography and masturbation. The only person he had ever been transparent with about this event was his wife. It affected his intimacy in his marriage, his self-confidence at work and hindered his spiritual growth. Mostly, Mike struggled with overeating, a behavior he used to medicate the spiritual and emotional shame of the molestation. His overeating had caused him to lose control of his weight and not long after the time he confessed, he was tipping the scales at well over 300 lbs.

    Confessing this long-held secret gave Mike a new freedom to live life with transparency on a daily basis. Seeing my personal transformation through the 12 Step work I was doing in Alcoholics Anonymous inspired him to address his weight issue in a similar manner. With the support and encouragement of the group, Mike started his own work in a 12 Step program with OA – Overeater's Anonymous. Today he has lost over 85 pounds. His marriage and family life is thriving and his relationship with God has grown to a deep intimacy he says he never could have imagined. Mike has a pastor's heart and gives of his time generously in helping other men find freedom from addiction and leading them through the 12 steps of recovery.

On a side note, Mike is my very best friend in the world and the one who waited for me to get released from jail. He picked me up that day and was there for me in my darkest hours. He is the kind of friend who was willing and courageous enough to gently, lovingly say the hard, even painful things to me that I needed to hear. I am eternally grateful for his invaluable friendship. I love you, bro!

TIM

About the time of my confession, Tim came forward with his own confession of a pornography addiction. He made a similarly painful full disclosure to his wife. With the encouragement and support of our group, he took action by going to a men's conference on sex and pornography addictions. He came back with a solid plan to stay accountable, receive counseling both individually and with his wife and started allowing God to put the pieces of his broken marriage back together.

Tim now walks in sobriety from pornography and over-eating as well. He also began attending OA and has lost over 50 lbs and is probably in the best physical shape of his life. He is a key man in our men's group and works personally with many other men that are struggling with addiction, leading them through the 12 steps.

One of the many things that inspires me about Tim is his commitment to do "whatever it takes" to live in freedom from his addictions. He is a brave man and takes his sobriety seriously. He is deeply committed to helping others and he has the experience and fruitfulness in his own life to back it up. Tim, like many of the men in our group, has what we like to refer to as "street cred" - an awesome story of God's redemptive power in his life. He willingly shares it with anyone in need.

Tim's commitment to do "whatever it takes" is so important to him that he had it inscribed on the inside of his wedding ring as a reminder. This past winter, we had the privilege of watching him renew his wedding vows with his wife as they celebrated their 25th wedding anniversary in a small, private ceremony of friends and family. Being transparent has brought amazing fruit back into Tim's life, his marriage, his family and his job. He has personally been a light of encouragement, support and guidance for me many times during my recovery and is one of my closest friends. His favorite saying to me that has gotten me through many dark times: "It's not always going to be like this, brother." Words of wisdom!

MARK

Several months after my confession, Mark hit his own rock bottom. He confessed to multiple emotional affairs and an unbreakable addiction to porn. His marriage was in tatters, his wife and he hated each other and he was ready to call it quits. She had no idea about the emotional affairs or the porn addiction. I remember the day he sat in a chair and wept as he came clean about the things he had also been hiding from everyone. He said he was ready to get a divorce and didn't know what to do. We all gathered around him, cried with him, laid our hands on him and prayed for God to deliver him from his addictions and to save his marriage.

We all counseled Mark to take some time to pray about confessing to his wife and coming clean with her. We encouraged him to set up a meeting with one of us present as he shared this kind of painful news with her. After seeing several of these kinds of confessions in our group, we knew it was best to have the support of a godly friend who could quietly pray and bring a level of calm to a difficult situation. In true manly fashion, Mark ignored our wise counsel and went home that afternoon and told his wife everything without anyone else present! It was a train wreck.

BUT, in spite of the devastation that his confession wrought upon his marriage, it set Mark on a new path. He also attended a men's conference to address his porn addiction and started working through a 12 Step program. Mark allowed our group to hold him accountable and he began walking the narrow, difficult path of recovery in the midst of a damaged marriage. He is walking in sobriety from porn and emotional affairs and devotes his time to helping others that struggle with similar addictions. His marriage is being rebuilt, trust re-established and he has learned to live life with the transparency of Bulletproof glass. Mark has also been a personal source of encouragement and support to me in my own recovery. Let's just say we have "talked each other off the proverbial ledge" multiple times. He is a valued, trusted friend that I love with my whole heart.

DAN

Dan came to our group as a new believer in Jesus. He was trying to figure out a difficult marriage to a woman struggling with her own addictions to pills, sex and alcohol. Dan left a life centered around strip clubs – he had managed several of them over the years. His wife was a former dancer and they both brought a significant load of baggage into their relationship. Sadly, Dan's marriage did not work out. As a group, we walked with him through the tough choices of divorce, alimony, child custody and the painful emotional challenges of leaving a spouse that refused to get help for her own addictions.

Dan struggled for years, since he was a young man, with pornography and anxiety. He found freedom and serenity by finally committing to doing his own 12 Step work. I had the privilege of helping Dan work the steps. The process gave him a completely new level of self-awareness and his entire character and personality have been transformed by God. I am absolutely AMAZED at the changes God has made in Dan's life through this process. He is a gentle, kind and encouraging friend that cares deeply for his brothers in our group. He is always available and always willing to pray for any of us when we are in need. I'm amazed at the man God is making out of you, Dan. Thanks for being a wonderful friend to all of us.

JERRY

Jerry is the quiet, steady pillar of reliability to all of us. He has been with our group for a long time and has seen all of us have our own wipe-outs of varying sorts. For the longest time, Jerry would just show up and listen, pray quietly for the guys in the group and give us the Cliff-notes version of what was going on in his life. I could always tell that Jerry was silently surveying our group to see if we were trustworthy and safe or not.

It took a while, but finally Jerry became comfortable enough with all of us to open up and let us into the details of his marriage, family, work and personal life. We've all watched God change him from a timid, introverted man into a strong, steady and courageous man of God that has a passion to help others in need. He has a heart of gold and is always praying for us, encouraging us, letting us know we are in his thoughts. Jerry's gifts are faithfulness and loyalty, things I have struggled to learn again as I went through my own recovery. I value Jerry as a great, loyal friend and his encouragement has often lifted me out of despair.

The Bulletproof Strong Community

So these are my "Bulletproof" brothers. I tell people that they are the guys that will someday carry my casket. These are men that have allowed God to change them into the men He originally intended when they were created. When God asks us to do something difficult to move our sobriety forward, to help someone in need or to examine a difficult part of our own hearts or lives, we say "YES!" If we have the willingness to move forward but lack the courage or the knowledge of how to proceed, we pray and ask God to give us courage and wisdom on what to do next and we rely on each other to navigate the situation. Saying "no" or sitting still is simply not an option.

We have learned a new way of living life together that allows us to experience God in ways that none of us ever thought possible. I think the idea of true "Christian friendship" has been lost in our culture. Being intimately known by other men and intimately knowing them as well has brought a new level of friendship none of us understood previously. "Iron sharpening iron" has taken on a whole new meaning in this group of men. I trust God IN each of these men and I reach out to them when I am in crisis or even just feeling a little "out of sorts." God uses them to keep me steady, moving forward on a path towards becoming the man He wants me to be. Over the years since my first days of "rock bottom" and the beginning of this group, God has often brought new men to us and He continues to do so now, almost weekly, and almost daily through the BrokentoBulletproof.com website and its social media channels.

ALL of us in this group give credit to God's use of TWO key elements in our lives for our recovery: TRANSPARENCY and COMMUNITY. Our transparency has come as we've walked through the 12 steps of recovery. The Big Book of Alcoholics Anonymous refers to the "triumphant arch" through which each of us walk into freedom. For us, this has been the process (within the context of ALL of the 12 Steps of Recovery) of taking a "searching and fearless moral inventory" (Step 4) and admitting "to God and to another human being the exact nature of our wrongs" (Step 5). These two steps involve a physical manifestation of two life-changing spiritual principles from the Bible that reach both vertically, UP to God and horizontally, OUT to our community of other men...

***UP:** "**If we confess our sins**, he is **faithful** and just and will forgive us our sins and purify us from all unrighteousness."*
- I John 1:9

and...

***OUT:** "Therefore **confess your sins to each other** and pray for each other so that you may be healed. The prayer of a righteous person is powerful and effective."*
- James 5:16

These two verses work together to produce the fruit of sobriety and emotional and spiritual health. For most of my adult life, I tried desperately to overcome my addictions through the use of the verse from I John 1:9. Whenever I failed and got drunk, took pills or acted out sexually in some way, I would confess these sins to God. I recognized these things were wrong and that I needed to stop doing them. Yes, I was forgiven, each and every time. God did not look at me any differently. He saw me as his beloved son. But by not being obedient to the instruction in James to "confess your sins to each other," I was MISSING the opportunity to BE HEALED. That's why I never got well. That's why I couldn't break my addictions on my own power - I REFUSED to be obedient to God's word. What a terrible and costly mistake! I GRIEVE the years I spent in this kind of disobedience.

We follow the 12 Steps as outlined in the Big Book of Alcoholics Anonymous and the 12 Steps and 12 Traditions as a guide to lead men through the journey of recovery – regardless of the addiction. We are able to help men that struggle, not only with alcohol, but with other addictive behaviors involving pornography, sex, emotional affairs, pills, anger, anxiety, over-eating, money issues and more. The 12 Steps are spiritual steps, a proven method of finding a proper relationship with God – life the way it was originally designed to be by our Creator.

Our group is comprised of men from different backgrounds, races, churches and addictions. What we have in common is one thing: we are all BROKEN men, desperately needing spiritual rescue by a power greater than ourselves. That power ultimately comes from our Lord, Jesus Christ.

"For in Him all things were created, things in heaven and on earth, visible and invisible, whether thrones or dominions or rulers or authorities. All things were created through Him and for Him. He is before all things, and in Him all things hold together."
- Colossians 1:16-17

We find this power daily now...in times of our own quiet solitude, study and prayer, in collective meetings together, at our own churches and places of worship...but mostly, through the simple, selfless acts of helping other men that struggle under the slavery of addiction and suffer the pain of broken relationships with God and others.

BULLETPROOF GLASS CHALLENGE:

Honest IN (Being authentic with myself, self-assess) –
- What is the ONE THING you've vowed not to tell ANYONE?
- What is keeping you from sharing it?

Honest UP (Being authentic with God, pray, confess) –
- Ask God to give you the courage you need to share this secret with someone you can trust, someone who is safe.
- Ask God for the opportunity to share it...and then be open to His guidance. God doesn't want us to keep secrets and it isn't until we've confessed that we can truly be healed.

Honest OUT (Being authentic with others, share, discuss) –
- Take a courageous step and tell your trusted friends, your "Bulletproof" brothers something you're struggling with that no one else knows about. Maybe this is in regards to your thought life, a secret behavior, an addiction...something that is producing a sense of guilt or shame in your life.
- Ask your friends to pray for you to learn how to allow God's strength into your struggle and commit to reach out to them the next time you find yourself dealing with it.

- Consider and discuss working the 12 Steps to help you with a particular struggle that is keeping you in bondage and pray with your friends for direction in taking action.

CHAPTER TWENTY FIVE

BULLETPROOF STRONG
Confess Your Sins to One Another

> *"Therefore confess your sins to each other and pray for each other so that you may be healed. The prayer of a righteous person is powerful and effective."*
>
> *- James 5:16*

Living in transparency with one another in this kind of group takes two things: willingness and courage. We all have to be willing to do whatever it takes to become the men God wants us to be AND we need to courage to take positive steps forward in the midst of difficult and confusing situations in life. It is MUCH EASIER to simply opt-out of calling a friend and giving him the details of a personal struggle and asking him to pray for you than it is to actually pick up that phone and DO IT. When you're in the middle of a nasty fight with your wife or under the strain of a difficult situation at work or any other number of hard things life throws at us, that telephone feels like it weighs 10,000 lbs. But when we have the willingness to reach UP and OUT, we make progress. That is what spiritual formation is all about - making spiritual progress, not striving for perfection. Here's an example of what that looks like in real life.

One night, I got a call from one of the guys in our group. His voice was elevated, tense. As best I can remember, the call went something like this...

Me: *"What's going on bro? You OK?"*
   Friend: *"Negative."*
Me: *"Where are you?"*
Friend: *"Out in front of the (XYZ) Motel."*
Me: *"That's not good. What happened?"*
Friend: *"I'm done man. I can't do this anymore. I am doing my best to get better (he was about a year sober from a porn addiction) but she keeps rubbing it in my face. I'm so pissed right now I can't see straight!"*
Me: *"O.K. So what's your game plan? Why are you at the hotel? Are you really going to go spend the night in there away from your family?"*
Friend: *"I haven't made up my mind yet. I was thinking about getting a six pack of beer before I decided. I figured a better idea was to call someone first."*
Me: *"Well, I'm sure glad you did!"*
Friend: Silent for a moment. *"Why's that?"*
Me: *"Cause I heard that hotel is TOTALLY infested with bedbugs, brother."*

He laughed. I asked him how he was feeling. He said he was feeling disrespected, angry, confused. We talked about those feelings and what was behind them – fear of losing his wife, his family. I prayed against this fear, anger, confusion, pride. I asked for God's wisdom, clarity and peace. I reminded him that she had a right to feel hurt, betrayed and that he needed to take responsibility for his part in the argument. He agreed. We made a game plan – he was going to drive around the block a couple of times to pray, bypass the liquor store and the hotel and then head home to listen to his wife.

He called me the next morning to tell me everything had worked out fine and told me thanks for helping him evade a bad case of the bed bugs. He had been in a tough spot - a spot I had been in several times myself. He was angry, confused and tired, yet he had the willingness to do REACH OUT. He had no idea what I was going to tell him. But because he TRUSTS me to speak God's word to him and he knows I care about him, he made the call anyway. Our brief conversation had given him the courage and patience he needed to listen well to his wife's heart. The thing is, we had had a similar conversation like this only a few weeks before and he was the one talking me out of doing something stupid!

This is just one example of how we care for each other in the Bulletproof Strong community. We have ALL been on both ends of similar conversations with other guys in our group. These are truly life-saving conversations. We did not develop this kind of trust and understanding overnight. Most of us have been meeting together for several years and we've seen each other through some wicked trials; a night in jail, a divorce, the sexual assault of one of the guy's spouses, the death of family members, massive job changes, lawsuits and other legal challenges. God has used each of us in different ways to minister to and carry each other through all of these things and more. Persevering together through trials like these have made our group "Bulletproof Strong."

Because we have all had the privilege of experiencing the intimate details of each other's lives, we have learned how to help each other in a powerful, effective way. This was not something we created, but this method really grew organically out of our mutual suffering and experience. It includes a commitment to three key principles:

HONEST IN: *We've learned how to be authentic with ourselves. We have each done the difficult soul searching to learn how to be self-aware, being able to recognize and understand our* own emotions, feelings, triggers and weaknesses. We are able to self-assess and recognize negative emotions like fear, anger, resentment, confusion, frustration, distraction, resignation, envy, jealousy, bitterness, pride, doubt, and a host of other emotions and spiritual forces when we experience them.

HONEST UP: We pray directly to our Creator as soon as we become aware of a problem and we allow our friends to pray with us, over us and for us and our families AT ANY TIME OF THE DAY OR NIGHT. We recognize our own powerlessness and rely on God's power in our weakness, depending on Him moment-by-moment, breath-by-breath for guidance, courage and strength.

HONEST OUT: We've all learned how to turn to God FIRST before we reach for something to medicate or appease these emotions or spiritual forces and we do so by calling in reinforcements. We all will freely text or call individuals or multiple guys (group text messages) to alert our friends that we have a problem and to ask for prayer. Nothing is held back. Our relationships are SAFE so everyone is free to share whatever intimate, graphic details they need to and they can use whatever type of language necessary so that none of us have to carry a secret failure or rebellious sin. There is complete trust and NO shame in these relationships.

Here's another REAL example of a text message string...and this kind of texting is pretty typical in our group:

Guy 1: "Guys sorry for the late hour I am at work and can't sleep due to an intense headache and nausea and with that I am exhausted and I've been battling some triggers. I just wanted to reach out before any of this slips into preoccupation. Thanks I love you guys." 3:47 am

Guy 2: "Praying for you." 4:02 am

Guy 3: "Praying too man. Good job reaching out." 4:35 am

Guy 4: "Praying bro. Great job. Jesus be the answer to what (Guy 1) desires and needs now Lord. He is turning to you instead of the world. You are worthy. Sustain him now and remove his headache, nausea, anxiety and fear." 5:04 am

Guy 5: "Great job (Guy 1)." 5:43 am

Guy 4: "Guys I could use some prayer also. Last night my wife was fearful, mistrustful and asked me if I ever had an account with an adult cheating website because of everything she has seen in the news. I never did but just the line of questioning is painful, opening up old wounds for both of us. On top of that, I'm getting ready to lead a recovery meeting this morning – major spiritual attack...especially with the big event coming next week. I'm in a good place spiritually but I know how fast it can go south so I would appreciate your prayers." 6:20 am

Guy 5: "Praying now"

Guy 2: "Praying for you bro"

Guy 1: "I will be praying also (Guy 4). Thank you guys for the prayers. The Lord is good!"

Guy 3: "Praying for you (Guy 4). I can definitely relate. My wife asked me the same thing out of fear and mistrust. It sucks. I know how difficult that is. Praying God helps you work through it and praying for your wife too. I know you'll do great leading the meeting!"

Look, here's the reality - this is NOT how most men talk with their friends. There is some true vulnerability going on here. It is where miracles happen for us every day. We've learned, as a group, to reach IN, reach UP and reach OUT and God is ALWAYS faithful. It completely rearranges things in my heart and mind when I know I have these guys praying for me. I can't think of a time when I've needed to hear from God and I reached out to one of these guys and DIDN'T hear God's voice in one way or another.

This is one of the most powerful and important ways we stay connected to God and experience His power in our lives. Each of us has had to make a personal commitment to stay involved, be available, and show up for meetings. We have several meetings each week which gives us multiple opportunities to connect with each other, plus, many of us attend the same churches and are able to connect there as well. They key is being willing to stay in contact with each other - take phone calls, send text messages and emails, and most importantly, meet face-to-face as often as possible. Isolation is NOT an option. If you start NOT showing up, you get hunted down and lovingly dragged back into community!

We've learned that we can't recover from addiction or grow to the deeper levels of our relationship with God OUTSIDE OF COMMUNITY - we need each other. God created us for fellowship with each other and He uses us in each other's lives to the extent that we'll allow him.

"Though one may be overpowered, two can defend themselves. A cord of three strands is not quickly broken."
– Ecclesiastes 4:12

"Iron sharpens iron, and one man sharpens another."
– Proverbs 27:17

BULLETPROOF GLASS CHALLENGE:

Honest IN (Being authentic with myself, self-assess) –
- Do you have a level of self-awareness that will allow you to recognize and name emotions like anger, fear, regret, resentment, confusion, disappointment?
- Do you have the self-discipline and self-control to turn FIRST to God or do you have a tendency to stuff, ignore or minimize your feelings or medicate their impact through a substance or negative behavior?

Honest UP (Being authentic with God, pray, confess) –
- Do you tend to think God isn't interested in the minute details of your life like petty emotions and so you neglect to talk to Him about them or are you willing to share honestly with Him about how you're really feeling in every situation?

Honest OUT (Being authentic with others, share, discuss) –
- Is there anything that God brought to mind in reading this post that you should discuss with a trusted friend, your "Bulletproof" brothers?
- Are you willing to be on both the giving (prayer, support, encouragement) and receiving end (reaching out, being prayed for) of true community like is described in this post?
- WILLINGNESS CHECK: Are you willing to step out in faith and seek out a group of men that you can be authentic with and serve through fellowship, prayer and support or do you have one already?

CHAPTER TWENTY SIX

IN JESUS, I AM

Maybe one of the most important aspects of maintaining the spiritual health of a disciple of Christ (not to mention a person in recovery) is to have a solid, proper understanding of HOW GOD VIEWS ME. Our sin nature creates in all of us a strong tendency towards self-centeredness and selfishness which in turn gives us a warped view of who God is and how we believe He sees us; as a harsh, angry judge, as aloof, uncaring and unknowable (agnosticism) or as non-existent (atheism). These are complete misunderstandings of who God is and how he sees us. The Bible says something totally different. When you are struggling with guilt, shame, condemnation, disappointment, grief, anxiety, fear or any other negative emotion (spiritual force), it is IMPERATIVE to remember the TRUTH of how your heavenly Father REALLY views his precious children:

In Jesus, I AM...
ACCEPTED • SECURE • SIGNIFICANT

ACCEPTED

- **I am God's Child:** *"Yet to all who did receive him, to those who believed in his name, he gave the right to become children of God"* John 1:12
- **I am God's Friend:** *"I no longer call you servants, because a servant does not know his master's business. Instead, I have called you friends, for everything that I learned from my Father I have made known to you."* John 15:15

- **I am Justified:** *"Therefore, since we have been justified through faith, we have peace with God through our Lord Jesus Christ" Romans 5:1*
- **I am United with him and one in spirit:** *"But the one who joins himself to the Lord is one spirit* **with Him.***"*

  1 Corinthians 6:17
- **I am not my own; I am bought with a price:** *"Or do you not know that your body is a temple of the Holy Spirit who is in you, whom you have from God, and that you are not your own? For you have been bought with a price: therefore glorify God in your body." 1 Corinthians 6:19-20*
- **I am member of Christ's body:** *"Now you are Christ's body, and individually members of it." 1 Corinthians 12:27*
- **I am chosen by God and adopted as his son:** *"Blessed* **be** *the God and Father of our Lord Jesus Christ, who has blessed us with every spiritual blessing in the heavenly* **places** *in Christ, just as He chosen us in Him before the foundation of the world, that we would be holy and blameless before Him. In love He predestined us to adoption as sons through Jesus Christ to Himself, according to the kind intention of His will, to the praise of the glory of His grace, which He freely bestowed on us in the Beloved. In Him we have redemption through His blood, the forgiveness of our trespasses, according to the riches of His grace which He lavished on us. Ephesians 1:3-8*
- **I am Redeemed and forgiven of all my sins:** *For He rescued us from the domain of darkness, and transferred us to the kingdom of His beloved Son, in whom we have redemption, the forgiveness of sins. Colossians 1:13-14*
- **I am Complete in Christ:** *"For in Him all the fullness of Deity dwells in bodily form, and in Him you have been made*

complete, and He is the head over all rule and authority." Colossians 2:9-10
- **I am given direct access to the throne of grace through Jesus:** *"Therefore, since we have a great high priest who has passed through the heavens, Jesus the Son of God, let us hold fast our confession. For we do not have a high priest who cannot sympathize with our weaknesses, but One who has been tempted in all things as* **we are, yet** *without sin. Therefore let us draw near with confidence to the throne of grace, so that we may receive mercy and find grace to help in time of need." Hebrews 4:14-16*

SECURE

- **I am free from condemnation:** *"Therefore there is now no condemnation for those who are in Christ Jesus. For the law of the Spirit of life in Christ Jesus has set you free from the law of sin and of death." Romans 8:1-2*
- **I am assured that God works for good in all circumstances:** *"And we know that in all things God works for the good of those who love him, who have been called according to his purpose." Romans 8:28*
- **I am free from any condemnation brought against me and I cannot be separated from the love of God**: *"What, then, shall we say in response to these things? If God is for us, who can be against us? He who did not spare his own Son, but gave him up for us all—how will he not also, along with him, graciously give us all things? Who will bring any charge against those whom God has chosen? It is God who justifies. Who then is the one who condemns? No one. Christ Jesus who died—more than that, who was raised to life—is at the*

right hand of God and is also interceding for us. Who shall separate us from the love of Christ? Shall trouble or hardship or persecution or famine or nakedness or danger or sword? As it is written: **"For your sake we face death all day long; we are considered as sheep to be slaughtered."** No, in all these things we are more than conquerors through him who loved us. For I am onvinced that neither death nor life, neither angels nor demons, neither the present nor the future, nor any powers, neither height nor depth, nor anything else in all creation, will be able to separate us from the love of God that is in Christ Jesus our Lord." Romans 8:31-39

- **I am established, anointed and sealed by God:** *"Now it is God who makes both us and you stand firm in Christ. He anointed us, set his seal of ownership on us, and put his Spirit in our hearts as a deposit, guaranteeing what is to come."* 2nd Corinthians 1:21-22
- **I am hidden with Christ in God:** *"Since, then, you have been raised with Christ, set your hearts on things above, where Christ is, seated at the right hand of God. Set your minds on things above, not on earthly things. For you died, and your life is now hidden with Christ in God. When Christ, who is your life, appears, then you also will appear with him in glory."* Colossians 3:1-4
- **I am confident that God will complete the good work He started in me:** *"being confident of this, that he who began a good work in you will carry it on to completion until the day of Christ Jesus."* Philippians 1:6
- **I am a citizen of heaven:** *"But our citizenship is in heaven. And we eagerly await a Savior from there, the Lord Jesus Christ"* Philippians 3:20

- **I am given a spirit of power, love and a sound mind – NOT of fear:** *"For you have not been given a spirit of fear but of power, love and a sound mind." 2nd Timothy 1:7*
- **I am established, anointed and sealed by God:** *"Now it is God who makes both us and you stand firm in Christ. He anointed us, set his seal of ownership on us, and put his Spirit in our hearts as a deposit, guaranteeing what is to come." 2nd Corinthians 1:21-22*
- **I am born of God and the evil one cannot touch me:** *"We know that no one who is born of God sins; but He who was born of God keeps him, and the evil one does not touch him." I John: 5:18*

SIGNIFICANT

- **I am a branch of Jesus Christ, the true vine, and a channel of His life:** *"I am the vine. You are the branches. If anyone remains joined to me, and I to him, he will bear a lot of fruit. You can't do anything without me." John 15:5*
- **I am chosen and appointed to bear fruit.** *"You did not choose me, but I chose you and appointed you so that you might go and bear fruit—fruit that will last—and so that whatever you ask in my name the Father will give you." John 15:16*
- **I am God's temple:** *"Don't you know that you yourselves are God's temple and that God's Spirit dwells in your midst?" 1 Corinthians 3:16*
- **I am a minister for reconciliation for God:** *"Therefore, if anyone is in Christ, the new creation has come: the old has gone, the new is here! All this is from God, who reconciled us to himself through Christ and gave us the ministry of*

reconciliation: that God was reconciling the world to himself in Christ, not counting people's sins against them. And he has committed to us the message of reconciliation. We are therefore Christ's ambassadors, as though God were making his appeal through us. We implore you on Christ's behalf: Be reconciled to God. God made him who had no sin to be sin for us, so that in him we might become the righteousness of God." 2 Corinthians 5:17-21

- **I am seated with Jesus Christ in the heavenly realm:** *"And God raised us up with Christ and seated us with him in the heavenly realms in Christ Jesus." Ephesians 2:6*
- **I am God's workmanship:** *"For we are God's handiwork, created in Christ Jesus to do good works, which God prepared in advance for us to do." Ephesians 2:10*
- **I am able to approach God with freedom and confidence**: *"In him and through faith in him we may approach God with freedom and confidence." Ephesians 3:12*
- **I am able to do all things through Christ, who strengthens me:** *"I can do all this through him who gives me strength." Philippians 4:13*

In Jesus, I AM FREE!

BULLETPROOF GLASS CHALLENGE:
Honest IN (Being authentic with myself, self-assess) –
- How do you REALLY think God views you?
- Do your actions, decisions and thoughts reflect that belief?
- How do you need to re-align your belief about the way God views you based on the verses above?

Honest UP (Being authentic with God, pray, confess) –
- Ask God to move the truth of the above verses from your head (knowledge) to your heart (belief & faith)
- Are you grateful to God for the way He sees you and do your actions and attitude reflect that?
- Do you need to ask God for forgiveness for believing something wrongly about the way He views you?
- Thank God for the truth of his word and what it reveals about His true feelings for you.

Honest OUT (Being authentic with others, share, discuss) –
- Do you need to share and discuss with one of your trusted friends a skewed belief that you've been holding about the way you think God views you?
- Is there someone you know that needs to be encouraged about the way God views THEM? How can you let them know how deeply God loves and cherishes them?

CHAPTER TWENTY SEVEN

BULLETPROOF MANHOOD
What Is a "Bulletproof Man"?

I started this book in the Introduction by posing the question, "What is a REAL man?" So I want to conclude with a more thorough explanation of how I have come to answer that question in my own life. It's an answer I've arrived at through my own personal journey of recovery and by experiencing the cost and pain of the negative consequences produced by the way I had been living. The answer to this question is going to be slightly different for every man because God has designed each and every one of us uniquely and vastly different. But there is one theme that will be common in the way each man finds this answer and it can be summed up in a single, two-word phrase:

BE TRUE.

I spoke earlier about an exercise I like to use in some of the groups I'm involved in which helps us learn how to reconcile our FALSE self with our TRUE self. First, we list out the different qualities of our FALSE self. What does it look like when I'm living falsely, in the flesh? The descriptions inevitably include adjectives like, "angry," "dishonest," "fake," "isolated," "self-absorbed," "lustful," "medicated," "resentful," "anxious," "ashamed," "disloyal," "fearful" and other similar negative terms. Then I ask the group, "Who would want to worship a god that created men and women to be like that? Based on these descriptions, would you say that we are 'good' or 'bad'?" They of course respond, "bad." Then my follow up question is, "Why would God MAKE us this way?"

The correct answer is, "He didn't."

God did not create man BADLY. He didn't make a mistake when he made us. No - when God created man, the crowning achievement in the story of Creation, He created us and declared that we were, not just "good" or "OK"...no, He declared us "VERY GOOD."

And God saw everything that he had made, and behold, it was very good. And there was evening and there was morning, the sixth day.

- Genesis 1:31

You know what happens next. Eve is **lied to.** She takes the fruit. She shares with her husband. They both eat it. God's perfect world becomes corrupted **by a lie.** History is changed. Still, God had created us and He had pronounced us "VERY GOOD." And so man is held in bondage for all time in this divided state of sin (being "BAD" or "unrighteous") yet still under God's original declaration of "VERY GOOD." It is an eternal dichotomy that we are condemned to...*if not for the rescue effort of Jesus.*

The reason I said I can sum up everything I learned in my journey to recovery in the words "BE TRUE" is because this is how God helped me to untangle the lies in my life. The lies about who I am. The lies about how my actions, achievements, looks, net worth and possessions somehow defined me. It took the 12 Steps to help me get there, but when I finally was able to realize that God had created me as someone quite different than the person I was spending all of my physical, emotional and spiritual effort trying to be, EVERYTHING CHANGED.

All I needed to do was to learn how to BE TRUE - true to the man God originally had in mind when he knit me together in my mother's womb. What does THAT man look like? That man is quite the opposite of the FALSE self. He is *"meek," "honest," "genuine," "connected," "selfless," "loving," "sober," "forgiving," "serene," "humble," "loyal" and "fearless."*

So here's the deal: since we are all ancestors of fallen Adam, we don't have the ability to become these things on our own power. We NEED that *"power greater than ourselves"* to do this. But God has made a way for us. He has promised He will make us into that TRUE MAN if we will only let Him. He has given us free will, so we must choose to allow Him..or not. This choice, this decision to say *"Yes, God. I will allow you to make me into the TRUE MAN you had in mind for me,"...is called* **WILLINGNESS.** If you want to become the TRUE MAN that God has planned for you, you **MUST** become WILLING. There is just no other way around it.

If you want to become the TRUE MAN that God has planned for you, you MUST become WILLING.

God is the source of LIFE. He desires so deeply to pour His life into us, to be intimate with us, to give his power and knowledge and wisdom to us. But most of us RESIST it. We REFUSE to allow God to make us into what He wants us to be. I imagine God pouring out showers of life upon us as men and we refuse to receive it and resist by putting up a spiritual umbrella to shield us from getting wet. And we wonder why we feel so dead!

Men have been spiritually and emotionally weakened through a barrage of cultural feminizing, passivity, emotional and spiritual emasculation, lies, fear, shame, and addiction. Those are all the lies in which the enemy and our fallen flesh try to define us. When I learned how to recognize that difference between my FALSE self and my TRUE self, I understood that I have an opportunity to choose to BE TRUE. To be REAL. To admit that I am broken and I need help from God and man. To admit that I don't have the ability to fix myself and remove all of my own shortcomings. I don't have the strength or the courage to go and make things right with all the people I've hurt. And I definitely don't have anything to offer someone else that is struggling the way I did.

BUT GOD DOES! He can do ALL of that in me and more...and HE WILL when I do my part and become willing to BE TRUE.

To me, a REAL MAN is someone who has learned how to BE TRUE to the man God intends for them to be. This is the life that a "Bulletproof man" pursues – true manhood as designed by God through being Honest In, Up and Out – authentic with self, God and others. Pursuing this kind of life produces vastly different behavior. GOOD behavior. GOOD results. GOOD fruit in our lives. Scripture encourages this in one of my favorite verses which I've mentioned before, Romans 13:12, using the term "armor of light"...

"The night is nearly over; the day is almost here. So let us put aside the deeds of darkness and put on the armor of light."

A Bulletproof man has nothing to hide. We hold no secrets with our trusted friends. We live in fulfillment of the code of "Esse quam videri" - "to be, rather than to appear." We are redeemed servants and disciples (students) of the Lord Jesus Christ. For me, this is what it means to live a "Bulletproof Strong" life.

What are the marks of a Bulletproof man? What does he look like? How would you know one when you meet him? Below is a description of what I think a "Bulletproof" man looks like. I call it the "Bulletproof Manifesto." But I want to first explain what this manifesto IS NOT. It is not a checklist of things to achieve in an effort to become a man. Please don't think that I'm suggesting that. Religious checklists are for people trying to accomplish their own righteousness. My righteousness, my *manhood,* comes ONLY from God through the work done by Jesus on the cross. Instead, I think of the Bulletproof Manifesto as a description of the *kind of fruit that God produces in the life of a man living in congruence with the way God designed him.* In that sense, it could and should be used as a gauge, a way to expose areas of potential growth to be pursued through prayer and counsel with other godly men, a way to recognize when I am failing to BE TRUE to my true self so that I can quickly get back on course.

In another sense, I look at it as a commitment, a way of life, a code of spiritual and physical conduct in which to honor God and others *through His power.* These principles are in accordance with scripture and describe a man living in authenticity, congruent with his TRUE self – the man God designed him to be.

THE BULLETPROOF MANIFESTO

Being "Bulletproof" is simple imagery for the spiritual concept of being transparent. We use the imagery of living our lives as a clear sheet of "Bulletproof glass" - we are what you see. Our hearts are strong, protected by God's Spirit and his word, not by our own power, strategies or strength.

Bulletproof men are not pretenders. We don't wear masks. We claim spiritual progress, not spiritual perfection. The marks of a Bulletproof man are not the product of self-powered striving, but the *fruit, the result* of *God's* work in his life. Here are the marks of a Bulletproof man...

WE ARE...
- Men that live without pretense, willing to pursue life in a constant state of emotional and spiritual truth with self, God and others – HONEST IN, UP & OUT.
- Men that honor God above all, in accordance to his word as communicated to the world through the Holy Bible.
- Men that honor others over self and are willing to sacrifice time, treasure and talents for the benefit of others.
- Men that honor women as God's daughters, his unique and beautiful creation – NOT as sexual objects designed for man's pleasure.
- Men that exhibit self-control over our own bodies, living life from a position of "strength under control" (meekness), discharging our God-given power in a manner that brings honor instead of shame.
- Men that are image-bearers of our Creator, active participants in the growth and flourishing of His kingdom here on earth.
- Men courageous enough to forge a few intimate, key relationships with a small circle of other men that we trust – our "Bulletproof" brothers.
- Men that honor our wives, children and family above self, friends and co-workers and are spiritual leaders in our homes.
- Men that allow God to bring about redemption, healing and success in our lives according to HIS will rather than striving for these things through our own "self-power".
- Men of courageous prayer, never afraid to pray for our wives, children, a relative, a friend, a stranger.
- Men of spiritual and emotional strength through God's Holy Spirit – not of our own devices.

- Men familiar with spiritual warfare, understanding how to wage war in the spiritual realm under the authority of Jesus.
- Men that periodically do a searching and fearless moral inventory, promptly admitting when wrong.
- Men who make amends to those we have wronged except when it would harm them or others.
- Men committed to helping others, especially other men with similar struggles and weaknesses.

Esse quam videri

*You can download a digital copy of the Bulletproof Manifesto at BrokentoBulletproof.com/media

BULLETPROOF GLASS CHALLENGE:
Honest IN (Being authentic with myself, self-assess) –
- When you read the *"**Bulletproof Man**ifesto,"* are there statements that give you an "uncomfortable" feeling? If so, which ones?
- Why?

Honest UP (Being authentic with God, pray, confess) –
- What would God have you do differently in dealing with the specific statements that make you uncomfortable?
- How is He possibly "inviting you" into a different way of life through the challenge of these statements?

Honest OUT (Being authentic with others, share, discuss) –
- Discuss the statements that make you feel uncomfortable with your trusted friends. Are you willing to hear their input or suggestions on how you might address these challenges?
- Pray with your friends and ask God to help you formulate specific steps you can take to move in the direction He wants you to go in relation to these challenges.

CHAPTER TWENTY EIGHT

EPILOGUE
What's Next

God has given men the gift of power. It was bestowed upon us in the Garden of Eden when the Creator charged Adam and Eve to RULE.

"God blessed them and said to them, "Be fruitful and increase in number; fill the earth and subdue it. Rule over the fish of the sea and birds of the air and over every living creature that moves on the ground."
– Genesis 1:28

The commands to "be fruitful," "increase," "fill the earth," "subdue" and "rule" are all commands which bestow the gift of power upon mankind. It is the greatest responsibility ever given unto man. God creates man in His own image, invites us into His story, and unleashes us into His creation as His own "image bearers." He ENTRUSTS us with the stewardship of His creation. What a massive responsibility and privileged charge of honor from the God of the universe, our Creator! So what did we do with this awesome responsibility?

We blew it!

And we continue to blow it because, since the fall of mankind in the garden, we are all fundamentally broken, every last one of us (see Romans 3:23 if you need to be reminded). In men like me, our brokenness shows up as addiction to alcohol, pills, pornography and sex. Others are broken in the way they eat or handle their money or how they relate to their spouse or child. Others are broken in the way they work or manage the business that they own. Some are broken in the way they direct their sexuality or gender role. Two things are for sure – we are ALL broken and our brokenness ALWAYS is born out of selfishness and self-centeredness. Righteousness is God's way. Selfishiness, self-centeredness is MY way.

> "There are none righteous. Not even one." – Romans 3:10

So what does your brokenness look like in your own life? Thank God that, in His infinite grace, love and mercy...He provides us a way to become "unbroken" once again...a way for us to be restored. By sending Jesus into this world, God lavishes upon His broken people the greatest gift of love ever given and He gives it with a promise of "making all things new" (Revelation 21:5). Jesus comes to RESTORE us into the original image bearers that we were back in the garden. He IS the way for us to become the true men and women that God originally created us to be. And with that restoration comes a confirmation of the gift of power and the responsibility to discharge it in ways that honor God's original command to be fruitful and multiply and to rule.

There is a scene in the movie, The Passion of the Christ that simultaneously haunts AND inspires me. It is near the end, as Jesus is struggling to carry his cross through the Via Dolorosa, towards Golgotha. He stumbles and falls under its weight as the apostle John and Mary, Jesus' mother watch on helplessly from a corridor along the road. The Roman soldiers whip him relentlessly, commanding Him to get up. Mary suddenly has a flashback from the past: Jesus as a young boy, stumbling and falling. She runs to his aid and cries out to Him in reassurance, "I am here!" She does the same for Him now as he lies bloodied and exhausted under the crushing cross there in the middle of the death-road. She runs to him in His greatest time of need and says the same thing to him again..."I am here!"

And here is the moment that moves me so deeply...Jesus, MY Lord, receives the encouragement from His mother, ignores his own pain and suffering and looks up at her, into her eyes and says...

"See, mother, I am making all things new!"

And then He marshals all of His physical and emotional resources, pulls himself up to His feet, picks up the cross and selflessly, sacrificially continues onward to His ultimate death. It is a scene in which terrifying tragedy, despair, pain and sorrow are momentarily suspended by hope and perseverance. I am in tears now just writing about it.

THIS is the single most important act in history – Jesus sacrificial death for us on the cross and subsequent resurrection. It is in this very pain-filled, blood drenched, horrific, murderous event that Jesus fulfills exactly what He promises. This is HOW He makes everything new. He is man's example of how a true "image bearer" of God acts – BY GIVING SELFLESSLY AND EXTRAVAGANTLY. Jesus is a giver. He gives food to the hungry. Freedom to those held captive. Sight to the blind. Feet and legs that actually work to the lame. His goes so far as to give even his own life which, in turn, gives LIFE to the dead. He is doing this as an example to us so that we will know what the responsible discharging of God's gift of power looks like.

Jesus is doing this so that we will know what the responsible discharging of God's gift of power looks like.

And this is what God calls US into as men (and women) who will dare to follow His Son. He asks us to GIVE AS JESUS GIVES because this is the way of His Father, the way in which we were originally created...and tragically, the way which we have turned our backs upon. He reminds us that we, on our own, are powerless to do really anything at ALL...and then He gives us the very power we need to fulfill what He is asking us to do.

How will we exert this tremendous gift of power that God has bestowed upon us as men? This is the question we are all faced with every day, every moment, isn't it? Will we unleash the resources that our extravagant Father has lavished upon us (our "talents") in ways that honor Him? Or will we squander our energy on our own pleasure, building our own kingdoms, demanding that we get "what I want, when I want, the way I want," like I did in the way I lived most of my own life? That was a life of selfishness and self-centeredness - the very root of all of my own addictions. It is unfaithful image-bearing, a wasted discharge of God's extravagant resources. I am the Prodigal son. I am Mary Magdalene. I am the servant who buried his talent in the ground. I am Lazarus...DEAD and in desperate need of LIFE.

THE DARE

I took my fair share of dares as a kid and even as a young man. You know, the kind of sophomoric challenges by the neighborhood knuckleheads designed to test your manhood. "I dare you to crawl through that concrete drainage pipe to the other end," or "I dare you to drink 30 packets of hot sauce at Del Taco," or "I dare you to try to jump your bike over 8 trash cans," or "I dare you to jump off that rock into the lake (an 80 foot jump!). I did ALL of those things, and many more; I have the scars to show! Why do all of those dares and so many others include the very real threat of some kind of physical maiming or pain? Because they are just that: physical dares. They focus on a physical action...all designed to solve my spiritual problem of needing to be validated as a man in the eyes of God and everyone else. But, as I've stated before, you can't solve a spiritual problem with a physical solution.

So, instead, I want to dare you "spiritually." I've included below a list of "spiritual" dares. None of these will result in physical pain or maiming, but they are all designed to move you closer to God in your relationship with Him, and MOST importantly, to move you towards becoming the TRUE man that He designed you to be from the very beginning.

- I dare you to PRAY for the "willingness" to do whatever it takes to become the TRUE man God has designed you to be.
- I dare you to FIND a small group of men you can trust and start meeting with them weekly.
- I dare you to ASK someone to help you journey through the 12 steps of recovery – whether you have an addiction or not, because we ALL need recovery from our sinful state of selfishness and self-centeredness.
- If your *are* struggling with an addiction, I dare you to ATTEND a local meeting of Alcoholics Anonymous (AA), Narcotics Anonymous (NA), Sexaholics Anonymous (SA), Codependants Anonymous (CODA), Overeaters Anonymous or Celebrate Recovery. There is more humility in the rooms of these kinds of meetings than any church in the world.

- I dare you to buy and READ the Big Book of Alcoholics Anonymous to give you a greater insight into addiction and idolatry and why the 12 steps works.
- If you're married, I dare you to ASK your wife what the one thing is that she wants most out of your marriage and then be willing to pursue accomplishing that through prayer with God and the help of your Bulletproof brothers.
- I dare you to FIND someone IN NEED, someone that struggles with the same kinds of things you've struggled with, and SERVE THEM by sharing your story with them.
- I dare you to ASK God to reveal how He wants you to discharge the power He has given you faithfully.
- I dare you to do that ONE HARD THING YOU DON'T WANT TO DO in pursuit of becoming the true man God created you to be.

That "one hard thing you don't want to do" is probably the exact thing that is keeping you from making progress. For me, it was finally making a full confession to my wife and friends, becoming transparent and willfully participating in a community of men that I trust. Become transparent. Join community. Help someone else. I dare you!

I want to close by quoting again the verse that continues to inspire to a life of transparency, community and helping others. It is the verse that God dropped on me in my darkest hours when he revealed the idea of "bulletproof glass."

"The night is nearly over; the day is almost here. So let us put aside the deeds of darkness and put on the armor of light."
- Romans 13:12

If you're serious about pursuing authentic manhood and willing to take the dare, I invite you to start your journey by partnering with me online at BrokentoBulletproof.com. You can become a part of our online community, explore more resources, make new connections and take the next important steps towards becoming the true man God created you to be. Plus, I would love to hear your comments about how you've been impacted by my story and this book. I look forward to meeting you there!

www.brokentobulletproof.com

BIBLIOGRAPHY

Chapter 1 - Jabbok
[1] Various quotes from the "Jabbok" sermon by Dr. David Wilkerson http://www.tscpulpitseries.org/english/undated/tsjabbok.html

Chapter 5 - Worthship
[2] Definition of "worship" - https://en.wikipedia.org/wiki/Worship - Wikipedia

Chapter 6 - Veritas
[3] Slick, Matt. "What is Truth?" http://carm.org/what-is-truth
[4] Willard, Dallas, "Renovation of the Heart", NavPress, 2012, pages 52, 53
[5] Crabb, Larry, "The Marriage Builder", Zondervan, 1992, page 35

Chapter 7 – Deceitful Desires
[6] "drawn way and enticed" - Clarke, Adam. "James 1:14 - Verse-by-Verse Bible Commentary." StudyLight.org. N.p., n.d. Web. 01 Feb. 2016. <http://www.studylight.org/commentary/james/1-14.html>.
[7] "Scarcity" – Daring Greatly, Chapter 1, Brene' Brown, PhD, Avery, 2012

Chapter 8 – The Magpie
[8] http://www.myersbriggs.org/my-mbti-personality-type/mbti-basics/

Chapter 9 - The Diamond
[9] "humility" - http://www.christianbiblereference.org/humility.htm

Chapter 10 – The Shamed
[10] Robert D. Caldwell, M.Div. - http://www.psychsight.com/ar-shame.html

Chapter 13 – The Jailers
[11] http://biblehub.com/greek/863.htm)

Chapter 14 – The Brave One
[12] *Love is Not a Fight – Warren Barfield*
https://play.google.com/music/preview/Teli33ozdk23tdwfvs5pyf5jjoq?lyrics=1&utm_source=google&utm_medium=search&utm_campaign=lyrics&pcampaignid=kp-songlyrics

Chapter 16 – WAR
[13] *Definition of "worship"* - https://en.wikipedia.org/wiki/Worship - Wikipedia

Chapter 21 – Appeasement
[14] http://www.tscpulpitseries.org/english/undated/tsjabbok.html

THE AUTHOR

TD (Tony) WILCOX is a Christ follower, husband, father, and friend. He is also a seasoned entrepreneur, mentor, speaker and author. He is the owner and president of his own marketing firm, The Atomic Group *(www.theatomicgroup.com)* which serves the automotive and other industries. Wilcox has recovered from his own life-long addictions to alcohol, pills, sex and pornography and is passionate about helping others. When he is not spending time with his wife, Celeste and their family, or pursuing outdoor adventures that include cross-country bike trips, fly fishing in the Colorado Rockies or climbing Mount Whitney, he discharges his God-given power by mentoring others caught in the cycle of addiction and searching for a deeper relationship with God.

Follow him online at...

www.brokentobulletproof.com
www.tdwilcox.com

Books by TD Wilcox

Broken to Bulletproof
Break It Now
Nails
The Joseph Scroll (the sequel to "Nails", coming soon!)
Tickle Spiders (children's)

For booking information/speaking engagements:

The Atomic Group - a division of Atomic Media Works, Inc.
P.O. Box 8007
Redlands, CA 92375
866.928.6642
twilcox@atomicmediaworks.com

NOTES:

NOTES:

NOTES:

www.ingramcontent.com/pod-product-compliance
Lightning Source LLC
LaVergne TN
LVHW011344080426
835511LV00005B/122